# ALC
# BEVERAGE
# CONTROL LAW
# OF *NEW YORK*



## 2003

**GOULD PUBLICATIONS**
**199 State Street**
**Binghamton, NY 13901-2782**

Published by
**GOULD PUBLICATIONS**
199 State Street
Binghamton, NY 13901-2782
(607) 724-3000
**World Wide Web**—http://www.gouldlaw.com
**E-mail**—info@gouldlaw.com

**ISBN** 0-87526-366-1



**Every attempt has been made to ensure the accuracy and the completeness of the law contained herein. No express or implied guarantees or warranties are made.**

**Since laws change very often and vary from jurisdiction to jurisdiction, it is very important to check the timeliness and applicability of the laws contained herein.**

# FOREWORD

The material presented herewith in convenient form is the **Alcoholic Beverage Control Law of New York**, asc currently amended to include the enactments of the 2002 Legislative Session, through Chapter 693, for use in 2003. All changes to these laws have been incorporated in text, and effective dates have been added where applicable.

An complete, up-to-date index is also included.

Comments from users of this book and ways to improve it to facilitate its use would be appreciated by the publisher.

This page intentionally left blank.

Printed in the U.S.A. ab

# 2002 Legislative Changes to the ALCOHOLIC BEVERAGE CONTROL LAW OF THE STATE OF NEW YORK

**(for use in 2003)**

| *Section (Subd.)* | *Change* | *Chapter (Section)* | *Effective Date* |
|---|---|---|---|
| 56 | Amend | 85(Z)(1) | 8/1/2002 |
| 58(4) | Amend | 85(Z)(2) | 8/1/2002 |
| 60(1-a) | New | 580(1) | 12/23/2002 |
| 61(1-a) | New | 580(2) | 12/23/2002 |
| 65(4) | Amend | 503(1) | On and after 1/1/2002 |
| 65-b | Amend | 503(1) | On and after 1/1/2002 |
| 66 | Amend | 85(Z)(3) | 8/1/2002 |
| 66(1-a) | New | 580(3) | 12/23/2002 |
| 67 | Amend | 85(Z)(4) | 8/1/2002 |
| 76-e | New | 133(1) | 10/21/2002 |
| 79-a(1) | Amend | 85(Z)(5) | 8/1/2002 |
| 79-b(1) | Amend | 85(Z)(6) | 8/1/2002 |
| 79-b(1-a) | Amend | 85(Z)(6) | 8/1/2002 |
| 81(3) | Amend | 627(1) | 10/9/2002 |
| 83 | Amend | 85(Z)(7) | 8/1/2002 |
| 91(3) | Amend | 85(Z)(8) | 8/1/2002 |
| 91-a(3)(open. par.) | Amend | 85(Z)(9) | 8/1/2002 |
| 92(3) | Amend | 85(Z)(10) | 8/1/2002 |
| 92-a(3) | Amend | 85(Z)(11) | 8/1/2002 |
| 92-a(4) | Amend | 85(Z)(11) | 8/1/2002 |
| 92-a(5) | Amend | 85(Z)(11) | 8/1/2002 |
| 92-a(6) | Amend | 85(Z)(11) | 8/1/2002 |
| 93(3) | Amend | 85(Z)(12) | 8/1/2002 |
| 93(4) | Amend | 85(Z)(12) | 8/1/2002 |
| 93-a(4) | Amend | 85(Z)(13) | 8/1/2002 |
| 94(2) | Amend | 85(Z)(14) | 8/1/2002 |
| 94(2-a) | Amend | 85(Z)(14) | 8/1/2002 |
| 95(4) | Amend | 85(Z)(15) | 8/1/2002 |
| 96(3) | Amend | 85(Z)(16) | 8/1/2002 |
| 96-a(4) | Amend | 85(Z)(17) | 8/1/2002 |
| 96-b(3) | Amend | 85(Z)(18) | 8/1/2002 |
| 97(1) | Amend | 85(Z)(19) | 8/1/2002 |
| 97(2) | Amend | 85(Z)(19) | 8/1/2002 |
| 97-a(1)(d) | Amend | 85(Z)(20) | 8/1/2002 |
| 97-a(2) | Amend | 85(Z)(20) | 8/1/2002 |
| 98(1) | Amend | 85(Z)(21) | 8/1/2002 |

Printed in the U.S.A.

# 2002 Legislative Changes to the ALCOHOLIC BEVERAGE CONTROL LAW OF THE STATE OF NEW YORK

*(Continued)*

| *Section (Subd.)* | *Change* | *Chapter (Section)* | *Effective Date* |
|---|---|---|---|
| 99(1) | Amend | 85(Z)(22) | 8/1/2002 |
| 99(2) | Amend | 85(Z)(22) | 8/1/2002 |
| 99-b(3) | Amend | 85(Z)(23) | 8/1/2002 |
| 99-d(2)(open. par.) | Amend | 85(Z)(24) | 8/1/2002 |
| 99-d(3) | Amend | 85(Z)(24) | 8/1/2002 |
| 99-f | Amend | 85(Z)(25) | 8/1/2002 |
| 99-g(2)(c) | Amend | 85(Z)(26) | 8/1/2002 |
| 100(2-a) | Amend | 249(1) | 7/30/2002 |
| 101(1)(a) | Amend | 105(1) | 6/28/2002 |
| 101(1)(a) | Amend | 407(1) | 8/13/2002 |
| 104(1)(a) | Amend | 223(1) | 7/30/2002 |
| 104(1)(d) | New | 223(1) | 7/30/2002 |
| 105(23) | New | 85(F)(1) | 5/29/2002 |
| 106(13) | Amend | 105(2) | 6/28/2002 |
| 117-a(1) | Amend | 289(1) | 12/4/2002 |
| 128-a | Amend | 678(1) | 12/20/2002 |

Printed in the U.S.A. ab

# TABLE OF CONTENTS

## ALCOHOLIC BEVERAGE CONTROL LAW OF NEW YORK

This page intentionally left blank.

# CHAPTER 3-B
# OF THE CONSOLIDATED LAWS

# ALCOHOLIC BEVERAGE CONTROL LAW

**Article**





## Article 1
## SHORT TITLE; POLICY OF STATE AND PURPOSE OF CHAPTER; DEFINITIONS

Sec.



### §1. Short title.

This chapter shall be known and may be cited and referred to as the "alcoholic beverage control law."

### §2. Policy of state and purpose of chapter.

It is hereby declared as the policy of the state that it is necessary to regulate and control the manufacture, sale and distribution within the state of alcoholic beverages for the purpose of fostering and promoting temperance in their consumption and respect for and obedience to law. It is hereby declared that such policy will best be carried out by empowering the liquor authority of the state to determine whether public convenience and advantage will be promoted by the issuance of licenses to traffic in alcoholic beverages, the increase or decrease in the number thereof and the location of premises licensed thereby, subject only to the right of judicial review hereinafter provided for. It is the purpose of this chapter to carry out that policy in the public interest. The restrictions, regulations and provisions contained in this chapter are enacted by the legislature for the protection, health, welfare and safety of the people of the state.

### §3. Definitions.

Whenever used in this chapter, unless the context requires otherwise:

1. "Alcoholic beverage" or "beverage" mean and include alcohol, spirits, liquor, wine, beer, cider and every liquid or solid, patented or not, containing alcohol, spirits, wine or beer and capable of being

consumed by a human being, and any warehouse receipt, certificate, contract or other document pertaining thereto; except that confectionery containing alcohol as provided by subdivision twelve of section two hundred of the agriculture and markets law shall not be regarded as an "alcoholic beverage" or "beverage" within the meaning of this section.

2. "Alcohol" means ethyl alcohol, hydrated oxide of ethyl or spirit of wine from whatever source or by whatever processes produced.

3. "Beer" means and includes any fermented beverages of any name or description manufactured from malt, wholly or in part, or from any substitute therefor.

3-a. "Biomass feedstock" shall mean any substance, other than oil, natural gas, coal, shale or products derived from any of these which is capable of being converted into alcohol, including but not be limited to wood and other forest materials, animal manure, municipal wastes, food crops and other agricultural materials.

4. "Brewery" means and includes any place or premises where beer is manufactured for sale; and all offices, granaries, mash-rooms, cooling-rooms, vaults, yards, and storerooms connected therewith or where any part of the process of manufacture of beer is carried on, or where any apparatus connected with such manufacture is kept or used, or where any of the products of brewing or fermentation are stored or kept, shall be deemed to be included in and to form part of the brewery to which they are attached or are appurtenant.

5. "Brewer" means any person who owns, occupies, carries on, works, or conducts any brewery, either by himself or by his agent.

❺6. "Board" or "local board" or "appropriate board" or "board having jurisdiction" shall mean the state liquor authority. ❺*(1995, chgd. by chap. 83, eff. 6/20/95.)*

7. "Building containing licensed premises" shall include the licensed premises and also any part of a building in which such premises is contained and any part of any other building connected with such building by direct access or by a common entrance.

7-a. "Catering establishment" means and includes any premises owned or operated by any person, firm, association, partnership or corporation who or which regularly and in a bona fide manner furnishes for hire therein one or more ballrooms, reception rooms, dining rooms, banquet halls, dancing halls or similar places of assemblage for a particular function, occasion or event and/or who or which furnishes provisions and service for consumption or use at such function, occasion or event. Such premises must have suitable and adequate facilities and accommodations to provide food and service for not less than fifty persons at any one function, occasion or event and shall in no event be deemed to include any taxi dance hall or any other premises at which public dances are regularly scheduled to be held daily, weekly or monthly and to which the general public is invited.

7-b. "Cider" means the partially or fully fermented juice of fresh, whole apples, containing more than three and two-tenths per centum but not more than seven per centum alcohol by volume, when used for beverage purposes, and to which nothing has been added to increase the alcoholic content produced by natural fermentation. Nothing contained in this subdivision shall be deemed to preclude the use of such methods or materials as may be necessary to encourage a normal alcoholic fermentation and to make a product that is free of microbiological activity at the time of sale. Cider may be sweetened after fermentation with apple juice, apple juice concentrate, or sugar, separately or in combination. Cider may contain retained or added carbon dioxide.

8. "Convicted" and "conviction" include and mean a finding of guilt resulting from a plea of guilty, the decision of a court or magistrate or the verdict of a jury, irrespective of the pronouncement of judgment or the suspension thereof.



❼9. "Club" shall mean an organization of persons incorporated pursuant to the provisions of the not-for-profit corporation law or the benevolent orders law, which is the owner, lessee or occupant of a building used exclusively for club proposes, and which does not traffic in alcoholic beverages for profit and is operated solely for a recreational, social, patriotic, political, benevolent or athletic purpose but not for pecuniary gain; except that where such club is located in an office or business building, or state armory, it may be licensed as such provided it otherwise qualifies as a "club" within the meaning of this subdivision. A "luncheon club" shall mean a club which is open only on week days during the hours between eleven o'clock in the morning and three o'clock in the afternoon. A "member" of a club shall mean a person who whether a charter member or admitted in agreement with the by-laws of the club, has become a bona fide member thereof, who maintains his membership by the payment of his annual dues in a bona fide manner in accordance with the by-laws and whose name and address is entered on the list of members. A club and a luncheon club shall appoint an alcoholic beverage officer from among its members who shall be responsible for filing all applications and other documents required to be submitted to the authority. The person appointed alcoholic beverage officer shall be subject to approval by the authority. ❼*(1997, chgd. by chap. 259, eff. 10/19/97.)*

10. "Distiller" means any person who owns, occupies, carries on, works, conducts or operates any distillery either by himself or by his agent.

11. "Distillery" means and includes any place or premises wherein any liquors are manufactured for sale.

12. "Drug store" means a place registered by the New York state board of pharmacy for the sale of drugs.

12-a. "Farm winery" means and includes any place or premises, located on a farm in New York state, in which wine is manufactured and sold.

12-b. "Felony" shall mean any criminal offense classified as a felony under the laws of this state or any criminal offense committed in any other state, district, or territory of the United States and classified as a felony therein which if committed within this state, would constitute a felony in this state.

12-c. "Government agency" means any department, division, board, bureau, commission, office, agency, authority or public corporation of the state or federal government or a county, city, town or village government within the state.

13. "Grocery store" means any retail establishment where foodstuffs are regularly and customarily sold in a bona fide manner for the consumption off the premises.

❶13-a. "Home vintner" means any person who manufactures in New York state no more than one hundred gallons of wine per year, but does not offer such wine for sale. ❶*(2001, added by chap. 32, eff. 5/14/2001; chgd. by chap. 138, eff. 8/6/2001, expires and deemed repealed 5/14/2002.)*

14. "Hotel" shall mean a building which is regularly used and kept open as such in bona fide manner for the feeding and lodging of guests, where all who conduct themselves properly and who are able and ready to pay for such services are received if there be accommodations for them. The term "hotel" shall also include an apartment hotel wherein apartments are rented for fixed periods of time, either furnished or unfurnished, where the keeper of such hotel regularly supplies food to the occupants thereof in a restaurant located in such hotel. "Hotel" shall also mean and include buildings (commonly called a motel) upon the same lot of land and owned or in possession under a lease in writing by the same person or firm who maintains such buildings for the lodging of guests and supplies them with food from a restaurant located upon the same premises.

15. "Liquor authority" and "authority" mean the state liquor authority provided for in this chapter.

❺16. ❺*(1995, repealed by chap. 83, eff. 6/20/95.)*

17. "License" means a license issued pursuant to this chapter.

18. "Licensee" means any person to whom a license has been issued pursuant to this chapter.

19. "Liquor" means and includes any and all distilled or rectified spirits, brandy, whiskey, rum, gin, cordials or similar distilled alcoholic beverages, including all dilutions and mixtures of one or more of the foregoing.

20. "Manufacturer" means and includes a distiller, brewer, vintner and rectifier; "Manufacture" means and includes distilling, rectifying, brewing and operating a winery.

❸20-a. "New York state labelled wine" means wine made from grapes, at least seventy-five percent the volume of which were grown in New York state. ❸*(1993, added by chap. 490, eff. 1/1/94.)*

Printed in the U.S.A. ab

21. "Permittee" means any person to whom a permit has been issued pursuant to this chapter.

●22. "Person" includes an individual, copartnership, corporations, society, joint stock company, alcoholic beverage officer appointed by a club or a luncheon club or limited liability company. ●*(1997, chgd. by chap. 259; 1998, chgd. by chap. 193, eff. 7/7/98.)*

23. "Population" means the number of inhabitants as determined by the last preceding federal census.

24. "Rectifier" means and includes any person who rectifies, purifies or refines distilled spirits or wines by any process other than as provided for on distillery premises and every person who, without rectifying, purifying or refining distilled spirits, shall, by mixing such spirits, wine or other liquor with water or any materials, manufactures any imitation of or compounds liquors for sale under the name of whiskey, brandy, gin, rum, wine, spirits, cordials, bitters or any other name.

25. "Retail sale" or "sale at retail" means a sale to a consumer or to any person for any purpose other than for resale.

26. "Retailer" means any person who sells at retail any beverage for the sale of which a license is required under the provisions of this chapter.

27. "Restaurant" shall mean a place which is regularly and in a bona fide manner used and kept open for the serving of meals to guests for compensation and which has suitable kitchen facilities connected therewith, containing conveniences for cooking an assortment of foods, which may be required for ordinary meals, the kitchen of which must, at all times, be in charge of a chef with the necessary help, and kept in a sanitary condition with the proper amount of refrigeration for keeping of food on said premises and must comply with all the regulations of the local department of health. "Meals" shall mean the usual assortment of foods commonly ordered at various hours of the day; the service of such food and victuals only as sandwiches or salads shall not be deemed a compliance with this requirement. "Guests" shall mean persons who, during the hours when meals are regularly served therein, come to a restaurant for the purpose of obtaining, and actually order and obtain at such time, in good faith, a meal therein. Nothing in this subdivision contained, however, shall be construed to require that any food be sold or purchased with any beverage.

28. "Sale" means any transfer, exchange or barter in any manner or by any means whatsoever for a consideration, and includes and means all sales made by any person, whether principal, proprietor, agent, servant or employee of any alcoholic beverage and/or a warehouse receipt pertaining thereto. "To sell" includes to solicit or receive an order for, to keep or expose for sale, and to keep with intent to sell and shall include the delivery of any alcoholic beverage in the state.

29. "Spirits" means any beverage which contains alcohol obtained by distillation mixed with drinkable water and other substances in solution.

30. "Traffic in" includes to manufacture and sell any alcoholic beverage at wholesale or retail.

31. "Vehicle" shall include any device in, upon or by which any person or property is or may be transported or drawn upon a public highway, road, street or public place.

32. "Vessel" includes any ship or boat of any kind whatsoever, whether propelled by steam or otherwise and whether used as a sea-going vessel or on inland waters which is properly equipped for the service of alcoholic beverages.

33. "Vintner" means any person who owns, occupies, carries on, works, conducts or operates any winery either by himself or by his agent.

34. "Wholesale sale" or "sale at wholesale" means a sale to any person for purposes of resale.

35. "Wholesaler" means any person who sells at wholesale any beverage for the sale of which a license is required under the provisions of this chapter.

36. "Wine" means the product of the normal alcoholic fermentation of the juice of fresh, sound, ripe grapes, with the usual cellar treatment and necessary additions to correct defects due to climatic, saccharine and seasonal conditions, including champagne, sparkling and fortified wine of an alcoholic content not to exceed twenty-four per centum by volume. No other product shall be called "wine" unless designated by appropriate prefixes descriptive of the fruit or other product from which the same was predominantly produced, or as artificial or imitation wine.

36-a. "Wine product" means a beverage containing wine to which is added concentrated or unconcentrated juice, flavoring material, water, citric acid, sugar and carbon dioxide and containing not more than six per centum alcohol by volume, to which nothing other than such wine has been added to increase the alcoholic content of such beverage.

37. "Winery" means and includes any place or premises wherein wines are manufactured from any fruit or brandies distilled as the by-product of wine or other fruit or cordials compounded and also includes a winery for the manufacture of wine in any state other than New York state and which has and maintains a branch factory, office or storeroom within the state of New York and receives wine in this state consigned to a United States government bonded winery, warehouse or storeroom located within the state.

38. "Warehouse" means and includes a place in which alcoholic beverages are housed or stored.

## Article 2
## LIQUOR AUTHORITY





### ❺§10. State liquor authority.

There shall continue to be in the executive department an alcoholic beverage control division, the head of which shall be the state liquor authority which shall consist of three members, who shall be known as commissioners, all of whom shall be citizens and residents of the state. The state alcoholic beverage control board created and appointed pursuant to chapter one hundred eighty of the laws of nineteen hundred thirty-three, as presently constituted, shall continue in existence and hereafter shall be known and designated as the state liquor authority. The terms "state alcoholic beverage control board", "state board", "liquor authority", or "authority", wherever occurring in any of the provisions of this chapter or of any other law, or in any official books, records, instruments, rules or papers, shall hereafter mean and refer to the state liquor authority provided for in this section. ❺*(1995, chgd. by chap. 83, eff. 6/20/95.)*

### ❺§11. Appointment of authority.

The members of the authority shall be appointed by the governor by and with the advice and consent of the senate. Not more than two members of the authority shall belong to the same political party. The chairman of the state alcoholic beverage control board heretofore appointed and designated by the governor and the remaining members of such board heretofore appointed by the governor shall continue to serve as chairman and members of the authority until the expiration of the respective terms for which they were appointed. Upon the expiration of such respective terms the successors of such chairman and members shall be appointed to serve for a term of three years each and until their successors have been appointed and qualified. ❺*(1995, chgd. by chap. 83, eff. 6/20/95.)*

### §12. Expenses.

Each member of the authority shall be entitled to his expenses actually and necessarily incurred by him in the performance of his duties.

### §13. Removal.

Any member of the authority may be removed by the governor for cause after an opportunity to be heard. A statement of the cause of his removal shall be filed by the governor in the office of the secretary of state.

**❺§14. Vacancies; quorum.**

In the event of a vacancy caused by the death, resignation, removal or disability of any member, the vacancy shall be filled by the governor by and with the advice and consent of the senate for the unexpired term. A majority of the members of the authority shall constitute a quorum for the purpose of conducting the business thereof and a majority vote of all the members in office shall be necessary for action. ❺*(1995, chgd. by chap. 83, eff. 6/20/95.)*

**❺§15. Officers; employees; offices.**

The authority shall have power to appoint any necessary deputies, counsels, assistants, investigators, and other employees within the limits provided by appropriation. Investigators so employed by the Authority shall be deemed to be peace officers for the purpose of enforcing the provisions of the alcoholic beverage control law or judgments or orders obtained for violation thereof, with all the powers set forth in section 2.20 of the criminal procedure law. The counsel, secretary, chief executive officer, assistant chief executive officers, confidential secretaries to commissioners and deputies shall be in the exempt class of the civil service. The other assistants, investigators and employees of the authority shall all be in the competitive class of the civil service. The authority shall continue to have its principal office in the city of Albany, and may maintain a branch office in the cities of New York and Buffalo and such other places as it may deem necessary.

❾The authority shall establish appropriate procedures to insure that hearing officers are shielded from ex parte communications with alleged violators and their attorneys and from other employees of the authority and shall take such other steps as it shall deem necessary and proper to shield its judicial processes from unwarranted and inappropriate communications and attempts to influence. ❾*(1999, added by chap. 403, eff. 7/27/99; chgd. by chap. 411(F), eff. 7/27/99.)*
❺*(1995, chgd. by chap. 83, eff. 6/20/95.)*

**§16. Disqualification of members and employees of authority.**

No member of the authority or any officer, deputy, assistant, inspector or employee thereof shall have any interest, direct or indirect, either proprietary or by means of any loan, mortgage or lien, or in any other manner, in or on any premises where alcoholic beverages are manufactured or sold; nor shall he have any interest, direct or indirect, in any business wholly or partially devoted to the manufacture, sale, transportation or storage of alcoholic beverages, or own any stock in any corporation which has any interest, proprietary or otherwise, direct or indirect, in any premises where alcoholic beverages are manufactured or sold, or in any business wholly or partially devoted to the manufacture, sale, transportation or storage of alcoholic beverages, or receive any commission or profit whatsoever, direct or indirect, from any person applying for or receiving any license or permit provided for in this chapter, or hold any other public office in the state or in any political subdivision except upon the written permission of the liquor authority, such member of the authority or officer, deputy, assistant, inspector or employee thereof may hold the public office of notary public or member of a community board of education in the city school district of the city of New York. Any one who violates any of the provisions of this section shall be removed.

**⊕§17. Powers of the authority.**

The authority shall have the following functions, powers and duties:

1. To issue or refuse to issue any license or permit provided for in this chapter.

2. To limit in its discretion the number of licenses of each class to be issued within the state or any political subdivision thereof, and in connection therewith to prohibit the acceptance of applications for such class or classes of licenses which have been so limited.

❖3. To revoke, cancel or suspend for cause any license or permit issued under this chapter and/or to impose a civil penalty for cause against any holder of a license or permit issued pursuant to this chapter. Any civil penalty so imposed shall not exceed the sum of ten thousand dollars as against the holder of any retail permit issued pursuant to sections ninety-five, ninety-seven, ninety-eight, ninety-nine-d and paragraph f of subdivision one of section ninety-nine-b of this chapter and as against the holder of any retail license issued pursuant to sections fifty-two, fifty-three-a, fifty-four, fifty-four-a, fifty-five, fifty-five-a, sixty-three, sixty-four, sixty-four-a, sixty-four-b, sixty-four-c, seventy-nine, eighty-one and eighty-one-a of this chapter, and the sum of thirty thousand dollars as against the holder of a license issued pursuant to sections fifty-three, seventy-six, seventy-six-a and seventy-eight of this chapter, provided that the civil penalty against the holder of a wholesale license issued pursuant to section fifty-three of this chapter shall not exceed the sum of ten thousand dollars where that licensee violates provisions of this chapter during the course of the sale of beer at retail to a person for consumption at home, and the sum of one hundred thousand dollars as against the holder of any license issued pursuant to sections fifty-one, sixty-one and sixty-two of this chapter. Any civil penalty so imposed shall be in addition to and separate and apart from the terms and provisions of the bond required pursuant to section one hundred twelve of this chapter. ❖*(2000, chgd. by chap. 114, eff. 7/11/2000.)*

4. To remove any employee of the authority for cause, after giving such employee a copy of the charges against him in writing, and an opportunity to be heard thereon. Any action taken under this subdivision shall be subject to and in accordance with the civil service law.

5. To fix by rule the standards of manufacture and fermentation in order to insure the use of proper ingredients and methods in the manufacture of alcoholic beverages to be sold or consumed in the state.

6. To hold hearings, subpoena witnesses, compel their attendance, administer oaths, to examine any person under oath and in connection

therewith to require the production of any books or papers relative to the inquiry. A subpoena issued under this section shall be regulated by the civil practice law and rules.

7. To prohibit, at any time of public emergency, without previous notice or advertisement, the sale of any or all alcoholic beverages for and during the period of such emergency.

8. To make an annual report to the governor and the legislature of its activities for the preceding year.

❶8-a. On and after January first, two thousand the report provided for in subdivision eight of this section shall include an evaluation of the effectiveness of the prohibition on the sale of alcohol to persons under the age of twenty-one as provided in section sixty-five-b of this chapter with particular emphasis on the provisions of subdivisions one, two, three, four and five of section sixty-five-b, subdivision five of section one hundred nineteen and subdivision six of section sixty-five of this chapter, paragraph (b) of subdivision seven of section 170.55 of the criminal procedure law and subdivision (f) of section 19.07 of the mental hygiene law. ❶*(1998, added by chap. 383; chgd. by chap. 652; 2001, chgd. by chap. 549, eff. 12/12/2001.)*

9. The powers provided in this section may be delegated by the authority to the chairman, or to such other officers or employees as may be designated by the chairman.

10. To appoint such advisory groups and committees as it deems necessary to provide assistance to the authority to carry out the purposes and objectives of this chapter.

11. Upon receipt of a resolution adopted by a board of supervisors or a county legislative body requesting further restriction of hours of sale of alcoholic beverages within such county, and upon notice and hearing within such county, to approve or disapprove such hours within such county.

❶12. To develop and establish minimum criteria for alcohol training awareness programs which may be given and administered by schools; other entities including trade associations whose members are engaged in or involved in the retail sale of alcoholic beverages; national and regional franchisors who have granted at least five franchises in the state which are licensed to sell beer at retail for off-premises consumption; licensees authorized to sell alcoholic beverages at retail for off-premises consumption operating five or more licensed premises; and persons interested, whether as an individual proprietor or partner or officer or member of a limited liability company, in five or more licensees authorized to sell alcoholic beverages at retail for off-premises consumption. The authority shall provide for the issuance of certificates of approval to all certified alcohol training awareness programs. Certificates of approval may be revoked by the authority for failure to adhere to the authority's rules and regulations. Such rules and regulations shall afford those who have been issued a certificate of approval an opportunity for a hearing prior to any determination of whether such certificate should be revoked.

No licensee shall be required to apply for any such certificate or renewal certificate and the licensee may voluntarily surrender such a certificate or renewal certificate at any time. A fee in the amount of nine hundred dollars shall be paid to the authority with each application for a certificate of approval or renewal certificate. The authority shall promptly refund such fee to an applicant whose application was denied. Each certificate of approval and renewal thereof shall be issued for a period of three years. To effectuate the provisions of this subdivision, the authority is empowered to require in connection with an application the submission of such information as the authority may direct; to prescribe forms of applications and of all reports which it deems necessary to be made by any applicant or certificate holder; to conduct investigations; to require the maintenance of such books and records as the authority may direct; to revoke, cancel, or suspend for cause any certificate provided for in this subdivision. Each entity authorized to give and administer an alcohol training awareness program shall issue certificates of completion to all licensees and employees who successfully complete such an approved alcohol training awareness program. Such entity shall regularly transmit to the authority the names, addresses and dates of attendance of all the licensees and employees of licensees who successfully complete an approved alcohol training awareness program. Such transmittal shall be in a form and manner prescribed by the authority. The authority shall adopt rules and regulations to effectuate the provisions of this subdivision, including the minimum requirements for the curriculum of each such training program and the regular ongoing training of employees holding certificates of completion or renewal certificates. Such rules and regulations shall include the minimum requirements for a separate curriculum for licensees and their employees authorized to sell alcoholic beverages at retail for off-premises consumption, minimum requirements for a separate curriculum for licensees and their employees authorized to sell alcoholic beverages at retail for on-premises consumption, and the form of a certificate of completion or renewal thereof to be issued in respect to each such type of program. A certificate of completion or renewal thereof issued by an entity authorized to give and administer an alcohol training awareness program pursuant to this subdivision to licensees and their employees authorized to sell alcoholic beverages at retail for off-premises consumption shall not be invalidated by a change of employment to another such licensee. A certificate of completion or renewal thereof issued by an entity authorized to give and administer an alcohol training awareness program pursuant to this subdivision to licensees and their employees authorized to sell alcoholic beverages at retail for on-premises consumption shall not be invalidated by a change of employment to another such licensee.

❶*(1998, added by chap. 383; chgd. by chap. 652; 1999, chgd. by chap. 481(2), (3); 2001, chgd. by chap. 549(1), (2), eff. 1/1/2002, 12/12/2001, respectively.)*

❾13. To study and report to the governor and the legislature bi-ennially* on or before February first of each year concerning:
**So in original. Probably should be "biennially".*

(a) recommendations to reduce the number and type of licenses, and to establish a uniform, statewide schedule of fees, such recommendations to include the development of a master application form for all licenses, with specific exhibits required for specific licenses, as appropriate, as well as recommendations on a non-refundable application fee set at a level which will cover the cost of the review and which would be applied against the first year license fee if the application is granted;

(b) recommendations to simplify license renewal procedures;

(c) recommendations to streamline the processing of applications and to eliminate duplication of reviews, such recommendations to include uniform standards for application review and decision which shall seek to assure that the review is as objective as possible and to narrow the discretion of the authority or of any reviewer employed by the authority;

(d) the extent to which quality of life issues, such as noise level, vehicular traffic and parking are considered in licensing decisions, particularly as such issues pertain to proceedings pursuant to subdivision seven of section sixty-four of this chapter;

(e) recommendations to improve enforcement methodologies in order to protect the health and safety of residents of communities experiencing persistent problems in the operation of retail establishments;

❾❾(f) recommendations concerning the addition of field enforcement personnel and the ratios of such field enforcement personnel to the total numbers of licensees that in the view of the authority would be appropriate to insure compliance with the law. Such study shall provide a detailed analysis of the costs and projected revenues to be obtained from the addition of such field enforcement personnel; and ❾❾*(1999, added by chap. 411(F), eff. 7/27/99.)*

❾❾(g) such other observations and recommendations concerning the activities of the authority as will improve its effectiveness and efficiency including the utilization of on-line services to provide information on a fee-for-service basis. ❾❾*(1999, relettered by chap. 411(F), eff. 7/27/99.)*

❾*(1999, added by chap. 403, eff. 7/27/99.)*

❺*(1995, chgd. by chap. 83, eff. 6/20/95.)*

**❺§18. Powers and duties of the chairman.**

The chairman shall have the following functions, powers and duties:

1. To exercise the powers and perform the duties in relation to the administration of the division of alcoholic beverage control as are not specifically vested by this chapter in the state liquor authority.

Printed in the U.S.A. ab

2. To preside at all meetings of the authority and perform the administrative functions of the authority.

3. To keep records in such form as he may prescribe of all licenses and permits issued and revoked within the state; such records shall be so kept as to provide ready information as to the identity of all licensees including the names of the officers and directors of corporate licensees and the location of all licensed premises. The chairman may, with the approval of the commissioner of taxation and finance, contract to furnish copies of the records of licenses and permits of each class and type issued within the state or any political subdivision thereof, for any license or permit year or term of years not exceeding five years.

4. To inspect or provide for the inspection of any premises where alcoholic beverages are manufactured or sold.

5. To prescribe forms of applications for licenses and permits under this chapter and of all reports deemed necessary by the authority.

6. To delegate to the officers and employees of the division such of his powers and duties as he may determine.

❺*(1995, added by chap. 83, eff. 6/20/95.)*

**❺§19. Oath of office.**

Each member of the authority shall, before entering upon his duties, take and file an oath of office as prescribed by section ten of the public officers law. ❺*(1995, renumbered by chap. 83, eff. 6/20/95.)*

## ❺Article 3
## LOCAL ALCOHOLIC BEVERAGE CONTROL BOARDS
❺*(1995, repealed by chap. 83, eff. 6/20/95.)*

## Article 4
## SPECIAL PROVISIONS RELATING TO BEER

## §50. Kinds of licenses.

The following kinds of licenses may be issued for the brewing and sale of beer:

1. Brewer's licenses;
2. Brewer's retail licenses;
3. Wholesaler's licenses;
4. Vendor's licenses;
5. Licenses to sell beer at retail for consumption off the premises; and
6. Licenses to sell beer at retail for consumption on the premises.

## §51. Brewer's license.

➍1. Any person may apply to the liquor authority for a license to brew beer within this state for sale. Such application shall be in writing and verified and shall contain such information as the liquor authority shall require. Such application shall be accompanied by a check or draft for the amount required by this article for such license. If the liquor authority shall grant the application, it shall issue a license in such form as shall be determined by its rules. Such license shall contain a description of the licensed premises and in form and in substance shall be a license to the person therein specifically designated to brew beer in the premises therein specifically licensed. ➍*(1994, chgd. by chap. 361, eff. 7/20/94.)*

2. Such a license shall authorize the sale from the licensed premises of the beer brewed by such licensee to duly licensed wholesalers, retailers and permittees in this state, and to sell or deliver such beer to persons outside the state pursuant to the laws of the place of such sale or delivery. A person holding a brewer's license may apply for a license to sell beer brewed by him at wholesale at premises other than those designated in the brewery license and the provisions of this article relative to wholesaler's licenses shall apply so far as applicable to such application.

3. A licensed brewer may, under such rules as may be adopted by the liquor authority, sell beer at retail in bulk by the keg, cask or barrel for consumption and not for resale at a clam-bake, barbecue, picnic, outing or other similar outdoor gathering at which more than fifty persons are assembled.

4. A licensed brewer may apply to the liquor authority for a license to sell beer, wine or liquor at retail for consumption on the premises in a restaurant owned by him and conducted and operated by him in or adjacent to the brewery for which he is licensed. All of the provisions of this chapter relative to licenses to sell beer, wine or liquor at retail for consumption on the premises shall apply so far as applicable to such application.

5. Except as otherwise provided in subdivisions three and four of this section and except as provided in section fifty-two no brewer shall sell any beer, wine or liquor at retail.

6. *(Repealed.)*

Printed in the U.S.A. ab

7. Notwithstanding any contrary provision of law or of any rule or regulation promulgated pursuant thereto, and in addition to the activities which may otherwise be carried on by any person licensed as a brewer under this chapter, such person may, on the premises designated in such license: (a) produce, package, bottle, sell and deliver soft drinks and other non-alcoholic beverages, vitamins, malt, malt syrup, and other by-products; (b) dry spent grain from the brewery; (c) recover carbon dioxide and yeast; (d) store bottles, packages and supplies necessary or incidental to all such operations; and (e) package, bottle, sell and deliver wine products. If any licensed brewer desires to engage in any of the foregoing activities which (a) require the use of by-products or wastage from the production of beer, or utilize buildings, room-areas or equipment not fully employed in the production of beer; or (b) are reasonably necessary to realize the maximum benefit from the premises and equipment and to reduce the overhead of the brewery; or (c) are in the public interest because of emergency conditions; or (d) involve experiments or research projects related to equipment, materials, processes, products, by-products or wastage of the brewery, he shall submit an application so to do to the liquor authority, on forms prescribed and furnished by it. If the authority determines that the activities specified in the application will not impede the effective administration of the alcoholic beverage control law, it may approve such application, subject to such restrictions or modifications, and in such manner and form as it may determine, and no brewer licensed under this chapter shall engage in any such activities without the prior approval of the authority. The liquor authority is hereby authorized to adopt such rules and regulations as it may determine necessary to effectuate the provisions of this subdivision.

**§52. Brewer's retail license.**

1. The liquor authority may in its discretion and upon such terms and conditions as it may by rule prescribe, issue to a licensed brewer upon his application therefor a license authorizing him to sell beer at retail to a person for consumption in his home.

❹2. Such application shall be in writing and verified and shall contain such information as the liquor authority shall require. Such application shall be accompanied by a check or draft for the amount required by this section for such license. If the liquor authority shall grant the application it shall issue a license in such manner as shall be determined by its rules. ❹*(1994, chgd. by chap. 361, eff. 7/20/94.)*

3. Such a license and the exercise of the privilege given thereunder may be subjected by the liquor authority to such requirements and restrictions as it may deem necessary to impose by rule.

4. For the exercise of the privilege granted by such license there is assessed a fee to be paid by the licensee in the sum of three hundred seventy-five dollars per year which license may be issued for semiannual periods and which fee shall be in addition to the fee provided for in this article for a brewer's license.

**❹§53. Wholesaler's license.**

Any person may apply to the liquor authority for a license to sell beer at wholesale. Such application shall be in writing and verified and shall contain such information as the liquor authority shall require. Such application shall be accompanied by a check or draft for the amount required by this article for such license. If the liquor authority shall grant the application it shall issue a license in such form as shall be determined by its rules. Such a license shall contain a description of the licensed premises and in form and in substance shall be a license to the person therein specifically designated to sell beer at wholesale in the premises therein specifically licensed to duly licensed wholesalers, retailers and permittees in this state, and to sell or deliver beer to persons outside the state pursuant to the laws of the place of such sale or delivery. A wholesaler's license issued or renewed prior to July first, nineteen hundred sixty, and thereafter renewed or transferred, shall authorize the holder thereof to sell beer at retail to a person for consumption in his home; provided, however, that regardless of the date issued, renewed or transferred, a wholesaler's license issued to a brewer or to the wholly-owned subsidiary of a brewer, shall authorize the holder thereof to sell beer at retail to a person for consumption in his home. ❹*(1994, chgd. by chap. 361, eff. 7/20/94.)*

**❹§53-a. Vendor's license.**

In cities having a population of one million or more, any individual person may apply for a license to sell beer as a vendor. Such application shall be in writing, and verified, and shall contain such information as the liquor authority shall require. Such application shall be accompanied by a check or draft for the amount required by this article for such license. If the liquor authority shall grant the application it shall issue a license in such form as shall be determined by its rules. Such a license shall contain a description of the licensed premises and in form and in substance shall be a license to the person therein specifically designated to sell beer as a vendor in cities having a population of one million or more only, from the premises therein specifically licensed. A vendor's license shall authorize the holder thereof to sell beer at retail to be delivered by such vendor to a person for consumption in his home and shall authorize the holder thereof to operate one vehicle for the delivery of beer, but shall not authorize the sale to any person or licensee for resale. ❹*(1994, chgd. by chap. 361, eff. 7/20/94.)*

**§54. License to sell beer at retail for consumption off the premises.**

❹1. Any person may apply to the appropriate board for a license to sell beer at retail not to be consumed upon the premises where sold. Such application shall be in writing and verified and shall contain such information as the liquor authority shall require. Such application shall be accompanied by a check or draft for the amount required by this article for such license. The term "premises" shall include any duly licensed supply ship operating in harbors in Lake Erie. ❹*(1994, chgd. by chap. 361, eff. 7/20/94.)*

❺2. In the event that the liquor authority issues such license it shall forward the same to the applicant.

❺3. If the authority shall disapprove an application for a license or permit, it shall state and file in its offices the reasons therefor and shall notify the applicant thereof. Such applicant may thereupon apply to the liquor authority for a review of such action in a manner to be prescribed by the rules of the liquor authority. A hearing upon notice to the applicant shall thereupon be held by the liquor authority or by one of its members at its office most conveniently situated to the office of its duly authorized representative in a manner to be prescribed in its rules; and on such hearing proof may be taken by oral testimony or by affidavit relative thereto. After such hearing, if the liquor authority confirms such disapproval, it shall endorse such application accordingly and shall send notice to the applicant of its action in such form as the liquor authority may prescribe. If the liquor authority does not confirm the disapproval action it may grant such application and issue such license.

❺*(1995, chgd. by chap. 83, eff. 6/20/95.)*

4. No such license shall be issued, however, to any person for any premises other than a grocery store, drug store, or duly licensed supply ship operating in harbors in Lake Erie.

5. Such license shall contain a description of the licensed premises and in form and in substance shall be a license to the person specifically designated therein to sell beer at retail in the premises specifically licensed, not to be consumed upon said premises.



**§54-a. License to sell beer and wine products at retail for consumption off the premises.**

❹1. Any person may apply to the appropriate board for a license to sell beer and wine products at retail not to be consumed upon the premises where sold. Such application shall be in writing and verified and shall contain such information as the liquor authority shall require. Such application shall be accompanied by a check or draft for the amount required by section fifty-six of this article for such license. The term "premises" shall include any duly licensed supply ship operating in harbors in Lake Erie. All the provisions contained in subdivisions two and three of section fifty-four of this article shall apply to the procedure relative to an application for a license under this section. ❹*(1994, chgd. by chap. 361, eff. 7/20/94.)*

2. No such license shall be issued, however, to any person for any premises other than a grocery store, drug store, or duly licensed supply ship operating in harbors in Lake Erie.

3. Such license shall contain a description of the licensed premises and in form and in substance shall be a license to the person specifically designated therein to sell beer and wine products at retail in the premises specifically licensed, not to be consumed on the premises.

**§55. License to sell beer at retail for consumption on the premises.**

❶1. Any person may make an application to the appropriate board for a license to sell beer at retail to be consumed upon the premises. Such application shall be in writing and verified and shall contain such information as the liquor authority shall require. Such application shall be accompanied by a check or draft for the amount required by this article for such license. All of the provisions contained in subdivisions two and three of the preceding section shall apply to the procedure relative to an application for a license under this section. ❶*(1994, chgd. by chap. 361, eff. 7/20/94.)*

2. Such a license shall contain a description of the licensed premises and in form and in substance shall be a license to the person therein specifically designated to sell beer in the premises therein specifically licensed, at retail, to be consumed upon such premises. Such license shall also include the privilege of selling beer at retail to be consumed off the premises.

❾2-a. Notwithstanding any other provision of this chapter, upon receipt in the city of New York of an application for a license under this section, an application for renewal under section one hundred nine of this chapter, or an application for an alteration to a premises licensed for consumption on the premises under section ninety-nine-d of this chapter, the applicant shall notify the community board established pursuant to section twenty-eight hundred of the New York city charter with jurisdiction over the area in which such licensed premises is to be located by certified mail, return receipt requested, wherein the prospective licensed premises is to be located or, in the case of an application for renewal, or alteration where it is presently located not less than thirty days prior to the submission of its application for a license under this section or for a renewal thereof pursuant to section one hundred nine of this chapter. Such community board may express an opinion for or against the granting of such license. Any such opinion shall be deemed part of the record upon which the liquor board makes its determination to grant or deny such license. ❾*(1999, added by chap. 582, eff. 9/1/99.)*

3. No such license shall be issued, however, to any person for any premises other than premises for which a license may be issued under section sixty-four or sixty-four-a of this chapter or a hotel or premises which are kept, used, maintained, advertised or held out to the public to be a place where food is prepared and served for consumption on the premises in such quantities as to satisfy the liquor authority that the sale of beer intended is incidental to and not the prime source of revenue from the operation of such premises. The foregoing provisions of this subdivision shall not apply to any premises located at, in, or on the area leased by the city of New York to New York World's Fair 1964 Corporation pursuant to the provisions of chapter four hundred twenty-eight of the laws of nineteen hundred sixty, as amended by a chapter of the laws of nineteen hundred sixty-one, during the term or

duration of such lease. Such license may also include such suitable space outside of the licensed premises and adjoining it as may be approved by the liquor authority.

**§55-a. License to sell beer at retail, in certain counties, for consumption at baseball parks, race tracks and outdoor athletic fields and stadia where admission fees are charged, in operation for certain periods of the year.**

❹1. Any person may make an application to the appropriate board for a license to sell beer to be consumed at baseball parks, race tracks, and other athletic fields and stadia where admission fees are charged, other than such parks, fields and stadia as are operated and maintained by educational institutions, to be consumed on the premises. Such application shall be in writing and verified and shall contain such information as the liquor authority shall require. Such application shall be accompanied by a check or draft for the amount required by this article for such license. All of the provisions contained in subdivisions two and three of section fifty-four shall apply to the procedure relative to an application for a license under this section. ❹*(1994, chgd. by chap. 361, eff. 7/20/94.)*

2. Such a license shall contain a description of the licensed premises and in form and substance shall be a license to the person therein specifically designated to sell beer on the premises therein specifically licensed, at retail, to be consumed upon such premises.

**§55-b. Manner of changing beer prices to wholesalers and retail licensees.**

1. It is hereby declared as the policy of the state that the sale and distribution of beer shall be subject to certain restrictions, prohibitions and regulations which tend to maintain an orderly market and prevent destructive competition. The necessity of the provisions of this section is therefore declared as a matter of legislative necessity.

2. No brewer or beer wholesaler may increase the price per case, draft package or special package of beer sold to beer wholesalers or retail licensees until at least one hundred eighty days have elapsed since his last price decrease on such case, draft package or special package, provided, however, that the brewer or beer wholesaler may increase any price established by him at any time in the amount of any direct tax increase on beer, or on containers thereof, actually paid by such brewer or beer wholesaler, and provided further, however, that if a brewer or beer wholesaler has increased his price to beer wholesalers at any time pursuant to the provisions hereof, the beer wholesaler may increase the price established by him on such package in an amount equal to the direct price increase to the beer wholesaler. The price per case, draft package or special package of beer sold to beer wholesalers or retail licensees on the first day of the month following the effective date of this act shall be deemed the base price, to or from which price increases or decreases may be made in accordance with the provisions of this section.

3. The authority is authorized and empowered to do such acts, prescribe such forms and adopt rules and regulations as it may deem necessary or proper to carry into effect the purpose and provisions of this section and to prevent circumvention or evasion thereof.

Without limiting the generality of the foregoing, and in addition to its other powers, the authority may, in its discretion, adopt rules or regulations:

a. Particularizing the standards of packaging which constitute a case, special package and draft package of beer.

b. Defining the guidelines relating to "price" within the purview of this section which guidelines may provide, without limitation thereto, that,

(1) Whenever a brewer or beer wholesaler decreases his price per case, draft package or special package of beer to beer wholesalers, the beer wholesaler may decrease his price to retail licensees on such reduced item or items by no more than the amount in dollars and cents by which the brewer or beer wholesaler has decreased the price per case, draft package or special package to the beer wholesaler.

(2) Whenever the price per case, draft package or special package of beer is increased to retail licensees by action of the brewer or beer wholesaler following a price decrease, the brewer or beer wholesaler may not increase its price to retailers on any item or items more than one-half of the price decrease previously granted, nor may the brewer or beer wholesaler selling such item or items to the beer wholesaler increase its price to such beer wholesaler more than one-half of the price decrease previously granted, provided, however, such restrictions on price increases by both brewers and beer wholesalers shall remain in effect for the period of one hundred eighty days.

(3) Whenever a brewer or beer wholesaler lowers its price per case, draft package or special package of beer to any beer wholesaler in New York state it must lower its price on each item or items by the same amount to all beer wholesalers throughout New York state to whom such item or items is offered for sale.

(4) Whenever a brewer or beer wholesaler, following a price decrease, raises its price per case, draft package or special package of beer to any beer wholesaler in New York state it must raise its price on each item or items by the same amount to all beer wholesalers throughout New York state to whom such item or items are offered for sale.

c. Providing that for good cause shown to its satisfaction, the authority may grant waivers to licensees adversely affected by this section, under such terms and conditions as the authority deems appropriate.

d. Requiring licensees to file with the authority reports certifying their prices of beer, the dates of any changes in the price of any item of beer, and such other matters as the authority may determine from time to time to be necessary to disclose accurately the price of beer during the previous twelve months and requiring licensees to keep forms, records and memoranda prescribed by the authority.

❾4. For the purpose of defraying the expenses incurred in the administration of this section, there shall be paid to the authority by each person hereafter applying for a license as brewer or beer wholesaler the following sums: brewer whose annual production is sixty thousand barrels per year or more, one thousand dollars; brewer whose annual production is less than sixty thousand barrels per year, one hundred dollars; beer wholesaler, one hundred dollars. A like sum shall be paid by each person hereafter applying for the issuance or renewal of any such license and such sum shall accompany the application and the license fee prescribed by this chapter for such license or renewal thereof, as the case may be. The sums prescribed by this subdivision shall not be pro-rated for any portion of the license fee and shall have no refund value. ❾*(1999, chgd. by chap. 176, eff. 8/5/99.)*

5. For any violation of any provision of this section or of any rule or regulation duly promulgated under this section the authority may revoke, cancel or suspend a license or recover, as provided in section one hundred twelve of this chapter, the penal sum of the bond filed by the licensee.



**❻§55-c. Agreements between brewers and beer wholesalers.**

1. Purpose. It is hereby declared to be the policy of this state, that the sale and delivery of beer by brewers to beer wholesalers shall be pursuant to a written agreement. That further, the regulation of business relations between brewers and beer wholesalers is necessary and appropriate to the general economy and tax base of this state and in the public interest.

2. Definitions. As used in this section, the following words shall have the following meanings:

(a) "Agreement" means any contract, agreement, arrangement, course of dealing or commercial relationship between a brewer and a beer wholesaler pursuant to which a beer wholesaler is granted the right to purchase, offer for sale, resell, warehouse or physically deliver beer sold by a brewer.

❼(b) "Brewer" means any person or entity engaged primarily in business as a brewer, manufacturer of alcoholic beverages, importer, marketer, broker or agent of any of the foregoing who sells or offers to sell beer to a beer wholesaler in this state or any successor to a brewer. ❼*(1997, chgd. by chap. 612, eff. 9/17/97.)*

(c) "Successor to a brewer" means any person or entity which acquires the business or beer brands of a brewer, without limitation, by way of the purchase, assignment, transfer, lease, or license or disposition of all or a portion of the assets, business or equity of a brewer in any transaction, including merger, corporate reorganization or consolidation or the formation of a partnership, joint venture or other joint marketing alliance.

(d) "Beer wholesaler" and "wholesaler" means the holder of a wholesaler's license pursuant to section fifty-three of this article who purchases, offers to sell, resells, markets, promotes, warehouses or physically distributes beer sold by a brewer.

❼(e) ❶"Good cause" means and shall be limited to:

❶(i) (A) The implementation by a brewer of a national or regional policy of consolidation which is reasonable, nondiscriminatory and essential. Such policy shall have been previously disclosed, in writing, in reasonable detail to the brewer's wholesalers, and shall result in a contemporaneous reduction in the number of a brewer's wholesalers not only for a brand in this state, but also for a brand in contiguous states or in a majority of the states in which the brewer sells the brand. All affected wholesalers and affected brewers shall be afforded ninety days prior notice of the implementation of such policy, and such notice shall be provided by the brewer implementing said policy. Further, an affected wholesaler who has actual knowledge of the intended implementation of such policy shall also notify each affected brewer. The term "affected brewers" means all other brewers with an agreement with an affected wholesaler who is a multiple brands wholesaler. The term "affected wholesalers" means wholesalers who may reasonably be expected to experience a loss or diminishment of a right to distribute a brand, in whole or in part, as a consequence of a proposed consolidation policy.

(B) An affected brewer receiving notice pursuant to this paragraph may, within one hundred twenty days after receiving such notice, terminate an agreement with a multiple brands wholesaler in the event: (1) the total case purchases computed in twenty-four twelve ounce equivalence units by the wholesaler of the products of the affected brewer amounted to two percent or less of the multiple brands wholesaler's total sales volume during the twelve month period preceding the notice; and (2) the affected brewer, prior to such termination, pays compensation to the multiple brands wholesaler.

❶*(2001, chgd. by chap. 346, eff. on and after 6/15/2001.)*

(ii) There is a failure by the beer wholesaler to comply with a material term of an agreement required by subdivision three of this section between the brewer and beer wholesaler, provided that: (A) the wholesaler was given written notice by the brewer of the failure to comply with the agreement as provided for in subdivision five of this section and in which the brewer states with particularity the basis for the brewer's determination of non-compliance, and upon the wholesaler's written request within ten days of receipt of the notice, the brewer has supplemented such notice by submitting to the wholesaler in writing the brewer's recommended plan of corrective action to cure the claimed defaults or deficiencies in a manner satisfactory to it; (B) the wholesaler was afforded a reasonable opportunity to assert good faith efforts to comply with the agreement by curing the claimed defaults or deficiencies specified in said notice within the time provided for in clause (C) of this subparagraph; and

(C) the wholesaler was afforded fifteen days after receipt of such notice to submit a written plan of corrective action to comply with the agreement by curing the claimed non-compliance and seventy-five days to cure such non-compliance in accordance with the plan. Provided, however, that such period for cure may be increased or reduced to a commercially reasonable period by an order of a court in this state entered after a hearing at which the brewer has the burden to demonstrate that the claimed defaults or deficiencies can be substantially rectified in the period of time afforded the wholesaler or that, after receipt of notice of default or deficiency as provided for in subdivision five of this section, the wholesaler has intentionally engaged in an affirmative course of conduct in which the brewer's current marketing plans and other trade secrets are disclosed to a third party without the prior consent of the brewer or in which the wholesaler acts or threatens to act to significantly impair, harm or dilute the reputation or competitive position of the brewer or otherwise irreparably injure the brewer, its brands or trademarks. Provided, further however: (1) that such period for cure need not exceed forty-five days if within the twelve months immediately following a cure, the wholesaler intentionally engages in conduct which repeats the same specified default and deficiency which the brewer had deemed cured; and (2) that such period for cure need not exceed sixty days in the event that during the twelve month period preceding the notice, the total case purchases by the wholesaler of the affected products of the brewer account for less than one-half of one percent of the wholesaler's aggregate case purchases from all sources or one thousand cases. For purposes of this subdivision, case purchases of affected products whether package or draught shall be computed in twenty-four twelve ounce equivalence units.
❼*(1997, chgd. by chap. 612, eff. 9/17/97.)*

(f) "Good faith" means honesty in fact and the observance of reasonable commercial standards in the trade.

(g) "Material modification" of an agreement or to "materially modify" means and includes a substantial and significant change in the competitive circumstances under which the agreement was entered into and is performed which is caused by a brewer without fault on the part of the wholesaler.

❼(h) "Multiple brands wholesaler" means a wholesaler which pursuant to agreements with different brewers holds the rights to purchase, resell, warehouse or physically deliver two or more competing products in substantially the same geographic area or to the same customer class. ❼*(1997, added by chap. 612, eff. 9/17/97.)*

❶(i) "Fair market value of distribution rights" means the amount a willing seller, under no compulsion to sell, would be willing to accept and a willing buyer, under no compulsion to purchase, would be willing to pay for the distribution rights. ❶*(2001, added by chap. 346, eff. on and after 6/15/2001.)*

❼3. Written agreement required. Except as provided for in subdivision ten of this section, beer offered for sale in this state by a brewer to a beer wholesaler shall be sold and delivered pursuant to a written agreement which conforms to the provisions of this section and which sets forth all essential and material terms, requirements, standards of performance and conditions of the business relationship between a brewer and a beer wholesaler. Such agreement may be cancelled, terminated, materially modified or not renewed for good cause as defined in this section, provided the brewer has acted in good faith.

❼4. Termination for cause and opportunity to cure. (a) No brewer may cancel, fail to renew, or terminate an agreement unless the party intending such action has good cause for such cancellation, failure to renew, or termination and in any case in which prior notification is required under this section, the party intending to act has furnished said prior notification as provided for in subdivision five of this section and the wholesaler has failed to cure such defaults or deficiencies after a period for cure, as provided for in clause (C) of subparagraph (ii) of paragraph (e) of subdivision two of this section.

(b) No brewer shall amend or materially modify or otherwise terminate any essential and material term or requirement of an agreement unless the brewer has good cause therefor and has furnished the affected party with at least fifteen days prior notification as required by subdivision five of this section.

❼*(1997, chgd. by chap. 612, eff. 9/17/97.)*

5. Notice of default or deficiency. (a) Except as provided in paragraph (d) of this subdivision, no brewer may cancel, fail to renew or terminate an agreement unless the brewer or beer wholesaler furnished prior notification in accordance with paragraph (c) of this subdivision.

(b) Notwithstanding any agreement, no brewer or beer wholesaler may materially amend or modify an essential and material term or requirement unless the brewer or beer wholesaler furnished prior notification in accordance with paragraph (c) of this subdivision.

(c) The notification required under paragraphs (a) and (b) of this subdivision shall be in writing and sent to the affected party by certified mail. Such notification shall contain:

(i) a statement of intent to cancel, not renew, otherwise terminate, materially amend or modify an agreement;

(ii) a statement of all reasons therefor, stated with particularity; and

(iii) the date on which such action shall take effect.

(d) A brewer or beer wholesaler may cancel, fail to renew or otherwise terminate an agreement without furnishing the prior notification required under this section only:

(i) in the event the affected party has made an assignment for the benefit of creditors or similar disposition of all or substantially all of the assets of such party's business;

Printed in the U.S.A. ab

(ii) in the event of a conviction or plea of guilty or no contest to a felony which in the reasonable judgment of the brewer may adversely affect the goodwill or interests of the wholesaler or brewer;

(iii) in the event of the revocation or suspension for thirty-one days or more of any license or permit required of the wholesaler for the normal operation of its business;

(iv) in the event there was fraudulent conduct on the part of the brewer or beer wholesaler in its dealings with the other party;

❼(v) in the event of the failure by either party to pay sums of money to the other party when due or if either the wholesaler or brewer takes any action which would provide grounds for immediate termination pursuant to the reasonable terms of a written enforceable agreement between them, which was freely entered into without threat of termination or other coercion or compulsion and was in full force and effect sixty days from the effective date of the chapter of the laws of nineteen hundred ninety-seven which amended this subparagraph; ❼*(1997, chgd. by chap. 612, eff. 9/17/97.)*

(vi) in the event the brewer and beer wholesaler voluntarily agree in writing to terminate the agreement.

❶6. Right of action. If a brewer fails to comply with the provisions of this section, a beer wholesaler may maintain a civil action in a court of competent jurisdiction within this state for damages sustained in accordance with the laws of this state which shall govern all disputes arising under an agreement or by reason of its making and performance. In any such action the court may grant such equitable relief as is necessary or appropriate, considering the purposes of this section, to remedy the effects of any failure to comply with the provisions of this section or the effects of conduct prohibited hereunder, including declaratory judgment, mandatory or prohibitive injunctive relief, or preliminary or other interim equitable relief; provided, however, that permanent injunctive relief shall not be granted to prohibit the effectiveness of a termination or non-renewal of an agreement in furtherance of a policy of consolidation that is in compliance with subparagraph (i) of paragraph (e) of subdivision two of this section. In any legal action challenging any cancellation, termination or failure to renew, or where an issue is the brewer's compliance with the provisions of subparagraph (i) of paragraph (e) of subdivision two of this section, the brewer shall have the burden of proof that its action was based upon good cause, provided however, the wholesaler shall retain the burden of proof in all other respects. The rights and remedies provided in this section to a beer wholesaler with respect to an agreement with a brewer and to an affected wholesaler or an affected brewer shall be intended to supplement and not be exclusive of any rights and remedies otherwise available pursuant to any other statute, or at law or equity. ❶*(1997, chgd. by chap. 612; 2001, chgd. by chap. 346, eff. on and after 6/15/2001.)*

❶7. Reasonable compensation. (a) Any brewer who shall implement a national or regional consolidation policy, pursuant to this section, shall not terminate its relationship with an affected wholesaler until compensation as provided for in this subdivision has been paid. Such brewer shall pay the affected beer wholesaler the fair market value of the distribution rights which will be lost or diminished by reason of the implementation of such policy, together with fair and reasonable compensation for other damages sustained.

(b) Every brewer who without good cause amends, cancels, terminates, materially modifies or fails to renew any agreement, or who in violation of this section causes a beer wholesaler to resign from an agreement or denies or withholds consent to any assignment, transfer or sale of a beer wholesaler's business assets or capital stock or other equity or debt securities, shall pay the affected beer wholesaler the fair market value of the beer wholesaler's business, including distribution rights, which have been lost or diminished as the result of the brewer's actions.

(c) In the event that the brewer and the beer wholesaler are unable to agree on the compensation to be paid for the value of the beer wholesaler's business and assets, the matter may with the consent of both the brewer and the beer wholesaler, be submitted to a neutral arbitrator to be selected by the parties; if they cannot agree on such an arbitrator, the same shall be selected by a judge of a court of competent jurisdiction. No brewer or beer wholesaler may impose binding arbitration of any issue as a term or condition of an agreement. Arbitration costs shall be equally divided by the beer wholesaler and the brewer. The award of the arbitrator shall be confirmed by a court of competent jurisdiction in this state, the judgment of which shall be binding.

❶*(2001, chgd. by chap. 346, eff. on and after 6/15/2001.)*

❼8. Sale and transfer of beer wholesaler's business. No brewer shall unreasonably withhold or delay its approval of any assignment, sale or transfer of all or any portion of beer wholesaler's corporate equity or debt or assets, including the beer wholesaler's rights and obligations under the terms of an agreement, whenever the person or persons to be substituted meet objectively reasonable standards imposed by the brewer. A wholesaler who sells, assigns or transfers an agreement made pursuant to this section shall provide written notice of such sale, assignment or transfer to all other brewers with whom it has entered agreements.

❼9. (a) A brewer qualified to do business in the state of New York may hold an interest in a limited partnership licensed by the authority as a wholesaler, when the brewer or its affiliate is a limited partner and the beer wholesaler is the general partner. Notwithstanding any other provision of law, such brewer may loan money to a general partner of an aforementioned limited partnership. Provided, however, any brewer or its affiliate who holds an interest in a limited partnership licensed by the authority as a wholesaler or who loans money to a general partner of such limited partnership may only exercise such control of the business as permitted by section 121-303 of the partnership law.

(b) Notwithstanding subdivision (a) of this subdivision, no brewer or its affiliate may acquire or hold an interest in or loan money to a general partner of a multiple brands wholesaler unless and until all other brewers having agreements with said multiple brands wholesaler have been afforded sixty days prior written notice of the particular terms and conditions of the limited partnership or loan agreement or of any change therein. A "loan" for purposes of this subdivision shall not include bona fide credit terms for product purchases customarily extended by a brewer to wholesalers in the normal course of business.



❶(c) For one hundred twenty days after the formation, licensing and commencement of operations as a beer wholesaler of a limited partnership or the making of a loan, and upon at least fifteen days prior notification as required by subdivision five of this section, a brewer may terminate an agreement with a multiple brands wholesaler in the event: (i) a competing brewer or its affiliate becomes a limited partner with or loans money to a general partner of a multiple brands wholesaler, (ii) by reason of said loan, the performance of a loan agreement, or the terms or conduct of the limited partnership, there is a reasonable likelihood that competition between brands of the competing brewers has been or may be significantly reduced in a relevant geographic area or market, and (iii) in lieu of other rights and remedies it might have under this chapter to terminate for good cause, the terminating brewer pays compensation to the multiple brands wholesaler. ❶*(2001, chgd. by chap. 346, eff. on and after 6/15/2001.)*
❼*(1997, chgd. by chap. 612, eff. 9/17/97.)*

10. Coverage. (a) This section shall not apply to written agreements that were in effect prior to the effective date of this section which set forth all terms and conditions of material significance governing the relationship between the brewer and beer wholesaler, including but not limited to the grounds and procedures which govern: (i) termination of the relationship; (ii) approval and disapproval of managers; (iii) change in ownership; and (iv) whether or not the wholesaler is entitled to compensation in the event the wholesaler is terminated for deficient performance under such agreement or without good cause. Provided, however, that this section shall apply to any agreement entered into, and renewals, extensions, amendments or conduct constituting a material modification of an agreement on or after the effective date of this section.

(b) Where an agreement between a brewer and beer wholesaler in effect prior to the effective date of this section is continuous in nature or has no specific duration or has no renewal provision and fails to set forth all terms and conditions of material significance governing the relationship between the brewer and beer wholesaler, including but not limited to the grounds and procedures which govern:

(i) termination of the relationship; (ii) approval and disapproval of managers; (iii) change in ownership; and (iv) whether or not the wholesaler is entitled to compensation in the event the wholesaler is terminated for deficient performance under such agreement or without good cause; such agreement shall be considered for purposes of this section to have been renewed sixty days after the effective date of this section.

❼11. The requirements of this section may not be altered, waived or modified by written or oral agreement in advance of a bona fide case and controversy arising under a written agreement complying with this section. ❼*(1997, added. by chap. 612, eff. 9/17/97.)*
❻*(1996, added by chap. 679, eff. 9/25/96.)*

**❷§56. License fees.**

1. The annual fee for a brewer's license shall be four thousand dollars, unless the annual production of the brewer is less than sixty thousand barrels per year, in which case the annual fee shall be three hundred twenty dollars.

2. The annual fee for a wholesaler's beer license shall be eight hundred dollars.

3. The annual fee for a vendor's license shall be one hundred forty-four dollars.

4. The annual fee for a license to sell beer at retail not to be consumed on the premises where sold shall be one hundred ten dollars. Where, however, the applicant is the holder of two such licenses, the annual fee for each additional license thereafter issued to such licensee shall be double the amount hereinabove set forth.

5. The annual fee for a license to sell beer at retail to be consumed on the premises where sold shall be three hundred twenty dollars in cities having a population of one hundred thousand or over, and one hundred sixty dollars elsewhere; provided, however, that where the premises to be licensed remain open only within the period commencing April first and ending October thirty-first of any one year or only within the period commencing October first and ending the following April thirtieth, the liquor authority, in its discretion, may grant a summer or winter license effective only for such appropriate period of time, for which an annual fee of one hundred sixty dollars shall be paid where the premises are located in cities having a population of one hundred thousand or over, and eighty dollars where such premises are located elsewhere.

6. The annual fee for selling beer upon any railroad car to be consumed on such car or any car connected therewith shall be ninety-six dollars for each railroad car licensed.

7. The annual fee for selling beer upon any vessel in this state, other than one regularly and exclusively engaged in the business of carrying passengers for hire, by charter or otherwise, for fishing purposes, to be consumed on such vessel, shall be one hundred sixty dollars for each vessel licensed. The annual fee for selling beer upon a vessel regularly and exclusively engaged in the business of carrying

passengers for hire, by charter or otherwise, for fishing purposes, to be consumed on such vessel, shall be forty dollars for each vessel licensed. The annual fee for selling beer for off-premise consumption upon a vessel regularly and exclusively engaged, as a duly licensed supply ship, in furnishing supplies to other vessels, shall be eighty dollars.

8. The annual fee for selling beer at any baseball park, race track or outdoor athletic field or stadium, to be consumed in any such baseball park, race track, or outdoor athletic field or stadium, shall be one hundred ninety-two dollars.

9. The annual fee for a license to sell beer and wine products at retail not to be consumed on the premises where sold shall be one hundred ninety-eight dollars.

10. The annual fee for a license to sell beer and wine products at retail not to be consumed on the premises where sold, when the applicant is the holder of two such licenses, the annual fee for each additional license thereafter issued to such licensee shall be three hundred fifty-two dollars.

*❷(1993, chgd. by chap. 535; 2002, chgd. by chap. 85(Z), eff. 8/1/2002.)*



**§56-a. Filing fees and refunds.**

1. In addition to the annual fees provided for in this chapter, there shall be paid to the authority with each initial application for a license filed pursuant to section fifty-one, fifty-three, fifty-eight, sixty-one, sixty-two, seventy-six or seventy-eight of this chapter, a filing fee of two hundred dollars with each initial application for a license filed pursuant to section sixty-three, sixty-four, sixty-four-a or sixty-four-b of this chapter, a filing fee of one hundred dollars; with each initial application for a license filed pursuant to section fifty-three-a, fifty-four, fifty-five, fifty-five-a, seventy-nine, eighty-one or eighty-one-a of this chapter, a filing fee of fifty dollars; with each initial application for a permit filed pursuant to section seventy-seven, ninety-one, ninety-one-a, ninety-two, ninety-two-a, ninety-three, ninety-three-a, if such permit is to be issued on a calendar year basis, ninety-four, ninety-five, ninety-six or ninety-six-a, or pursuant to subdivisions b, c, e or j of section ninety-nine-b if such permit is to be issued on a calendar year basis, or for an additional bar pursuant to subdivision four of section one hundred of this chapter, a filing fee of ten dollars; and with each application for a permit under section ninety-three-a, other than a permit to be issued on a calendar year basis, ninety-seven, ninety-eight, ninety-nine, or ninety-nine-b of this chapter, other than a permit to be issued pursuant to subdivisions b, c, e or j of said section ninety-nine-b on a calendar year basis, a filing fee of five dollars.

2. In addition to the annual fees provided for in this chapter, there shall be paid to the authority with each renewal application for a license filed pursuant to section fifty-one, fifty-three, fifty-eight, sixty-one, sixty-two, seventy-six or seventy-eight of this chapter, a filing fee of one hundred dollars; with each renewal application for a license filed pursuant to section sixty-three, sixty-four, sixty-four-a or

sixty-four-b of this chapter, a filing fee of ninety dollars; with each renewal application for a license filed pursuant to section seventy-nine, eighty-one or eighty-one-a of this chapter, a filing fee of twenty-five dollars; and with each renewal application for a license or permit filed pursuant to section fifty-three-a, fifty-four, fifty-five, fifty-five-a, seventy-seven, ninety-one, ninety-one-a, ninety-two, ninety-two-a, ninety-three, ninety-three-a, if such permit is issued on a calendar year basis, ninety-four, ninety-five, ninety-six or ninety-six-a of this chapter or pursuant to subdivisions b, c, e or j of section ninety-nine-b, if such permit is issued on a calendar year basis, or with each renewal application for an additional bar pursuant to subdivision four of section one hundred of this chapter, a filing fee of thirty dollars.

3. If the authority shall deny an application filed pursuant to this chapter it shall return the annual fee to the applicant and retain the filing fee.

**§57. License fees; when due and payable; fee for part of year.**

1. (a) Except as otherwise provided pursuant to section fifty-seven-a, each license issued pursuant to this article other than the one specified in paragraph (b) of this subdivision shall be effective for a license year expiring on the thirtieth day of June following the date of its issuance and the license fee prescribed therefor shall be the license fee due and payable therefor and shall be paid in advance at the time of the application as provided for in this article.

(b) Each license issued pursuant to section fifty-five-a of this article shall be effective for a license year expiring on the thirty-first day of March following the date of its issuance and the license fee prescribed therefor shall be the license fee due and payable therefor and shall be paid in advance of the time of the application as provided for in this article.

2. When application for any license under this article is made after the commencement of the license year hereinbefore provided the license fee therefor shall, for the balance of the license year, be in proportion as the remainder of such year shall bear to the whole year, except that it shall in no case be for less than one-half of such year.

**§57-a. Change in duration of licenses.**

The liquor authority is authorized to change the periods during which the licenses authorized by sections fifty-three-a, fifty-four, fifty-five and fifty-five-a shall be effective and to establish the commencement dates, duration and expiration dates thereof, provided that no such license shall be effective for a period in excess of three years. When any change or changes are made in the duration of any such license, the license fee shall be equal to the annual license fee specified in this article multiplied by the number of years for which such license is issued. The liquor authority may make such rules as shall be appropriate to carry out the purpose of this section.

# Article 4-A
# SPECIAL PROVISIONS RELATING TO CIDER





## ⊕§58. Cider producers' or wholesalers' license.

1. Any person may apply to the liquor authority for a cider producers' or wholesalers' license as provided for in this subdivision. Such application shall be in writing and shall contain such information as the liquor authority shall require. Such application shall be accompanied by a check or draft for the amount required by this subdivision for such license. If the liquor authority shall grant the application it shall issue a license in such form as shall be determined by its rules. A license issued under this subdivision shall authorize the licensee to manufacture cider within the licensed premises in this state for sale in bottles, barrels or casks to beer, wine and liquor retail licensee and/or to sell cider at wholesale from the licensed premises to such licensees and to holders of licenses under this section in bottles, barrels or casks and to sell and deliver cider to persons outside the state pursuant to the laws of the place of such sale or delivery. The annual fee for such a license shall be one hundred twenty-five dollars. The provisions contained in section sixty-seven of this chapter shall apply to all licenses issued pursuant to this article.

2. (a) Any person licensed pursuant to subdivision one of this section may conduct cider tastings of New York state labelled ciders in establishments licensed pursuant to section sixty-three of this chapter to sell alcoholic beverages for off-premises consumption. Such cider producer or wholesaler may charge a fee of not more than twenty-five cents for each cider sample tasted. The liquor authority shall promulgate rules and regulations relating to the conduct of such tastings.

(b) Any person licensed pursuant to subdivision one of this section may conduct cider tastings of New York state labelled ciders and apply to the liquor authority for a permit to sell cider produced by such cider producer or wholesaler, by the bottle, during such tastings in establishments licensed pursuant to section sixty-four of this chapter to sell alcoholic beverages for consumption on the premises. Such cider producer or wholesaler may charge a fee of not more than twenty-five cents for each cider sample tasted. The liquor authority shall promulgate rules and regulations relating to the conduct of tastings.

(c) Cider tastings shall be conducted subject to the following limitations:

(i) cider tastings shall be conducted by an official agent, representative or solicitor of one or more cider producers or wholesalers. Such agent, representative or solicitor shall be physically present at all times during the conduct of the tastings; and

(ii) any liability stemming from a right of action resulting from a cider tasting as authorized pursuant to this subdivision and in accordance with the provisions of sections 11-100 and 11-101 of the general obligations law, shall accrue to the cider producer or wholesaler licensee.

3. Notwithstanding any provision of this chapter to the contrary, a licensed cider producer or wholesaler may apply to the liquor authority for a permit to sell New York state labelled cider by the bottle and conduct cider tastings at the state fair, at recognized county fairs and at farmers markets operated on a not-for-profit basis. As a condition of such permit, an agent, representative or solicitor from the cider producer or wholesaler shall be present at the time of sale or tastings.

❷4. Notwithstanding any provision of this chapter to the contrary, any one or more cider producer or wholesaler licensee, singly or jointly, may apply to the liquor authority for a license or licenses to sell cider at retail for consumption off the premises. The duration of such license shall be coextensive with the duration of such licensee's cider producer or wholesaler license, and the fee therefor shall be six hundred forty dollars if such retail premises is located in cities having a population of one million or more; in cities having less than one million population and more than one hundred thousand, three hundred twenty dollars; and elsewhere, the sum of one hundred sixty dollars. Such license shall entitle the holder thereof to sell at retail for consumption off the premises any New York state labelled cider. Such license shall also entitle the holder thereof to conduct cider tastings on such licensed premises and charge for such tastings. Not more than five such licenses shall be issued to any licensed cider producer or wholesaler. All other provisions of this chapter relative to licenses to sell cider at retail for consumption off the premises shall apply so far as applicable to such application. The liquor authority is hereby authorized to adopt such rules as it may deem necessary to carry out the purpose of this subdivision, provided that all licenses issued pursuant to this subdivision shall be subject to the same rules and regulations as are applicable to the sale of cider at retail for consumption off the premises of the cider producer or wholesaler licensee. ❷*(2002, chgd. by chap. 85(Z), eff. 8/1/2002.)*

❾*(1994, chgd. by chap. 361; 1999, chgd. by chap. 347, eff. 7/27/99.)*

### §58-a. Sale of cider by wholesale beer licensees.

A wholesale beer licensee, as defined under this chapter shall, upon the payment of an additional annual license fee of one hundred twenty-five dollars, be permitted to sell cider as defined under this chapter at wholesale from duly licensed premises, to duly licensed beer, wine and liquor retailers and to other holders of licenses under this chapter, in bottles, barrels or casks, and to sell and deliver cider to persons outside the state pursuant to the laws of the place of such delivery. The provisions of section fifty-seven shall apply to licenses issued hereunder to sell cider at wholesale pursuant to the provisions of this section.

### Φ§58-b. Retail sale of cider by wholesale licensees.

1. Notwithstanding any other law upon payment to the liquor authority of an additional annual fee of one hundred twenty-five dollars, the liquor authority may in its discretion and upon such terms and conditions as it may prescribe, issue to a licensed cider producer upon application therefor a certificate authorizing such producer to sell cider at retail in sealed containers to a householder for consumption in his home, but no sale to such householder shall be in quantities aggregating more than fifteen gallons. Revenues received by any such licensed cider producer from the sale of cider at retail to householders under such a certificate during the term thereof shall not exceed five per centum of all the revenues derived by such licensee from the sale of apples and cider during such term.

2. No retail licensee of cider authorized by this section shall keep or permit to be kept upon the licensed premises, any cider in any unsealed bottle or other unsealed container, except for the purpose of cider tasting or sampling by any person pursuant to authorization to conduct such a sampling or tasting pursuant to subdivision two of section fifty-eight of this article, except to those persons to whom sales are prohibited in section sixty-five of this chapter.

Φ*(1999, chgd. by chap. 347, eff. 7/27/99.)*



### §59. Authorization for sale of cider by retail licensees.

Each retail licensee under this chapter shall have the right, by virtue of his license and without being required to pay any additional fee for the privilege, to sell at retail for consumption on or off the premises, as the case may be, cider purchased from a person licensed to produce or sell cider at wholesale under this chapter.

## Article 5
## SPECIAL PROVISIONS RELATING TO LIQUOR

## §60. Kinds of licenses.

The following kinds of licenses may be issued for the manufacture and sale of liquor, alcohol and spirits, to wit:

1. Distiller's license, class A.

❷1-a. Distiller's license, class A-1. ❷*(2002, added by chap. 580, eff. 12/23/2002.)*

2. Distiller's license, class B.

2-a. Distiller's license, class C.

❻2-b. Distiller's license, class B-1. ❻*(1996, added by chap. 479, eff. 12/6/96.)*

3. Wholesaler's license.

4. License to sell liquor at retail for consumption off the premises.

5. License to sell liquor at retail for consumption on the premises.

6. Special license to sell liquor at retail for consumption on the premises.

## §61. Distiller's licenses.

1. A class A distiller's license shall authorize the holder thereof to operate a distillery for the manufacture of liquors by distillation or redistillation at the premises specifically designated in the license. Such a license shall also authorize the sale in bulk by such licensee from the licensed premises of the products manufactured under such license to any person holding a distiller's class A license, a distiller's class B license or a permittee engaged in the manufacture of products which are unfit for beverage use. It shall also authorize the sale from the licensed premises and from one other location in the state of New York of any liquor whether or not manufactured by such licensee to a wholesale or retail liquor licensee or permittee in sealed containers of not more than one quart each. Such license shall also include the privilege to operate a rectifying plant under the same terms and conditions as the holder of a class B distiller's license without the payment of any additional fee.

❷1-a. A class A-1 distiller's license shall authorize the holder thereof to operate a distillery which has a production capacity of no more than 35,000 gallons per year for the manufacture of liquors by distillation or redistillation at the premises specifically designated in the license. Such a license shall also authorize the sale in bulk by such licensee from the licensed premises of the products manufactured under such license to any person holding a distiller's class A license, a distiller's class B license or a permittee engaged in the manufacture of products which are unfit for beverage use. It shall also authorize the sale from the licensed premises and from one other location in the state of New York of liquors manufactured by such licensee to a wholesale or retail liquor licensee or permittee in sealed containers of not more than one quart each. Such license shall also include the privilege to operate a rectifying plant under the same terms and conditions as the holder of a class B-1 distiller's license without the payment of any additional fee. ❷*(2002, added by chap. 580, eff. 12/23/2002.)*

2. A class B distiller's license shall authorize the holder thereof to operate a rectifying plant for the manufacture of the products of rectification by purifying or combining alcohol, spirits, wine or beer and the manufacture of gin and cordials by the redistillation of alcohol or spirits over or with any materials. Such a license shall also authorize the holder thereof to blend, reduce proof and bottle on his licensed premises or in a United States customs bonded warehouse for which a warehouse permit has been issued under this chapter for wholesale liquor licensees or for persons authorized to sell liquor at wholesale pursuant to the laws and regulation of any other state, territorial possession of the United States or foreign country liquor received in bulk by such wholesalers from other states, territorial possessions of the United States or a foreign country, and to rebottle or recondition for wholesale liquor or wine licensees or for persons authorized to sell liquor or wine at wholesale pursuant to the laws and regulations of any other state, territorial possession of the United States or foreign country, liquor or wine manufactured outside the state, which was purchased and received by such wholesalers in sealed containers not exceeding one quart each of liquor or fifteen gallons each of wine. Such a license shall also authorize the sale from the licensed premises of the products manufactured by such licensee to a wholesale or retail licensee in sealed containers of not more than one quart each.



2-a. A class C distiller's license shall authorize the holder thereof to operate a distillery for the manufacture only of fruit brandy and the sale of such product by such licensee to a wholesale or retail licensee in sealed containers of not more than one quart each. Such a license shall also authorize the sale in bulk of fruit brandy to a winery licensee, to the holder of a class B distiller's license or to a permittee engaged in the manufacture of products which are unfit for beverage use. It shall also authorize the sale from the licensed premises and from one other location in the state of any fruit brandy whether or not manufactured by such licensee to a wholesale or retail liquor licensee or permittee in sealed containers of not more than one quart each.

⑥2-b. A class B-1 distiller's license shall authorize the holder thereof to operate a rectifying plant which has a production capacity of no more than thirty-five thousand gallons per year for the manufacture of the products of rectification by purifying or combining alcohol, spirits, wine, or beer and the manufacture of cordials by the redistillation of alcohol or spirits over or with any materials. Such a license shall also authorize the holder thereof to blend, reduce proof and bottle on his licensed premises or in a United States customs bonded warehouse for which a warehouse permit has been issued under this chapter for wholesale liquor licensees or for persons authorized to sell liquor at wholesale pursuant to the laws and regulation of any other state, territorial possession of the United States or foreign country liquor received in bulk by such wholesalers from other states, territorial possessions of the United States or a foreign country, and to rebottle or recondition for wholesale liquor or wine licensees or for persons authorized to sell liquor or wine at wholesale pursuant to the laws and regulations of any other state, territorial possession of the United States or foreign country, liquor or wine manufactured outside the state, which was purchased and received by such wholesalers in sealed containers not exceeding one quart each of liquor or fifteen gallons each of wine. Such a license shall also authorize the sale from the licensed premises of the products manufactured by such licensee to a wholesale or retail licensee in sealed containers of not more than one quart each. ❻*(1996, added by chap. 479, eff. 12/6/96.)*

3. A distiller's license of any class shall not authorize more than one of said activities, namely, that of a distillery, a rectifying plant or a fruit brandy distillery, and a separate license shall be required for each such activity, except as provided in subdivision one of this section.

❹4. Any person may apply to the liquor authority for a distiller's license as provided for in this section. Such application shall be in writing and verified and shall contain such information as the liquor authority shall require. Such application shall be accompanied by a check or draft for the amount required by this article for such license. If the liquor authority shall grant the application it shall issue a license in such form as shall be determined by its rules. ❹*(1994, chgd. by chap. 361, eff. 7/20/94.)*

5. No distiller shall be engaged in any other business on the licensed premises. No distiller shall sell or agree to sell any liquor, alcohol or spirits to any wholesaler or any retailer who is not duly licensed under this article to sell liquor, alcohol or spirits at wholesale or retail at the time of such agreement and sale or sell or agree to sell any liquor, alcohol or spirits to persons outside the state except pursuant to the laws of the place of such sale or delivery.

**❹§62. Wholesaler's liquor license.**

Any person may apply to the liquor authority for a license to sell liquor at wholesale. Such application shall be in writing and verified and shall contain such information as the liquor authority shall require. Such application shall be accompanied by a check or draft for the amount required by this article for such license. If the liquor authority shall grant the application it shall issue a license in such form as shall be determined by its rules. Such license shall contain a description of the licensed premises and in form and in substance shall be a license to the person therein specifically designated to sell liquors at wholesale in the premises therein specifically licensed to duly licensed wholesalers, retailers and permittees in this state, and to sell liquor in bulk to a licensed rectifier or to a permittee engaged in the manufacture of products which are unfit for beverage use, for use in the manufacture of products produced and sold by such rectifier or permittee, and to sell or deliver liquor to persons outside the state pursuant to the laws of the place of such sale or delivery. Such a license shall also include the privilege to sell wine at wholesale under the same terms and conditions without the payment of any additional fee. ❹*(1994, chgd. by chap. 361, eff. 7/20/94.)*

**§63. License to sell liquor at retail for consumption off the premises.**

❶1. Any person may make an application to the appropriate board for a license to sell liquor at retail not to be consumed upon the premises where sold. Such application shall be in such form and shall contain such information as shall be required by the rules of the liquor authority and shall be accompanied by a check or draft in the amount required by this article for such license. ❶*(1994, chgd. by chap. 361, eff. 7/20/94.)*

2. Section fifty-four shall control so far as is applicable the procedure in connection with such applications.

3. Such license shall in form and in substance be a license to the person specifically designated therein to sell liquor in the premises specifically licensed at retail for off-premise consumption and shall also include the privilege to sell wine under the same terms and conditions without the payment of any additional fee.

❸4. No licensee under this section shall be engaged in any other business on the licensed premises. The sale of lottery tickets, when duly authorized and lawfully conducted, the sale of corkscrews or the sale of ice or the sale of publications, including prerecorded video and/or audio cassette tapes, designed to help educate consumers in their knowledge and appreciation of wine and wine products, as defined in section three of this chapter, or the sale of non-carbonated, non-flavored mineral waters, spring waters and drinking waters or the sale of glasses designed for the consumption of wine, racks designed for the storage of wine, and devices designed to minimize oxidation in bottles of wine which have been uncorked, shall not constitute engaging in another business within the meaning of this subdivision. ❸*(1995, chgd. by chap. 357, 358; 1998, chgd. by chap. 237, eff. 9/1/98.)*

5. Not more than one license shall be granted to any person under this section.

6. Determinations under this section with respect to the issuance of a new license or under section one hundred eleven with respect to the transfer to any other premises of a license issued hereunder, shall be made in accordance with public convenience and advantage.

**❶§63-a. Liquor tasting.**

1. Any person licensed pursuant to section sixty-one or sixty-two of this article may conduct consumer tastings of liquor in establishments licensed under section sixty-three of this article to sell alcoholic beverages for off-premises consumption.

2. All consumer tastings of liquor shall be conducted subject to the following limitations:

(a) tastings of liquor shall be conducted by an official agent of one or more persons licensed pursuant to section sixty-one or sixty-two of this article. Such agent shall be physically present upon the premises at all times during the conducting of the consumer tasting of liquor.

(b) no such person or persons licensed pursuant to section sixty-one or sixty-two of this article, and no official agent thereof, may provide, directly or indirectly: (i) more than a total of three samples of liquor for tasting to a person in one calendar day; or (ii) a sample of liquor for tasting equal to more than one-quarter fluid ounce.

(c) any liability stemming from a right of action resulting from a consumer tasting of liquor authorized by this section and in accordance with the provisions of sections 11-100 and 11-101 of the general obligations law, shall accrue to the persons licensed pursuant to section sixty-one or sixty-two of this article, who conducted such tasting.

3. The state liquor authority shall promulgate rules and regulations regarding liquor tastings as provided for in this section. ❶*(2001, added by chap. 272, eff. 12/4/2001.)*

**§64. License to sell liquor at retail for consumption on the premises.**

1. Notwithstanding the provisions of subdivision two of section seventeen of this chapter, any person may make an application to the appropriate board for a license to sell liquor at retail to be consumed on the premises where sold, and such licenses shall be issued to all applicants except for good cause shown.

❹2. Such application shall be in such form and shall contain such information as shall be required by the rules of the liquor authority and shall be accompanied by a check or draft in the amount required by this article for such license. ❹*(1994, chgd. by chap. 361, eff. 7/20/94.)*

❺2-a. Notwithstanding any other provision of this chapter, upon receipt of an application for a license under this section, an application for renewal under section one hundred nine of this chapter, or an application for an alteration to a premises licensed for consumption on the premises under section ninety-nine-d of this chapter, the applicant shall notify the clerk of the village, town or city, as the case may be, by certified mail, return receipt requested, wherein the prospective licensed premises is to be located or, in the case of an application for renewal, or alteration where it is presently located not less than thirty days prior to the submission of its application for a license under this section or for a renewal thereof pursuant to section one hundred nine of this chapter. For the purposes of the preceding sentence notification need only be given to the clerk of a village when such premises is to be located within the boundaries of the village. In the city of New York, the community board established pursuant to section twenty-eight hundred of the New York city charter with jurisdiction over the area in which such licensed premises is to be located shall be considered the appropriate public body to which notification shall be given. Such municipality or community board, as the case may be, may express an opinion for or against the granting of such license. Any such opinion shall be deemed part of the record upon which the liquor board makes its determination to grant or deny such license. ❺*(1995, chgd. by chap. 83, eff. 6/20/95.)*

3. Section fifty-four shall control so far as applicable the procedure in connection with such application.

4. Such license shall in form and in substance be a license to the person specifically licensed to sell liquors at retail, to be consumed upon the premises. Such license shall also be deemed to include a license to sell wine and beer at retail to be consumed under the same terms and conditions, without the payment of any additional fee.

5. No retail license under this section shall be granted except for such premises as are being conducted as a bona fide hotel provided that a restaurant is operated in such premises, restaurant, catering establishment, club, railroad car, vessel or aircraft being operated on regularly scheduled flights by a United States certificated airline.

6. Where an on-premise license shall be granted to the owner of a hotel situated in a town or village the liquor authority may in its discretion grant to such owner the right to sell liquor and wine for off-premise consumption under the same terms and conditions as apply to off-premise licenses upon the payment of an additional fee of sixty-two dollars and fifty cents; provided, however, that this permission shall not be granted if an off-premise license has been granted for premises located within eight miles of such hotel.



6-a. The authority may consider any or all of the following in determining whether public convenience and advantage and the public interest will be promoted by the granting of licenses and permits for the sale of alcoholic beverages at a particular unlicensed location:

(a) The number, classes and character of licenses in proximity to the location and in the particular municipality or subdivision thereof.

(b) Evidence that all necessary licenses and permits have been obtained from the state and all other governing bodies.

(c) Effect of the grant of the license on vehicular traffic and parking in proximity to the location.

(d) The existing noise level at the location and any increase in noise level that would be generated by the proposed premises.

(e) The history of liquor violations and reported criminal activity at the proposed premises.

(f) Any other factors specified by law or regulation that are relevant to determine the public convenience and advantage and public interest of the community.

*(1993, added by chap. 670, eff. 9/3/93.)*

❻7. No retail license for on-premises consumption shall be granted for any premises which shall be

(a) on the same street or avenue and within two hundred feet of a building occupied exclusively as a school, church, synagogue or other place of worship or

(b) in a city, town or village having a population of twenty thousand or more within five hundred feet of three or more existing premises licensed and operating pursuant to the provisions of this section;

(c) the measurements in paragraphs (a) and (b) of this subdivision are to be taken in straight lines from the center of the nearest entrance of the premises sought to be licensed to the center of the nearest entrance of such school, church, synagogue or other place of worship or to the center of the nearest entrance of each such premises licensed and operating pursuant to the provisions of this section; except, however, that no renewal license shall be denied because of such restriction to any premises so located which were maintained as a bona fide hotel, restaurant, catering establishment or club on or prior to December fifth, nineteen hundred thirty-three; and, except that no license shall be denied to any premises at which a license under this chapter has been in existence continuously from a date prior to the date when a building on the same street or avenue and within two hundred feet of said premises has been occupied exclusively as a school, church, synagogue or other place of worship; and except that no license shall be denied to any premises, which is within five hundred feet of three or more existing premises licensed and operating pursuant to the provisions of this section, at which a license under this chapter has been in existence continuously on or prior to November first, nineteen hundred ninety-three; and except that this subdivision shall not be deemed to restrict the issuance of a hotel liquor license to a building used as a hotel and in which a restaurant liquor license currently exists for premises which serve as a dining room for guests of the hotel and a caterer's license to a person using the permanent catering facilities of a church, synagogue or other place of worship pursuant to a written agreement between such person and the authorities in charge of such facilities. The liquor authority, in its discretion, may authorize the removal of any such licensed premises to a different location on the same street or avenue, within two hundred feet of said school, church, synagogue or other place of worship, provided that such new location is not within a closer distance to such school, church, synagogue or other place of worship.

(d) Within the context of this subdivision, the word "entrance" shall mean a door of a school, of a house of worship, or premises licensed and operating pursuant to the provisions of this section or of the premises sought to be licensed, regularly used to give ingress to students of the school, to the general public attending the place of worship, and to patrons or guests of the premises licensed and operating pursuant to the provisions of this section or of the premises sought to be licensed, except that where a school or house of worship or premises licensed and operating pursuant to the provisions of this section is set back from a public thoroughfare, the walkway or stairs leading to any such door shall be deemed an entrance; and the measurement shall be taken to the center of the walkway or stairs at the point where it meets the building line or public thoroughfare. A door which has no exterior hardware, or which is used solely as an emergency or fire exit, or for maintenance purposes, or which leads directly to a part of a building not regularly used by the general public or patrons, is not deemed an "entrance".

(e) Notwithstanding the provisions of this chapter to the contrary, the authority may issue a license to sell liquor at retail to be consumed on premises to a club as such term is defined in subdivision nine of

Printed in the U.S.A. ab

section three of this chapter whether or not the building in which the premises for which such license is to be issued is used exclusively for club purposes and whether or not such premises is within two hundred feet of a building used exclusively as a school, church, synagogue or place of worship if such club is affiliated or associated with such school, church, synagogue or place of worship and the governing body of such school, church, synagogue or other place of worship has filed written notice with the authority that it has no objection to the issuance of such license.

❾(f) Notwithstanding the provisions of paragraph (b) of this subdivision, the authority may issue a retail license for on-premises consumption for a premises which shall be within five hundred feet of three or more existing premises licensed and operating pursuant to the provisions of this section if, after consultation with the municipality or community board, it determines that granting such license would be in the public interest. Before it may issue any such license, the authority shall conduct a hearing, upon notice to the applicant and the municipality or community board, and shall state and file in its office its reasons therefor. Notice to the municipality or community board shall mean written notice mailed by the authority to such municipality or community board at least fifteen days in advance of any hearing scheduled pursuant to this paragraph. Upon the request of the authority, any municipality or community board may waive the fifteen day notice requirement. No premises having been granted a license pursuant to this section shall be denied a renewal of such license upon the grounds that such premises are within five hundred feet of a building or buildings wherein three or more premises are operating and licensed pursuant to this section. ❾*(1999, chgd. by chap. 602, eff. 1/1/2000.)*

❻*(1993, chgd. by chaps. 183, 720; 1996, chgd. by chap. 177, eff. 6/18/96.)*

8. A license issued for such premises as are being conducted as a catering establishment shall authorize the holder thereof to sell alcoholic beverages at retail during such period of time as a function, occasion or event is in progress therein and then only to persons invited to and attending such function, occasion or event and only for consumption on the premises where sold.

9. A retail license under this section may be granted for a premises being conducted as a restaurant and located in the area leased by the city of New York to the New York World's Fair 1964-1965 pursuant to the provisions of chapter four hundred twenty-eight of the laws of nineteen hundred sixty as amended by chapter nine hundred nine of the laws of nineteen hundred sixty-one during the term or duration of such lease, notwithstanding the fact that said premises is not open to the general public as required by this chapter provided that such premises has been designated as an authorized facility of the New York World's Fair 1964-1965 Corporation and has been certified to the liquor authority by said corporation as such.

**§64-a. Special license to sell liquor at retail for consumption on the premises.**

1. On or before September first, nineteen hundred sixty-nine, any license issued under section sixty-four of this article may be converted into a special on-premises license under this section upon the granting of a request for conversion filed with the liquor authority by the holder of said license. Such a request shall be granted by the authority except for good cause shown. The granting of such a request shall constitute conversion of said license into a special on-premises license subject to the provisions of this chapter applicable to special on-premises licenses issued under this section.

2. On or after October first, nineteen hundred sixty-four, any person may make an application to the appropriate board for a special license to sell liquor at retail to be consumed on the premises where sold.

❹3. Such application shall be in such form and shall contain such information as shall be required by the rules of the liquor authority and shall be accompanied by a check or draft in the amount required by this article for such license. ❹*(1994, chgd. by chap. 361, eff. 7/20/94.)*

4. Section fifty-four shall control so far as applicable the procedure in connection with such application.

5. Such special license shall in form and in substance be a license to the person specifically licensed to sell liquor at retail to be consumed on the premises specifically licensed. Such license shall also be deemed to include a license to sell wine and beer at retail to be consumed under the same terms and conditions, without the payment of any additional fee.

6. No special on-premises license shall be granted except for premises in which the principal business shall be (a) the sale of food or beverages at retail for consumption on the premises or (b) the operation of a legitimate theatre or such other lawful adult entertainment or recreational facility as the liquor authority, giving due regard to the convenience of the public and the strict avoidance of sales prohibited by this chapter, shall by regulation classify for eligibility. Nothing contained in this subdivision shall be deemed to authorize the issuance of a license to a motion picture theatre.

❻7. (a) No special on-premises license shall be granted for any premises which shall be

(i) on the same street or avenue and within two hundred feet of a building occupied exclusively as a school, church, synagogue or other place of worship or

(ii) in a city, town or village having a population of twenty thousand or more within five hundred feet of three or more existing premises licensed and operating pursuant to the provisions of this section;

(iii) the measurements in subparagraphs (i) and (ii) of this paragraph are to be taken in straight lines from the center of the nearest entrance of the premises sought to be licensed to the center of the nearest entrance of such school, church, synagogue or other place of

Printed in the U.S.A. ab

worship or to the center of the nearest entrance of each such premises licensed and operating pursuant to the provisions of this section; except that no license shall be denied to any premises at which a license under this chapter has been in existence continuously from a date prior to the date when a building on the same street or avenue and within two hundred feet of said premises has been occupied exclusively as a school, church, synagogue or other place of worship and except that no license shall be denied to any premises, which is within five hundred feet of three or more existing premises licensed and operating pursuant to the provisions of this section, at which a license under this chapter has been in existence continuously on or prior to November first, nineteen hundred ninety-three.

(b) Within the context of this subdivision, the word "entrance" shall mean a door of a school, of a house of worship, or premises licensed and operating pursuant to the provisions of this section or of the premises sought to be licensed, regularly used to give ingress to students of the school, to the general public attending the place of worship, and to patrons or guests of the premises licensed and operating pursuant to the provisions of this section or of the premises sought to be licensed, except that where a school or house of worship or premises licensed and operating pursuant to the provisions of this section is set back from a public thoroughfare, the walkway or stairs leading to any such door shall be deemed an entrance; and the measurement shall be taken to the center of the walkway or stairs at the point where it meets the building line or public thoroughfare. A door which has no exterior hardware, or which is used solely as an emergency or fire exit, or for maintenance purposes, or which leads directly to a part of a building not regularly used by the general public or patrons, is not deemed an "entrance".

(c) Notwithstanding paragraph (a) of this subdivision, a special on-premises license for a premises in which the principal business shall be the operation of a legitimate theater by a corporation organized pursuant to the not-for-profit corporation law may be granted notwithstanding the proximity of such premises to any school, provided that the availability of alcoholic beverages on such premises shall not be advertised in any way at such premises in any manner visible from such street or avenue.

(d) Notwithstanding the provisions of subparagraph (ii) of paragraph (a) of this subdivision, the authority may issue a retail license for on-premises consumption for a premises which shall be within five hundred feet of three or more existing premises licensed and operating pursuant to the provisions of this section if, after consultation with the municipality or community board, it determines that granting such license would be in the public interest. Before it may issue any such license, the authority shall conduct a hearing, upon notice to the applicant and the municipality or community board, and shall state and file in its office its reasons therefor. No premises having been granted a license pursuant to this section shall be denied a renewal of

such license upon the grounds that such premises are within five hundred feet of a building or buildings wherein three or more premises are operating and licensed pursuant to this section.
❻*(1993, chgd. by chaps. 183, 720; 1996, chgd. by chap. 177, eff. 6/18/96.)*

8. Every special on-premises licensee shall regularly keep food available for sale to its customers for consumption on the premises. The availability of sandwiches, soups or other foods, whether fresh, processed, pre-cooked or frozen, shall be deemed compliance with this requirement. The licensed premises shall comply at all times with all the regulations of the local department of health. Nothing contained in this subdivision, however, shall be construed to require that any food be sold or purchased with any liquor, nor shall any rule, regulation or standard be promulgated or enforced requiring that the sale of food be substantial or that the receipts of the business other than from the sale of liquor equal any set percentage of total receipts from sales made therein.

9. The liquor authority may make such rules as it deems necessary to carry out the provisions of this section.



**§64-b. License to sell liquor on premises commonly known as a bottle club.**

1. It shall be unlawful for any person, partnership or corporation operating a place for profit or pecuniary gain, with a capacity for the assemblage of twenty or more persons to permit a person or persons to come to the place of assembly for the purpose of consuming alcoholic beverages on said premises, which alcoholic beverages are either provided by the operator of the place of assembly, his agents, servants or employees, or are brought onto said premises by the person or persons assembling at such place, unless an appropriate license has first been obtained from the state liquor authority by the operator of said place of assembly. Nothing in this section shall be construed as affecting the definition of place of assembly in this chapter or any other law. Nothing contained herein shall prohibit or restrict the leasing or use of such place of assemblage as defined herein by any organization or club enumerated in subdivision seven hereof.

2. Upon or after the effective date hereof any person may make an application to the appropriate board for a special license to operate a bottle club.

❹3. Such application shall be in such form and shall contain such information as shall be required by the rules of the liquor authority and shall be accompanied by a check or draft in the amount required by this article for such license. ❹*(1994, chgd. by chap. 361, eff. 7/20/94.)*

4. Section fifty-four of this chapter shall control so far as applicable the procedure in connection with such application.

5. No bottle club license shall be granted for any premises which shall be on the same street or avenue and within two hundred feet of a building occupied exclusively as a school, church, synagogue or other

place of worship; the measurements to be taken in a straight line from the center of the nearest entrance of such school, church, synagogue or other place of worship to the center of the nearest entrance of the premises to be licensed; except that no license shall be denied to any premises at which a license under this chapter has been in existence continuously from a date prior to the date when a building on the same street or avenue and within two hundred feet of said premises has been occupied exclusively as a school, church, synagogue or other place of worship.

6. The liquor authority may make such rules as it deems necessary to carry out the provisions of this section.

7. This section shall not apply to any non-profit religious, charitable, or fraternal organization nor to a club as defined in section three, subdivision nine of this chapter, nor to a duly recognized political club, except that it shall be unlawful for any of the above to permit consumption of alcoholic beverages during the hours prohibited by or pursuant to section one hundred six of the alcoholic beverage control law.



**❼§64-c. License to manufacture and sell alcoholic beverages in a premises commonly known as a restaurant-brewer.**

1. Any person may make an application to the state liquor authority for a license to operate a restaurant-brewer.

2. Such application shall be in such form and shall contain such information as shall be required by the liquor authority and shall be accompanied by a check or draft in the amount required by this section for such license.

3. Upon receipt of an original or a renewal application for a license under this section, the applicant shall notify the clerk of the village, town or city, as the case may be, by certified mail, return receipt requested, wherein the prospective licensed premises is to be located or, in the case of an application for renewal, where it is presently located not less than thirty days prior to the submission of its application for a license under this section or for a renewal thereof. For the purposes of the preceding sentence notification need only be given to the clerk of a village when such premises is to be located within the boundaries of the village. In the city of New York, the community board established pursuant to section twenty-eight hundred of the New York city charter with jurisdiction over the area in which such licensed premises is to be located shall be considered the appropriate public body to which notification shall be given. Such municipality or community board, as the case may be, may express an opinion for or against the granting of such license. Any such opinion shall be deemed part of the record upon which the liquor authority makes its determination to grant or deny such license.

4. Section fifty-four of this chapter shall control so far as applicable the procedure in connection with such application.

5. Such restaurant-brewer license shall in form and in substance be a license to the person specifically licensed to operate a restaurant and sell liquor at retail to be consumed on the premises specifically licensed. Such license shall also be deemed to include a license to sell wine and beer at retail to be consumed under the same terms and conditions, without the payment of any additional fee.

6. A license under this section may only be granted to a person who regularly and in a bona fide manner brews beer on the premises.

7. Not more than five licenses shall be granted to any person under this section.

8. Not more than five thousand barrels of beer per year may be brewed on any premises licensed under this section nor may any person who holds multiple licenses under this section brew, in the aggregate, more than twenty thousand barrels of beer per year.

9. On or within thirty days of the effective date of this section, any person who holds a brewer's license under section fifty-one of this chapter as well as a license to sell beer, wine and liquor at retail for consumption on the premises may file an application with the liquor authority to convert those licenses into a license under this section. Such an application shall be granted by the authority except for good cause shown. The granting of such an application shall constitute conversion of said license into a restaurant-brewer license subject to the provisions of this chapter applicable to restaurant-brewers licenses issued under this section.

10. Except as provided in subdivisions seven, eight, nine, twelve, thirteen, fourteen and sixteen of this section, no person licensed under this section may be interested directly or indirectly in any other premises in this state where alcoholic beverages are manufactured or sold. Any person who has an interest in premises eligible for conversion under subdivision nine of this section shall not be issued any license under this section unless and until a conversion application has been filed with and approved by the authority.

11. (a) No restaurant-brewer license shall be granted for any premises which shall be:

(i) on the same street or avenue and within two hundred feet of a building occupied exclusively as a school, church, synagogue or other place of worship; or

(ii) in a city, town or village having a population of twenty thousand or more within five hundred feet of three or more existing premises licensed and operating pursuant to the provisions of this section or section sixty-four or sixty-four-a of this article; or

(iii) the measurements in subparagraphs (i) and (ii) of this paragraph are to be taken in straight lines from the center of the nearest entrance of the premises sought to be licensed to the center of the nearest entrance of such school, church, synagogue or other place of worship or to the center of the nearest entrance of each such premises licensed and operating pursuant to the provisions of this section; except that no license shall be denied to any premises at which a license

Printed in the U.S.A. ab

under this chapter has been in existence continuously from a date prior to the date when a building on the same street or avenue and within two hundred feet of said premises has been occupied exclusively as a school, church, synagogue or other place of worship and except that no license shall be denied to any premises, which is within five hundred feet of three or more existing premises licensed and operating pursuant to the provisions of this section or section sixty-four or sixty-four-a of this article, at which a license under this chapter has been in existence continuously on or prior to November first, nineteen hundred ninety-three.

(b) Within the context of this subdivision, the word "entrance" shall mean a door of a school, of a house of worship, or premises licensed and operating pursuant to the provisions of this section or of the premises sought to be licensed, regularly used to give ingress to students of the school, to the general public attending the place of worship, and to patrons or guests of the premises licensed and operating pursuant to the provisions of this section or of the premises sought to be licensed, except that where a school or house of worship or premises licensed and operating pursuant to the provisions of this section is set back from a public thoroughfare, the walkway or stairs leading to any such door shall be deemed an entrance; and the measurement shall be taken to the center of the walkway or stairs at the point where it meets the building line or public thoroughfare. A door which has no exterior hardware, or which is used solely as an emergency or fire exit, or for maintenance purposes, or which leads directly to a part of a building not regularly used by the general public or patrons, is not deemed an "entrance".

(c) Notwithstanding the provisions of subparagraph (ii) of paragraph (a) of this subdivision, the authority may issue a license pursuant to this section which shall be within five hundred feet of three or more existing premises licensed and operating pursuant to the provisions of this section or section sixty-four or sixty-four-a of this article if, after consultation with the municipality or community board, it determines that granting such license would be in the public interest. Before it may issue any such license, the authority shall conduct a hearing, upon notice to the applicant and the municipality or community board, and shall state and file in its office its reasons therefor. No premises having been granted a license pursuant to this section shall be denied a renewal of such license upon the grounds that such premises are within five hundred feet of a building or buildings where three or more premises are operating and licensed pursuant to this section or section sixty-four or sixty-four-a of this article.

12. The liquor authority may in its discretion and upon such terms and conditions as it may prescribe, issue to a licensed restaurant-brewer upon his application therefor a supplemental license authorizing the restaurant-brewer to sell beer brewed on the licensed premises at retail to a person for consumption in his home, at retail in

bulk by the keg, cask or barrel for consumption and not for resale at a clambake, barbecue, picnic, outing or other similar outdoor gathering at which more than fifty persons are assembled and at wholesale. Such additional license shall permit the sale of up to two hundred fifty barrels of beer per year. No person, who holds multiple licenses under this section and applies for and receives multiple supplemental licenses, may sell, under those supplemental licenses, in the aggregate more than one thousand barrels of beer per year.

13. For the exercise of the privilege granted by such supplemental license issued under subdivision twelve of this section there is assessed a fee to be paid by the licensee in the sum of eleven hundred twenty-five dollars per three-year period plus a one hundred dollar filing fee and which fee shall be in addition to the fee provided for in this section for a restaurant-brewer license.

14. An application for a supplemental license under subdivision thirteen of this section shall be in such form and shall contain such information as shall be required by the liquor authority and shall be accompanied by a check or draft in the amount required by subdivision thirteen of this section.

15. The fee for an original and a renewal restaurant-brewer license shall be fifty-eight hundred fifty dollars in the counties of New York, Kings, Bronx and Queens; forty-three hundred fifty dollars in the county of Richmond and in cities having a population of more than one hundred thousand and less than one million; thirty-six hundred dollars in cities having a population of more than fifty thousand and less than one hundred thousand; and the sum of twenty-eight hundred fifty dollars elsewhere. Said license shall run for a period of three years. In addition to the license fees provided for in this subdivision, there shall be paid to the authority with each initial application a filing fee of two hundred dollars and with each renewal application a filing fee of one hundred dollars.

16. A restaurant-brewer license issued under this section and a supplemental license issued under this section shall run concurrently.
❼*(1997, added by chap. 538, eff. 9/3/97.)*

**❾§64-d. License to sell liquor on premises commonly known as a cabaret.**

1. Any person may make an application to the state liquor authority to operate a cabaret.

2. Such application shall be in such form and shall contain such information as shall be required by the liquor authority and shall be accompanied by a check or draft in the amount required by this article for such license.

3. Upon receipt of an original or a renewal application for a license under this section, the applicant shall notify the clerk of the village, town or city, as the case may be, by certified mail, return receipt requested, wherein the prospective licensed premises is to be located or, in the case of an application for renewal, where it is presently located,

not less than thirty days prior to the submission of its application for a license under this section or for a renewal thereof. For the purposes of the preceding sentence notification need only be given to the clerk of a village when such premises is to be located within the boundaries of the village. In the city of New York, the community board established pursuant to section twenty-eight hundred of the New York city charter with jurisdiction over the area in which such licensed premises is to be located shall be considered the appropriate public body to which notification shall be given. Such municipality or community board, as the case may be, may express an opinion for or against the granting of such license. Any such opinion shall be deemed part of the record upon which the liquor authority makes its determination to grant or deny such license.

4. Section fifty-four of this chapter shall control so far as applicable the procedure in connection with such application.

5. Such cabaret license shall in form and in substance be a license to the person specifically licensed to operate a cabaret and sell liquor at retail to be consumed on the premises specifically licensed. Such license shall also be deemed to include a license to sell wine and beer at retail to be consumed under the same terms and conditions, without the payment of any additional fee.

◆6. A license under this section shall be required of any licensee upon whose premises musical entertainment, singing, dancing or other forms of entertainment is permitted; provided, however, that this section shall only apply to licensees whose premises have a capacity for the assemblage of six hundred or more persons. Nothing contained in this subdivision shall be construed as requiring a license under this section by an establishment licensed under section sixty-four or paragraph (b) of subdivision six of section sixty-four-a of this article. ◆*(2000, chgd. by chap. 114, eff. 9/9/2000.)*

7. The authority shall consider all of the following in determining whether public convenience and advantage and the public interest will be promoted by the granting of a license pursuant to this section:

(a) the number, classes and character of licenses in proximity to the location and in the particular municipality or subdivision thereof;

(b) evidence that applicants have secured all necessary licenses and permits from the state and all other governing bodies;

(c) the effect that the granting of the license will have on vehicular traffic and parking in the proximity of the location;

(d) the existing noise level at the location and any increase in noise level that would be generated by the proposed premises;

(e) the history of liquor violations and reported criminal activity at the proposed premises; and

(f) any other factors specified by law or regulation that are relevant to determine the public convenience or advantage and necessary to find that the granting of such license shall be in the public interest.

8. No cabaret license shall be granted for any premises which shall be:

(a) on the same street or avenue and within two hundred feet of a building occupied exclusively as a school, church, synagogue or other place of worship or

(b) in a city, town or village having a population of twenty thousand or more within five hundred feet of an existing premises licensed and operating pursuant to the provisions of this section, or within five hundred feet of three or more existing premises licensed and operating pursuant to sections sixty-four and sixty-four-c of this article.

The measurements in paragraphs (a) and (b) of this subdivision shall be taken in accordance with the provisions of subdivision seven of section sixty-four of this article.

9. On or within ninety days of the effective date of this section, any person who holds a license under section sixty-four of this article to sell beer, wine and liquor at retail for consumption on the premises and who operates pursuant to the provisions of subdivision six of this section shall file an application with the liquor authority to convert such license into a license under this section. Such an application shall be granted by the authority except for good cause shown. The granting of such an application shall constitute conversion of said license into a cabaret license subject to the provisions of this chapter applicable to cabaret licenses issued under this section; provided, however, that no licensee applying for such conversion shall be denied on the grounds that such application fails to meet the requirements of subdivision eight of this section.

10. All other provisions of this chapter relative to licenses to sell liquor at retail for consumption on the premises shall apply as far as applicable.

⑨*(1999, added by chap. 602, eff. 1/1/2000.)*

**§65. Prohibited sales.**

No person shall sell, deliver or give away or cause or permit or procure to be sold, delivered or given away any alcoholic beverages to

1. Any person, actually or apparently, under the age of twenty-one years;

2. Any visibly intoxicated person;

3. Any habitual drunkard known to be such to the person authorized to dispense any alcoholic beverages.

❷4. Neither such person so refusing to sell or deliver under this section nor his employer shall be liable in any civil or criminal action or for any fine or penalty based upon such refusal, except that such sale or delivery shall not be refused, withheld from or denied to any person on account of race, creed, color or national origin. In any proceeding pursuant to subdivision one of this section, it shall be an affirmative defense that such person had produced a photographic identification card apparently issued by a governmental entity and that the alcoholic beverage had been sold, delivered or given to such person in reasonable reliance upon such identification. In evaluating the applicability of such affirmative defense, the authority shall take into consideration any written policy adopted and implemented by the seller to carry out the provision of paragraph (b) of subdivision [one] *two* of section sixty-five-b of this article. ❷*(1999, chgd. by chap. 519; 2002, chgd. by chap. 503, eff. on and after 1/1/2002, expires and deemed repealed 1/1/2004. Matter in italics expires and deemed repealed 1/1/2004. Matter in brackets eff. 1/1/2004.)*

5. The provisions of subdivision one of this section shall not apply to a person who gives or causes to be given any such alcoholic beverage to a person under the age of twenty-one years, who is a student in a curriculum licensed or registered by the state education department and is required to taste or imbibe alcoholic beverages in courses which are part of the required curriculum, provided such alcoholic beverages are used only for instructional purposes during classes conducted pursuant to such curriculum.



❶6. In any proceeding pursuant to section one hundred eighteen of this chapter to revoke, cancel or suspend a license to sell alcoholic beverages at retail, in which proceeding it is alleged that a person violated subdivision one of this section, it shall be an affirmative defense that at the time of such violation such person who committed such alleged violation held a valid certificate of completion or renewal from an entity authorized to give and administer an alcohol training awareness program pursuant to subdivision twelve of section seventeen of this chapter. Such licensee shall have diligently implemented and complied with all of the provisions of the approved training program. In such proceeding to revoke, cancel or suspend a license pursuant to section one hundred eighteen of this chapter, the licensee must prove each element of such affirmative defense by a preponderance of the credible evidence. Evidence of three unlawful sales of alcoholic beverages by any employee of a licensee to persons under twenty-one years of age, within a two year period, shall be considered by the authority in determining whether the licensee had diligently implemented such an approved program. Such affirmative defense shall not preclude the recovery of the penal sum of a bond as provided in sections one hundred twelve and one hundred eighteen of this chapter. ❶*(1998, added by chap. 383; chgd. by chap. 652; 1999, chgd. by chap. 481(1), (3); 2001, chgd. by chap. 549, eff. 12/12/2001.)*

## §65-a. Procuring alcoholic beverages for persons under the age of twenty-one years.

Any person who misrepresents the age of a person under the age of twenty-one years for the purpose of inducing the sale of any alcoholic beverage, as defined in the alcoholic beverage control law, to such person, is guilty of an offense and upon conviction thereof shall be punished by a fine of not more than two hundred dollars, or by imprisonment for not more than five days, or by both such fine and imprisonment.

**§65-b. Offense for one under age of twenty-one years to purchase or attempt to purchase an alcoholic beverage through fraudulent means.**

1. As used in this section: (a) "A device capable of deciphering any electronically readable format" or "device" shall mean any commercial device or combination of devices used at a point of sale or entry that is capable of reading the information encoded on the magnetic strip or bar code of a driver's license or non-driver identification card issued by the commissioner of motor vehicles;

(b) "Card holder" means any person presenting a driver's license or non-driver identification card to a licensee, or to the agent or employee of such licensee under this chapter; and

(c) "Transaction scan" means the process involving a device capable of deciphering any electronically readable format by which a licensee, or agent or employee of a licensee under this chapter reviews a driver's license or non-driver identification card presented as a precondition for the purchase of an alcoholic beverage as required by subdivision two of this section or as a precondition for admission to an establishment licensed for the on-premises sale of alcoholic beverages where admission is restricted to persons twenty-one years or older.

2. (a) No person under the age of twenty-one years shall present or offer to any licensee under this chapter, or to the agent or employee of such licensee, any written evidence of age which is false, fraudulent or not actually his own, for the purpose of purchasing or attempting to purchase any alcoholic beverage.

(b) No licensee, or agent or employee of such licensee shall accept as written evidence of age by any such person for the purchase of any alcoholic beverage, any documentation other than: (i) a valid driver's license or non-driver identification card issued by the commissioner of motor vehicles, the federal government, any United States territory, commonwealth or possession, the District of Columbia, a state government within the United States or a provincial government of the dominion of Canada, or (ii) a valid passport issued by the United States government or any other country, or (iii) an identification card issued by the armed forces of the United States. Upon the presentation of such driver's license or non-driver identification card issued by a governmental entity, such licensee or agent or employee thereof may perform a transaction scan as a precondition to the sale of any alcoholic beverage. Nothing in this section shall prohibit a licensee or agent or employee from performing such a transaction scan on any of the other documents listed in this subdivision if such documents include a bar code or magnetic strip that that* may be scanned by a device capable of deciphering any electronically readable format.

**So in original. Probably the second "that" should be deleted.*

(c) In instances where the information deciphered by the transaction scan fails to match the information printed on the driver's license or non-driver identification card presented by the card holder, or if the transaction scan indicates that the information is false or fraudulent, the attempted purchase of the alcoholic beverage shall be denied.

3. A person violating the provisions of paragraph (a) of subdivision two of this section shall be guilty of a violation and shall be sentenced in accordance with the following:

(a) For a first violation, the court shall order payment of a fine of not more than one hundred dollars and/or an appropriate amount of community service not to exceed thirty hours. In addition, the court may order completion of an alcohol awareness program established pursuant to section 19.25 of the mental hygiene law.

(b) For a second violation, the court shall order payment of a fine of not less than fifty dollars nor more than three hundred fifty dollars and/or an appropriate amount of community service not to exceed thirty hours. The court also shall order completion of an alcohol awareness program as referenced in paragraph (a) of this subdivision if such program has not previously been completed by the offender, unless the court determines that attendance at such program is not feasible due to the lack of availability of such program within a reasonably close proximity to the locality in which the offender resides or matriculates, as appropriate.

(c) For third and subsequent violations, the court shall order payment of a fine of not less than fifty dollars nor more than seven hundred fifty dollars and/or an appropriate amount of community service not to exceed thirty hours. The court also shall order that such person submit to an evaluation by an appropriate agency certified or licensed by the office of alcoholism and substance abuse services to determine whether the person suffers from the disease of alcoholism or alcohol abuse, unless the court determines that under the circumstances presented such an evaluation is not necessary, in which case the court shall state on the record the basis for such determination. Payment for such evaluation shall be made by such person. If, based on such evaluation, a need for treatment is indicated, such person may choose to participate in a treatment plan developed by an agency certified or licensed by the office of alcoholism and substance abuse services. If such person elects to participate in recommended treatment, the court shall order that payment of such fine and community service be suspended pending the completion of such treatment.

(d) Evaluation procedures. For purposes of this subdivision, the following shall apply:

(i) The contents of an evaluation pursuant to paragraph (c) of this subdivision shall be used for the sole purpose of determining if such person suffers from the disease of alcoholism or alcohol abuse.

(ii) The agency designated by the court to perform such evaluation shall conduct the evaluation and return the results to the court within thirty days, subject to any state or federal confidentiality law, rule or regulation governing the confidentiality of alcohol and substance abuse treatment records.

(iii) The office of alcoholism and substance abuse services shall make available to each supreme court law library in this state, or, if no supreme court law library is available in a certain county, to the county court law library of such county, a list of agencies certified to perform evaluations as required by subdivision (f) of section 19.07 of the mental hygiene law.

(iv) All evaluations required under this subdivision shall be in writing and the person so evaluated or his or her counsel shall receive a copy of such evaluation prior to its use by the court.

(v) A minor evaluated under this subdivision shall have, and shall be informed by the court of, the right to obtain a second opinion regarding his or her need for alcoholism treatment.

4. A person violating the provisions of paragraph (b) of subdivision two of this section shall be guilty of a violation punishable by a fine of not more than one hundred dollars, and/or an appropriate amount of community service not to exceed thirty hours. In addition, the court may order completion of an alcohol training awareness program established pursuant to subdivision twelve of section seventeen of this chapter where such program is located within a reasonably close proximity to the locality in which the offender is employed or resides.

5. No determination of guilt pursuant to this section shall operate as a disqualification of any such person subsequently to hold public office, public employment, or as a forfeiture of any right or privilege or to receive any license granted by public authority; and no such person shall be denominated a criminal by reason of such determination.

6. ❖In addition to the penalties otherwise provided in subdivision three of this section, if a determination is made sustaining a charge of illegally purchasing or attempting to illegally purchase an alcoholic beverage, the court may suspend such person's license to drive a motor vehicle and the privilege of an unlicensed person of obtaining such license, in accordance with the following and for the following periods, if it is found that a driver's license was used for the purpose of such illegal purchase or attempt to illegally purchase; provided, however, that where a person is sentenced pursuant to paragraph (b) or (c) of subdivision three of this section, the court shall impose such license suspension if it is found that a driver's license was used for the purpose of such illegal purchase or attempt to illegally purchase: ❖*(2000, chgd. by chap. 503, eff. 9/1/2001.)*

(a) For a first violation of paragraph (a) of subdivision two of this section, a three month suspension.

(b) For a second violation of paragraph (a) of subdivision two of this section, a six month suspension.

(c) For a third or subsequent violation of paragraph (a) of subdivision two of this section, a suspension for one year or until the holder reaches the age of twenty-one, whichever is the greater period of time.

Such person may thereafter apply for and be issued a restricted use license in accordance with the provisions of section five hundred thirty of the vehicle and traffic law.

7. (a) In any proceeding pursuant to subdivision one of section sixty-five of this article, it shall be an affirmative defense that such person had produced a driver's license or non-driver identification card apparently issued by a governmental entity, successfully completed the transaction scan, and that the alcoholic beverage had been sold, delivered or given to such person in reasonable reliance upon such identification and transaction scan. In evaluating the applicability of such affirmative defense, the liquor authority shall take into consideration any written policy adopted and implemented by the seller to carry out the provisions of this chapter. Use of a transaction scan shall not excuse any licensee under this chapter, or agent or employee of such licensee, from the exercise of reasonable diligence otherwise required by this section. Notwithstanding the above provisions, any such affirmative defense shall not be applicable in any other civil or criminal proceeding, or in any other forum.

(b) A licensee or agent or employee of a licensee may electronically or mechanically record and maintain only the information from a transaction scan necessary to effectuate the purposes of this section. Such information shall be limited to the following: (i) name, (ii) date of birth, (iii) driver's license or non-driver identification number, and (iv) expiration date. The liquor authority and the state commissioner of motor vehicles shall jointly promulgate any regulation necessary to govern the recording and maintenance of these records by a licensee under this chapter. The liquor authority and the commissioner of health shall jointly promulgate any regulations necessary to ensure quality control in the use of transaction scan devices.

8. A licensee or agent or employee of such licensee shall only use the information recorded and maintained through the use of such devices for the purposes contained in paragraph (a) of subdivision seven of this section, and shall only use such devices for the purposes contained in subdivision two of this section. No licensee or agent or employee of a licensee shall resell or disseminate the information recorded during such scan to any third person. Such prohibited resale or dissemination includes, but is not limited to, any advertising, marketing or promotional activities. Notwithstanding the restrictions imposed by this subdivision, such records may be released pursuant to a court ordered subpoena or pursuant to any other statute that specifically authorizes the release of such information. Each violation of this subdivision shall be punishable by a civil penalty of not more than one thousand dollars.

*❷(1998, chgd. by chaps. 383, 652; 1999, chgd. by chap. 519; 2001, chgd. by chap. 549; 2002, chgd. by chap. 503, eff. on and after 1/1/2002, expires and deemed repealed 1/1/2004. See other section 65-b below, eff. 1/1/2004.)*

**❷§65-b. Offense for one under age of twenty-one years to purchase or attempt to purchase an alcoholic beverage through fraudulent means.**

1. (a) No person under the age of twenty-one years shall present or offer to any licensee under this chapter, or to the agent or employee of such licensee, any written evidence of age which is false, fraudulent or not actually his own, for the purpose of purchasing or attempting to purchase any alcoholic beverage.

(b) No licensee, or agent or employee of such licensee shall accept as written evidence of age by any such person for the purchase of any alcoholic beverage, any documentation other than: (i) a valid driver's license or non-driver identification card issued by the commissioner of motor vehicles, the federal government, any United States territory, commonwealth or possession, the District of Columbia, a state government within the United States or a provincial government of the dominion of Canada, or (ii) a valid passport issued by the United States government or any other country, or (iii) an identification card issued by the armed forces of the United States.

2. A person violating the provisions of paragraph (a) of subdivision one of this section shall be guilty of a violation and shall be sentenced in accordance with the following:

(a) For a first violation, the court shall order payment of a fine of not more than one hundred dollars and/or an appropriate amount of community service not to exceed thirty hours. In addition, the court may order completion of an alcohol awareness program established pursuant to section 19.25 of the mental hygiene law.

(b) For a second violation, the court shall order payment of a fine of not less than fifty dollars nor more than three hundred fifty dollars and/or an appropriate amount of community service not to exceed thirty hours. The court also shall order completion of an alcohol awareness program as referenced in paragraph (a) of this subdivision if such program has not previously been completed by the offender, unless the court determines that attendance at such program is not feasible due to the lack of availability of such program within a reasonably close proximity to the locality in which the offender resides or matriculates, as appropriate.

(c) For third and subsequent violations, the court shall order payment of a fine of not less than fifty dollars nor more than seven hundred fifty dollars and/or an appropriate amount of community service not to exceed thirty hours. The court also shall order that such person submit to an evaluation by an appropriate agency certified or licensed by the office of alcoholism and substance abuse services to determine whether the person suffers from the disease of alcoholism or alcohol abuse, unless the court determines that under the circumstances presented such an evaluation is not necessary, in which case the court shall state on the record the basis for such determination. Payment for such evaluation shall be made by such person. If, based on such evaluation, a need for treatment is indicated, such person may choose to participate in a treatment plan developed by an agency certified or licensed by the office of alcoholism and substance abuse services. If such person elects to participate in recommended treatment, the court shall order that payment of such fine and community service be suspended pending the completion of such treatment.

(d) Evaluation procedures. For purposes of this subdivision, the following shall apply:

(i) The contents of an evaluation pursuant to paragraph (c) of this subdivision shall be used for the sole purpose of determining if such person suffers from the disease of alcoholism or alcohol abuse.

(ii) The agency designated by the court to perform such evaluation shall conduct the evaluation and return the results to the court within thirty days, subject to any state or federal confidentiality law, rule or regulation governing the confidentiality of alcohol and substance abuse treatment records.

(iii) The office of alcoholism and substance abuse services shall make available to each supreme court law library in this state, or, if no supreme court law library is available in a certain county, to the county court law library of such county, a list of agencies certified to perform evaluations as required by subdivision (f) of section 19.07 of the mental hygiene law.

(iv) All evaluations required under this subdivision shall be in writing and the person so evaluated or his or her counsel shall receive a copy of such evaluation prior to its use by the court.

(v) A minor evaluated under this subdivision shall have, and shall be informed by the court of, the right to obtain a second opinion regarding his or her need for alcoholism treatment.

3. A person violating the provisions of paragraph (b) of subdivision one of this section shall be guilty of a violation punishable by a fine of not more than one hundred dollars, and/or an appropriate amount of community service not to exceed thirty hours. In addition, the court may order completion of an alcohol training awareness program established pursuant to subdivision twelve of section seventeen of this chapter where such program is located within a reasonably close proximity to the locality in which the offender is employed or resides.

4. No determination of guilt pursuant to this section shall operate as a disqualification of any such person subsequently to hold public office, public employment, or as a forfeiture of any right or privilege or to receive any license granted by public authority; and no such person shall be denominated a criminal by reason of such determination.

5. In addition to the penalties otherwise provided in subdivision two of this section, if a determination is made sustaining a charge of illegally purchasing or attempting to illegally purchase an alcoholic beverage, the court may suspend such person's license to drive a motor vehicle and the privilege of an unlicensed person of obtaining such license, in accordance with the following and for the following periods, if it is found that a driver's license was used for the purpose of such illegal purchase or attempt to illegally purchase; provided, however, that

where a person is sentenced pursuant to paragraph (b) or (c) of subdivision two of this section, the court shall impose such license suspension if it is found that a driver's license was used for the purpose of such illegal purchase or attempt to illegally purchase:

(a) For a first violation of paragraph (a) of subdivision one of this section, a three month suspension.

(b) For a second violation of paragraph (a) of subdivision one of this section, a six month suspension.

(c) For a third or subsequent violation of paragraph (a) of subdivision one of this section, a suspension for one year or until the holder reaches the age of twenty-one, whichever is the greater period of time.

Such person may thereafter apply for and be issued a restricted use license in accordance with the provisions of section five hundred thirty of the vehicle and traffic law.

❷*(1998, chgd. by chaps. 383, 652; 1999, chgd. by chap. 519; 2000, chgd. by chap. 503; 2001, chgd. by chap. 549; 2002, chgd. by chap. 503, eff. 1/1/2004. See other section 65-b above, expires and deemed repealed 1/1/2004.)*

**§65-c. Unlawful possession of an alcoholic beverage with the intent to consume by persons under the age of twenty-one years.**

1. Except as hereinafter provided, no person under the age of twenty-one years shall possess any alcoholic beverage, as defined in this chapter, with the intent to consume such beverage.

2. A person under the age of twenty-one years may possess any alcoholic beverage with intent to consume if the alcoholic beverage is given:

(a) to a person who is a student in a curriculum licensed or registered by the state education department and the student is required to taste or imbibe alcoholic beverages in courses which are a part of the required curriculum, provided such alcoholic beverages are used only for instructional purposes during class conducted pursuant to such curriculum; or

(b) to the person under twenty-one years of age by that person's parent or guardian.

❶3. Any person who unlawfully possesses an alcoholic beverage with intent to consume may be summoned before and examined by a court having jurisdiction of that charge; provided, however, that nothing contained herein shall authorize, or be construed to authorize, a peace officer as defined in subdivision thirty-three of section 1.20 of the criminal procedure law or a police officer as defined in subdivision thirty-four of section 1.20 of such law to arrest a person who unlawfully possesses an alcoholic beverage with intent to consume. If a determination is made sustaining such charge the court may impose a fine not exceeding fifty dollars and/or completion of an alcohol awareness program established pursuant to section 19.25 of the mental hygiene law and/or an appropriate amount of community service not to exceed thirty hours. ❶*(1993, chgd. by chap. 389; 2001, chgd. by chap. 137, eff. 8/6/2001.)*

4. No such determination shall operate as a disqualification of any such person subsequently to hold public office, public employment, or as a forfeiture of any right or privilege or to receive any license granted by public authority; and no such person shall be denominated a criminal by reason of such determination, nor shall such determination be deemed a conviction.

5. Whenever a peace officer as defined in subdivision thirty-three of section 1.20 of the criminal procedure law or police officer as defined in subdivision thirty-four of section 1.20 of the criminal procedure law shall observe a person under twenty-one years of age openly in possession of an alcoholic beverage as defined in this chapter, with the intent to consume such beverage in violation of this section, said officer may seize the beverage, and shall deliver it to the custody of his or her department.



6. Any alcoholic beverage seized in violation of this section is hereby declared a nuisance. The official to whom the beverage has been delivered shall, no earlier than three days following the return date for initial appearance on the summons, dispose of or destroy the alcoholic beverage seized or cause it to be disposed of or destroyed. Any person claiming ownership of an alcoholic beverage seized under this section may, on the initial return date of the summons or earlier on five days notice to the official or department in possession of the beverage, apply to the court for an order preventing the destruction or disposal of the alcoholic beverage seized and ordering the return of that beverage. The court may order the beverage returned if it is determined that return of the beverage would be in the interest of justice or that the beverage was improperly seized.

**§65-d. Posting of signs.**

1. The authority shall prepare, have printed and distribute across the state to all persons with a license to sell alcoholic beverages for consumption on the premises or a license to sell alcoholic beverages for consumption off the premises a sign or poster with conspicuous lettering that states the following:

"No person shall sell or give away any alcoholic beverages to:

1. any person under the age of twenty-one years; or

2. any visibly intoxicated person.

IT IS A VIOLATION PUNISHABLE UNDER LAW FOR ANY PERSON UNDER THE AGE OF TWENTY-ONE TO PRESENT ANY WRITTEN EVIDENCE OF AGE WHICH IS FALSE, FRAUDULENT OR NOT ACTUALLY HIS OWN FOR THE PURPOSE OF ATTEMPTING TO PURCHASE ANY ALCOHOLIC BEVERAGE".

Such sign or poster shall be captioned with the word "warning" in at least two inch lettering.

2. All persons with a license to sell alcoholic beverages for consumption on the premises or a license to sell alcoholic beverages for consumption off the premises shall display, in an upright position and in a conspicuous place, where it can be easily read by the clientele of the establishment, the sign or poster upon receiving it from the authority.

3. Any person with such license who violates the provisions of this section shall be subject to a civil penalty, not to exceed one hundred dollars for each day of violation.

**❷§66. License fees.**

1. The annual fee for a distiller's license, class A, shall be twelve thousand dollars.

❷❷1-a. The annual fee for a distiller's license, class A-1, shall be two hundred fifty dollars. ❷❷*(2002, added by chap. 580, eff. 12/23/2002.)*

2. The annual fee for a distiller's license, class B, shall be eight thousand dollars.

2-a. The annual fee for a distiller's license, class C, shall be one hundred twenty-eight dollars.

2-b. The annual fee for a distiller's license, class B-1, shall be three hundred twenty dollars.

3. The annual fee for a license to sell liquor at wholesale shall be sixty-four hundred dollars.

4. The annual fee for a license, under section sixty-four or sixty-four-a, to sell liquor at retail to be consumed on the premises where sold shall be twenty-one hundred seventy-six dollars in the counties of New York, Kings, Bronx and Queens; fifteen hundred thirty-six dollars in the county of Richmond and in cities having a population of more than one hundred thousand and less than one million; twelve hundred sixteen dollars in cities having a population of more than fifty thousand and less than one hundred thousand; and the sum of eight hundred ninety-six dollars elsewhere; except that the license fees for catering establishments shall be two-thirds the license fee specified herein and for clubs, except luncheon clubs and golf clubs, shall be seven hundred fifty dollars in counties of New York, Kings, Bronx and Queens; five hundred dollars in the county of Richmond and in cities having a population of more than one hundred thousand and less than one million; three hundred fifty dollars in cities having a population of more than fifty thousand and less than one hundred thousand; and the sum of two hundred fifty dollars elsewhere. The annual fees for luncheon clubs shall be three hundred seventy-five dollars, and for golf clubs in the counties of New York, Kings, Bronx, Queens, Nassau, Richmond and Westchester, two hundred fifty dollars, and elsewhere one hundred eighty-seven dollars and fifty cents. Notwithstanding any other provision of law to the contrary, there shall be no annual fee for a license, under section sixty-four, to sell liquor at retail to be consumed on the premises where the applicant is an organization organized under section two hundred sixty of the military law and incorporated pursuant to the not-for-profit corporation law. Provided, however, that where any premises for which a license is issued pursuant to section sixty-four or sixty-four-a of this article remain open only within the period commencing April first and ending October thirty-first of any one year, or only within the period commencing October first and ending the following April thirtieth, the liquor authority may, in its discretion, grant a

summer or winter license effective only for such appropriate period of time, for which a license fee shall be paid to be prorated for the period for which such license is effective, at the rate provided for in the city, town or village in which such premises are located, except that no such license fee shall be less than one-half of the regular annual license fee; provided further that where the premises to be licensed are a race track or a golf course or are licensed pursuant to section sixty-four or sixty-four-a of this chapter, the period of such summer license may commence March first and end November thirtieth.

Where a hotel, restaurant, club, golf course or race track is open prior to April first and/or subsequent to October thirty-first by reason of the issuance of a caterer's permit or permits issued by the authority, such fact alone shall not affect the eligibility of the premises or the person owning or operating such hotel, restaurant, club, golf course or race track for a summer license.

5. The annual fee for a license to sell liquor at retail not to be consumed on the premises where sold shall be thirteen hundred sixty-six dollars in the counties of New York, Kings, Bronx and Queens; eight hundred fifty-four dollars in the county of Richmond and in cities having a population of more than one hundred thousand and less than one million; and elsewhere the sum of five hundred twelve dollars.

6. The annual fee for a license to sell liquor upon any railroad car to be consumed on such car or any car connected therewith shall be one hundred ninety-two dollars for each railroad car licensed.

7. The annual fee for a license to sell liquor upon any vessel in this state to be consumed upon such vessel shall be sixteen hundred dollars for each vessel licensed, provided, however, that where a vessel is operated only within the period commencing April first and ending October thirty-first of any one year, the liquor authority may, in its discretion, grant for such vessel a summer license effective only for such period of time, for which a license fee of four hundred forty-eight dollars shall be paid.

8. The annual fee for a license to sell liquor upon an aircraft being operated on regularly scheduled flights by a United States certificated airline in this state shall be nineteen hundred twenty dollars per annum for an airline company operating up to and including twenty such aircraft and twenty-five hundred sixty dollars for such an airline operating more than twenty such aircraft.

9. The annual fee for a license for a bottle club shall be the same as the annual fee for a special license to sell liquor at retail to be consumed on the premises, as set forth in subdivision four of this section.
❷*(1996, added by chap. 479; 1995, chgd. by chap. 149; 2002, chgd. by chap. 85(Z), eff. 8/1/2002.)*

**❷§67. License fees, duration of licenses; fee for part of year.**

Effective April first, nineteen hundred eighty-three, licenses issued pursuant to sections sixty-one, sixty-two, sixty-three, sixty-four, sixty-four-a and sixty-four-b of this article shall be effective for three years at three times that annual fee, except that, in implementing the purposes of this section, the liquor authority shall schedule the commencement dates, duration and expiration dates thereof to provide for an equal cycle of license renewals issued under each such section through the course of the fiscal year. Effective December first, nineteen hundred ninety-eight, licenses issued pursuant to sections sixty-four, sixty-four-a and sixty-four-b of this article shall be effective for two years at two times that annual fee, except that, in implementing the purposes of this section, the liquor authority shall schedule the commencement dates, duration and expiration dates thereof to provide for an equal cycle of license renewals issued under each such section through the course of the fiscal year. Notwithstanding the foregoing, commencing on December first, nineteen hundred ninety-eight and concluding on July thirty-first, two thousand two, a licensee issued a license pursuant to section sixty-four, sixty-four-a or sixty-four-b of this article may elect to remit the fee for such license in equal annual installments. Such installments shall be due on dates established by the liquor authority and the failure of a licensee to have remitted such annual installments after a due date shall be a violation of this chapter. For licenses issued for less than the three-year licensing period, the license fee shall be levied on a pro-rated basis. The entire license fee shall be due and payable at the time of application. The liquor authority may make such rules as shall be appropriate to carry out the purpose of this section. ❷*(1997, chgd. by chap. 389; 2002, chgd. by chap. 85(Z), eff. 8/1/2002.)*

## Article 6
## SPECIAL PROVISIONS RELATING TO WINE

**§75. Kinds of licenses.**

The following licenses may be issued for the manufacture and sale of wine, to wit:

1. Winery license;

1-a. Farm winery license;

❸1-b. Temporary winery or farm winery permit; ❸*(1993, added by chap. 332, eff. 1/1/94.)*

2. Wholesaler's license;

3. License to sell wine at retail for consumption off the premises;

4. License to sell wine at retail for consumption on the premises.

**§76. Winery license.**

❹1. Any person may apply to the liquor authority for a winery license as provided for in this article. Such application shall be in writing and verified and shall contain such information as the liquor authority shall require. Such application shall be accompanied by a check or draft for the amount required by this article for such license. If the liquor authority shall grant the application it shall issue a license in such form as shall be determined by its rules. ❹*(1994, chgd. by chap. 361, eff. 7/20/94.)*

❸2. ❾(a) Any person having applied for and received a license as a winery or farm winery under this section or section seventy-six-a of this article may conduct wine tastings of New York state labelled wines in establishments licensed under section sixty-three of this chapter to sell alcoholic beverages for off-premises consumption. Such winery or farm winery may charge a fee for each wine sample tasted. The state liquor authority shall promulgate rules and regulations regarding such tastings as provided for in this subdivision. ❾*(1999, chgd. by chap. 539, eff. 11/4/99.)*

❼(a-1) Any person having applied for and received a license as a winery or farm winery under this section or section seventy-six-a of this article may conduct wine tastings of New York state labelled wines and apply to the liquor authority for a permit to sell wine produced by such winery or farm winery, by the bottle, during such tastings in establishments licensed under section sixty-four of this chapter to sell alcoholic beverages for consumption on the premises. Such winery or farm winery may charge a fee of no more than twenty-five cents for each wine sample tasted. The state liquor authority shall promulgate rules and regulations regarding such tastings as provided for in this subdivision. ❼*(1997, added by chap. 438, eff. 8/20/97.)*

(b) Tastings shall be conducted subject to the following limitations: (i) wine tastings shall be conducted by an official agent, representative or solicitor of one or more wineries or farm wineries. Such agent, representative or solicitor shall be physically present at all times during the conduct of the tastings; and

(ii) any liability stemming from a right of action resulting from a wine tasting as authorized herein and in accordance with the provisions

of sections 11-100 and 11-101 of the general obligations law, shall accrue to the farm winery or winery licensee.
❽*(1993, chgd. by chap. 490, eff. 1/1/94.)*

❾3. A licensed winery may apply to the liquor authority for a license to sell wine at retail for consumption on the premises. All the provisions of this chapter relative to licenses to sell wine at retail for consumption on the premises shall apply so far as applicable to such application. ❾*(1993, chgd. by chap. 321; 1999, chgd. by chap. 539, eff. 11/4/99.)*

❽4. Notwithstanding any provision of this chapter to the contrary, any one or more winery licensees or farm winery licensees, singly or jointly, may apply to the liquor authority for a license or licenses to sell wine at retail for consumption off the premises. The duration of such license shall be coextensive with the duration of such licensee's winery license or farm winery license, and the fee therefor shall be five hundred dollars if such retail premises is located in cities having a population of one million or more; in cities having less than one million population and more than one hundred thousand, two hundred fifty dollars; and elsewhere, the sum of one hundred twenty-five dollars. Such license shall entitle the holder thereof to sell at retail for consumption off the premises any New York state labelled wine. Such license shall also entitle the holder thereof to conduct winetastings* and engage in any of the activities authorized by paragraphs (a), (b) and (c) of subdivision four of section seventy-seven of this article on such licensed premises. Such license shall also authorize the sale by the holder thereof of New York state labelled wine, in sealed containers for off-premises consumption, from the specially licensed premises of any person licensed pursuant to section eighty-one-a of this article to sell wine at retail for consumption on premises in which the principal business is the operation of a legitimate theater or such other lawful adult entertainment or recreational facility as the liquor authority may classify for eligibility pursuant to subdivision six of section sixty-four-a of this chapter. Not more than five such licenses shall be issued to any licensed winery or farm winery. All other provisions of this chapter relative to licenses to sell wine at retail for consumption off the premises shall apply so far as applicable to such application. The liquor authority is hereby authorized to adopt such rules as it may deem necessary to carry out the purpose of this subdivision, provided that all licenses issued pursuant to this subdivision shall be subject to the same rules and regulations as are applicable to the sale of wine at retail for consumption off the premises of the winery licensee or farm winery licensee. ❽*(1993, chgd. by chap. 490, eff. 1/1/94.)*
**So in original. Probably should be "wine tastings".*

5. Any winery licensed pursuant to this section is authorized to engage in what is commonly known as wine by wire services whereby a winery within the state may make deliveries on behalf of other wineries within the state. *(See other subd. 5 below.)*

❸5. Notwithstanding any provision of this chapter to the contrary, a licensed winery or a licensed farm winery may apply to the liquor authority for a permit to sell New York state labelled wine, by the bottle, at the state fair, at recognized county fairs and at farmers markets operated on a not-for-profit basis. As a condition of the permit, an agent, representative, or solicitor from the winery must be present at the time of sale. ❸*(1993, chgd. by chap. 490, eff. 1/1/94. See other subd. 5 above.)*

**§76-a. Farm winery license.**

❶1. Any person may apply to the liquor authority for a farm winery license as provided for in this article. Such application shall be in writing and verified and shall contain such information as the liquor authority shall require. Such application shall be accompanied by a check or draft for the amount required by this article for such license. If the liquor authority shall grant the application it shall issue a license in such form as shall be determined by its rules. ❶*(1994, chgd. by chap. 361, eff. 7/20/94.)*

2. *(Repealed.)*

❾3. A farm winery license shall authorize the holder thereof to operate a farm winery for the manufacture of wine at the premises specifically designated in the license. Such a license shall also authorize the sale in bulk by such licensee from the licensed premises of the products manufactured under such license to any winery licensee, any other farm winery licensee, any distiller licensee or to a permittee engaged in the manufacture of products which are unfit for beverage use and to sell or deliver such wine to persons outside the state pursuant to the laws of the place of such sale or delivery. It shall also authorize the holder thereof to sell from the licensed premises to a licensed wholesaler or retailer, or to a corporation operating railroad cars or aircraft for consumption on such carriers, or at retail for consumption off the premises, wine manufactured by the licensee as above set forth and to sell or deliver such wine to persons outside the state pursuant to the laws of the place of such sale or delivery. All wine sold by such licensee for consumption off the premises shall be securely sealed and have attached thereto a label setting forth such information as shall be required by this chapter. Such license shall also be deemed to include authorization to sell cider and wine at retail for consumption on or off the premises; and to sell wine at retail for consumption on the premises of a restaurant, conference center, inn, bed and breakfast or hotel business owned and operated by the licensee in or adjacent to the farm winery for which the licensee is licensed. A licensee who operates a restaurant, conference center, inn, bed and breakfast or hotel pursuant to such authority shall comply with all applicable provisions of this chapter which relate to licenses to sell wine at retail for consumption on the premises. ❾*(1993, chgd. by chap. 321; 1995, chgd. by chap. 348; 1999, chgd. by chap. 539, eff. 11/4/99.)*

4. (a) A farm winery license shall authorize the holder thereof to manufacture, bottle and sell fruit juice, fruit jellies and fruit preserves, tonics and unpotable wine cooking sauces on and from the licensed premises.

(b) Such license shall authorize the holder thereof to store and sell gift items in a tax-paid room upon the licensed premises. These gift items shall be limited to the following categories:

(1) Wine supplies, which shall include any item utilized for the storage, serving or consumption of wine. These supplies may be sold as single items or may be combined into a package sold as a unit item or may be combined into a package containing wine or a wine product;

(2) Food items, which shall include any food or food product not specifically prepared for immediate consumption upon the premises. Such food items may be combined into a package containing wine or a wine product;

(3) Souvenirs, which shall include any item which can be construed to represent or serve as a memento of the licensed premises or of the state of New York.

●(4) New York state labelled wine produced or manufactured by any other New York state winery or farm winery licensee. Such wine may be purchased outright by the licensee from a New York winery or farm winery licensee or obtained on a consignment basis pursuant to a written agreement between the selling and purchasing licensee. ●*(1993, added by chap. 490, eff. 1/1/94.)*

(c) The authority is hereby authorized to promulgate rules and regulations to effectuate the purposes of this subdivision.

●(d) A licensed farm winery may engage in any other business on the licensed premises subject to such rules and regulations as the liquor authority may prescribe. In prescribing such rules and regulations, the liquor authority shall promote the expansion and profitability of wine production and of tourism in New York, thereby promoting the conservation, production and enhancement of New York state agricultural lands. Further, such rules and regulations shall determine which businesses will be compatible with the policy and purposes of this chapter and shall consider the effect of particular businesses on the community and area in the vicinity of the farm winery licensee. ●*(1993, chgd. by chap. 490, eff. 1/1/94.)*

5. No licensed farm winery shall manufacture or sell any wine not produced exclusively from grapes or other fruits or agricultural products grown or produced in New York state.

●6. Notwithstanding any other provision of this chapter, a farm winery license shall authorize the holder thereof to:

(a) Offer for sale or solicit any order in the state for the sale of any New York state labelled wine manufactured by the licensee or any other winery or farm winery licensed pursuant to this article.

(b) Engage as a broker in the purchase and sale of New York state labelled wines for a fee or commission for or on behalf of any winery or farm winery licensed pursuant to this article.

(c) Maintain a warehouse on the premises pursuant to section ninety-six of this chapter for the warehousing of any New York state labelled wines manufactured by any winery or farm winery licensed pursuant to this article. Any winery or farm winery that maintains such a warehouse must comply with the provisions of section ninety-six of this chapter.

(d) Deliver or transport any New York state labelled wine manufactured or produced by the licensee or any other winery or farm winery licensed pursuant to this article in any vehicle owned, leased or hired by the licensee. The New York state labelled wine can be delivered, transported or sold by the licensee to any holder of: (i) a winery or farm winery license, (ii) a license to sell alcoholic beverages for consumption on the premises, (iii) a license to sell alcoholic beverages for consumption off the premises, (iv) or any person that can receive or purchase wine from a farm winery. The licensee is not required to obtain from the liquor authority a trucking permit or pay any fees pursuant to section ninety-four of this chapter.

❸*(1993, added by chap. 490, eff. 1/1/94.)*

7. No licensed farm winery shall manufacture in excess of one hundred fifty thousand finished gallons of wine annually.

**❸§76-b. Temporary winery or farm winery permit.**

❹1. Any person may apply to the liquor authority for a temporary winery or farm winery permit. Such application shall be in writing and verified and shall contain information as the liquor authority shall require. Such application shall be accompanied by a check or draft for the amount required by this article for such permit. Such application fee shall offset any subsequently assessed fees required by this article for the issuance of a winery or farm winery license to such applicant.

❹*(1994, chgd. by chap. 361, eff. 7/20/94.)*

2. Upon application, the liquor authority shall issue a temporary winery or farm winery permit when the applicant:

(a) either requires a license to establish a winery to produce or manufacture wine or has a winery or farm winery license application pending before the liquor authority, and the beginning of the harvest season for grapes or any other fruit or product necessary for the production or manufacture of wine at that facility will occur within thirty days; or

(b) is in good faith negotiating with or has entered into an agreement with a winery or farm winery licensee to purchase, obtain or acquire part or full ownership rights in the assets or stock of an existing and operating winery facility; or

(c) due to unforeseen circumstances or an emergency situation is in need of a permit to ensure the continued or future operation of an existing winery facility.

3. The liquor authority in granting such permit shall ensure that:

(a) issuance of the permit will not inordinately hinder the operation or effective administration of this article.

(b) the applicant would in all likelihood be able to ultimately obtain a permanent winery or farm winery license.

(c) the applicant has substantially complied with the requirements necessary to obtain a winery or farm winery license.

(d) upon issuance of the temporary permit, the winery or farm winery license for said premises shall have been surrendered into safekeeping pursuant to rules of the liquor authority.

(e) the applicant for the temporary permit shall have filed concurrently with the liquor authority an application for a permanent winery or farm winery license at such premises.

4. The application for a permit shall be approved or denied by the liquor authority within forty-five days after the receipt of such application.

5. A temporary winery or farm winery permit shall authorize the holder thereof to operate a winery or farm winery, as the case may be, for the manufacture and sale of wine at the premises specifically designated in the permit. Further, it shall authorize the holder of a temporary winery permit or a temporary farm winery permit to conduct any of the activities permitted, respectively, by section seventy-six, section seventy-six-a or seventy-seven of this chapter.

6. Such temporary permit shall remain in effect for six months or until the permittee is issued a permanent winery or farm winery license, whichever is shorter. Such permit may be extended at the discretion of the authority for an additional three month period of time upon payment of an additional fee of fifty dollars. Notwithstanding any other provision of law, a temporary permit may be summarily cancelled or suspended at any time if the liquor authority determines that good cause for such cancellation or suspension exists. The liquor authority shall promptly notify the holder of such permit in writing of such cancellation or suspension and shall set forth the reasons for such action.

7. The liquor authority in reviewing such application shall review the entire record and grant it unless good cause is otherwise shown. A decision on an application shall be based on substantial evidence in the record and supported by a preponderance of the evidence in favor of the applicant.

❸*(1993, added by chap. 332, eff. 1/1/94.)*

**❹§76-c. Special winery license.**

1. Any person may apply to the liquor authority for a license to operate a winery on the premises of a winery licensee. Such application shall be in writing and verified and shall contain such information as the liquor authority shall require. Such application shall be accompanied by a check or draft for the amount required by this article for such license. If the liquor authority shall grant the application it shall issue a license in such form as shall be determined by its rules.

2. (a) Any person having applied for and received a license under this section or section seventy-six-d of this article may conduct wine tastings of New York state labelled wines in establishments licensed

under section sixty-three of this chapter to sell alcoholic beverages for off-premises consumption. The state liquor authority shall promulgate rules and regulations regarding such tastings as provided for in this subdivision.

(b) Tastings shall be conducted subject to the following limitations: (i) wine tastings shall be conducted by an official agent of one or more wineries or farm wineries. Such agent shall be physically present at all times during the conduct of the tastings; and

(ii) any liability stemming from a right of action resulting from a wine tasting as authorized herein and in accordance with the provisions of sections 11-100 and 11-101 of the general obligations law, shall accrue to the farm winery operator or winery licensee operator.



3. Special winery licensees licensed under the provisions of this section may apply to the liquor authority for a license to sell wine at retail for consumption on the premises in a restaurant owned by the licensee and conducted and operated by the licensee in or adjacent to the winery for which the licensee is licensed. All the provisions of this chapter relative to licensure to sell wine at retail for consumption on the premises shall apply so far as applicable to such application.

4. Notwithstanding any provision of this chapter to the contrary, any one or more special winery licensees licensed under the provisions of this section or a special farm winery licensee licensed pursuant to section seventy-six-d of this article, singly or jointly, may apply to the liquor authority for a license or licenses to sell wine at retail for consumption off the premises. The duration of such license shall be coextensive with the duration of such licensee's winery license or farm winery license under the provisions of this section. Such license shall also entitle the holder thereof to conduct wine tastings and engage in any of the activities authorized by paragraphs (a), (b) and (c) of subdivision four of section seventy-seven of this article on such licensed premises. Such license shall also authorize the sale by the holder thereof of New York state labelled wine, in sealed containers for off-premises consumption, from the specially licensed premises of any person licensed pursuant to section eighty-one-a of this article to sell wine at retail for consumption on premises in which the principal business is the operation of a legitimate theater or such other lawful adult entertainment or recreational facility as the liquor authority may classify for eligibility pursuant to subdivision six of section sixty-four-a of this chapter. Not more than five such licenses shall be issued to any special winery licensee or special farm winery licensee licensed under the provisions of this section. All other provisions of this chapter relative to licenses to sell wine at retail for consumption off the premises shall apply so far as applicable to such application. The liquor authority is hereby authorized to adopt such rules as it may deem necessary to carry out the purpose of this subdivision, provided that all licenses issued pursuant to this subdivision shall be subject to the same rules and regulations as are applicable to the sale of wine at retail for consumption off the premises of a winery licensee or a farm winery licensee.

For purposes of this subdivision, New York state labelled wine shall mean wine made from grapes, at least seventy-five percent the volume of which were grown in New York state.

5. Notwithstanding any provision of this chapter to the contrary, a special winery licensee or a special farm winery licensee may apply to the liquor authority for a permit to sell New York state labelled wine, by the bottle, at the state fair, at recognized county fairs and at farmers' markets operated on a not-for-profit basis. As a condition of the permit, a representative from the winery must be present at the time of sale.

6. Any special farm winery licensee licensed pursuant to this section is authorized to engage in what is commonly known as wine by wire services whereby a special farm winery licensee within the state may make deliveries on behalf of other wineries within the state.

7. The provisions of section seventy-seven of this article relating to the manufacture and sale of wine in bulk shall also apply as far as practicable to the holder of a license under this section.

❶*(1993, added by chap. 489; 1994, renumbered and chgd. by chap. 361, eff. 7/20/94.)*

**❶§76-d. Special farm winery license.**

1. Any person may apply to the liquor authority for a special farm winery license to operate on the premises of an existing licensee as provided for in this article. Such application shall be in writing and verified and shall contain such information as the liquor authority shall require. Such application shall be accompanied by a check or draft for the amount required by this article for such license. If the liquor authority shall grant the application it shall issue a license in such form as shall be determined by its rules.

2. A special farm winery license shall authorize the holder thereof to operate a farm winery upon the preexisting licensed premises of another farm winery or winery licensee. Such license shall authorize the holder thereof to all the operating privileges provided in sections seventy-six-a and seventy-six-c of this article so far as applicable to such licensee.

❶*(1993, added by chap. 489; 1994, renumbered and chgd. by chap. 361, eff. 7/20/94.)*

**❷§76-e. Special provisions relating to wineries and farm wineries holding a distiller's license.**

1. Any person who holds a winery license pursuant to section seventy-six of this article or a farm winery license pursuant to section seventy-six-a of this article and, in addition to such license, holds a distiller's license pursuant to section sixty-one of this chapter, and who conducts wine tastings pursuant to the provisions of such sections seventy-six and seventy-six-a of this article, shall be authorized to conduct tastings of brandy manufactured by such licensed winery or licensed farm winery, at such wine tastings.

2. All consumer tastings of brandy shall be conducted subject to the following limitations:

(a) Tastings of brandy shall be conducted by an official agent of one or more persons licensed pursuant to section sixty-one of this chapter. Such agent shall be physically present upon the premises at all times during the conducting of the consumer tasting of brandy.

(b) No such person or persons licensed pursuant to section sixty-one of this chapter, and no official agent thereof, may provide, directly or indirectly: (i) more than a total of three samples of brandy for tasting to a person in one calendar day; or (ii) a sample of brandy for tasting equal to more than one-quarter fluid ounce.

(c) Any liability stemming from a right of action resulting from a consumer tasting of brandy authorized by this section and in accordance with the provisions of sections 11-100 and 11-101 of the general obligations law, shall accrue to the persons licensed pursuant to section sixty-one of this chapter, who conducted such tasting.

3. The state liquor authority shall promulgate rules and regulations regarding brandy tastings as provided for in this section.

4. Any person who holds a winery license pursuant to section seventy-six of this article or a farm winery license pursuant to section seventy-six-a of this article, and who is authorized to sell wine for consumption off the premises pursuant to the provisions of such sections seventy-six and seventy-six-a of this article, shall be authorized to sell brandy manufactured by such licensed winery or licensed farm winery for consumption off the premises. Such sale of brandy for consumption off the premises shall only occur at the licensed winery or farm winery and not at any other off-premises locations licensed to the winery or farm winery, pursuant to subdivision four of section seventy-six of this article. The sale of brandy at a winery or farm winery shall also be subjected to the same hours of operation as set forth for the sale of wine at a winery or farm winery. The authority shall promulgate rules and regulations for the sale of brandy at wineries or farm wineries for off-premises consumption.

❷*(2002, added by chap. 133, eff. 10/21/2002.)*

### §77. Sale of wine in bulk.

1. A winery license shall authorize the holder thereof to operate a winery for the manufacture of wine at the premises specifically designated in the license and to receive and possess wine from other states consigned to a United States government bonded winery, warehouse or storeroom located within the state. Such a license shall also authorize the sale in bulk by such licensee from the licensed premises of the products manufactured under such license and wine received by such licensee from any other state to any winery licensee, any distiller licensee or to a permittee engaged in the manufacturer* of products which are unfit for beverage use and to sell or deliver such wine to persons outside the state pursuant to the laws of the place of such sale or delivery. It shall also authorize the holders thereof to sell from the licensed

premises to a licensed wholesaler or retailer, or to a corporation operating railroad cars or aircraft for consumption on such carriers, wine manufactured or received by the licensee as above set forth in the original sealed containers of not more than fifteen gallons each and to sell or deliver such wine to persons outside the state pursuant to the laws of the place of such sale or delivery. All wine sold by such licensee shall be securely sealed and have attached thereto a label setting forth such information as shall be required by this chapter.

**So in original. Probably should be "manufacture".*

2. Notwithstanding any provision of this chapter to the contrary, and upon payment to the liquor authority of an additional annual fee of one hundred twenty-five dollars, the liquor authority may in its discretion and upon such terms and conditions as it may prescribe, issue to a licensed winery upon application therefor a certificate authorizing such winery to sell wine at retail in sealed containers to a regularly organized church, synagogue or religious organization for sacramental purposes, and to a householder for consumption in his home.

3. *(Repealed.)*

4. (a) A licensed winery may manufacture, bottle and sell fruit juice, fruit jellies and fruit preserves, tonics and unpotable wine cooking sauces on and from licensed premises, provided that the winery license number does not appear on the labels of such products, and operate a restaurant on the premises.

(b) Such license shall authorize the holder thereof to store and sell gift items in a tax-paid room upon the licensed premises. These gift items shall be limited to the following categories:

(1) Wine supplies, which shall include any item utilized for the storage, serving or consumption of wine. These supplies may be sold as single items or may be combined into a package sold as a unit item or may be combined into a package containing wine or a wine product;

(2) Food items, which shall include any food or food product not specifically prepared for immediate consumption upon the premises. Such food items may be combined into a package containing wine or a wine product;

(3) Souvenirs, which shall include any item which can be construed to represent or serve as a memento of the licensed premises or of the state of New York.

❸(4) New York state labelled wine produced or manufactured by any other New York state winery or farm winery licensee. Such wine may be purchased outright by the licensee from a New York winery or farm winery licensee or obtained on a consignment basis pursuant to a written agreement between the selling and purchasing licensee. ❸*(1993, added by chap. 490, eff. 1/1/94.)*

(c) Notwithstanding any provision of this chapter to the contrary, any winery licensee or farm winery licensee may charge:

(1) For tours of their premises; and

(2) For any wine tastings.

(d) Wine grape growers or wine producer organizations or associations, incorporated within the state for the purpose of wine or wine grape promotion may hold wine tastings for purposes of education in the production and proper use of wine products under the same rules applying to winery licensees.

(e) The authority is hereby authorized to promulgate rules and regulations to effectuate the purposes of this subdivision.

❸(f) A licensed winery may engage in any other business on the licensed premises subject to such rules and regulations as the liquor authority may prescribe. In prescribing such rules and regulations, the liquor authority shall promote the expansion and profitability of wine production and of tourism in New York, thereby promoting the conservation, production and enhancement of New York state agricultural lands. Further, such rules and regulations shall determine which businesses will be compatible with the policy and purposes of this chapter and shall consider the effect of particular businesses on the community and area in the vicinity of the winery licensee. ❸*(1993, chgd. by chap. 490, eff. 1/1/94.)*



❺5. A licensed winery shall be permitted to remain open for the purposes of selling its products, in accordance with the provisions of subdivisions two and three of this section, and/or of conducting public tours of its winery and/or to sell New York state labelled wine, by the bottle, at the state fair, at recognized county fairs and at farmers markets operated on a not-for-profit basis in accordance with the provisions of section seventy-six of this article on Sunday between the hours of ten o'clock in the morning and midnight.

The authority is hereby authorized to promulgate rules and regulations to effectuate the purposes of this subdivision.
❺*(1995, chgd. by chap. 455, eff. 8/2/95.)*

**§78. Wholesaler's wine license.**

1. The procedure contained in section sixty-two hereof shall apply so far as applicable to applications for a wholesaler's wine license. Such license shall contain a description of the licensed premises and in form and in substance shall be a license to the person therein specifically designated to sell wine at wholesale in the premises therein specifically licensed in the original sealed containers of not more than fifteen gallons each to duly licensed manufacturers, wholesalers, retailers and permittees in this state, and to sell or deliver such wine to persons outside the state pursuant to the laws of the place of such sale or delivery.

2. Upon payment to the liquor authority of an additional annual fee of one hundred twenty-five dollars, the liquor authority may in its discretion and upon such terms and conditions as it may prescribe, issue to a wholesale wine licensee upon application therefor a certificate authorizing such wholesaler to sell wine at retail in sealed containers to a regularly organized church, synagogue or religious organization for sacramental purposes.

## §79. License to sell wine at retail for consumption off the premises.

1. The procedure set forth in section sixty-three hereof shall apply so far as applicable to applications for licenses to sell wine at retail for off-premise consumption. Such license shall in form and in substance be a license to the person specifically licensed to sell wine at retail for off-premise consumption.

2. Not more than one license shall be granted to any person under this section.

3. No licensee under this section shall be engaged in any other business in the premises licensed. The sale of those items specifically enumerated in subdivision four of section sixty-three of this chapter shall not constitute engaging in another business within the meaning of this subdivision.

4. Determinations under this section with respect to the issuance of a new license or under section one hundred eleven with respect to the transfer to any other premises of a license issued hereunder shall be made in accordance with public convenience and advantage.



## §79-a. Authorization to sell wine products by certain licensees for consumption off the premises.

❷1. Any person licensed to sell beer at retail for consumption off the premises, pursuant to section fifty-four of this chapter, shall, by virtue of such license and upon payment to the liquor authority of an additional fee in the sum of one hundred sixty-five dollars in cities having a population of one hundred thousand or over and eighty-three dollars elsewhere, be granted authorization to sell from the licensed premises wine products in sealed containers for consumption off such premises. Upon receipt of such additional fee, the liquor authority shall promptly issue a permit authorizing such sales by the licensee. ❷*(2002, chgd. by chap. 85(Z), eff. 8/1/2002.)*

2. Notwithstanding any other provisions of this chapter, any person receiving a permit pursuant to this section shall be subject to such provisions of this chapter as are applicable to persons licensed pursuant to section fifty-four of this chapter, and not to those provisions which are applicable only to persons licensed pursuant to sections sixty-three and seventy-nine of this chapter.

## §79-b. Authorization to sell wine products by certain licensees for consumption on the premises.

❷1. Any person licensed to sell beer at retail for consumption on the premises, pursuant to section fifty-five of this chapter, shall, by virtue of such license and upon payment to the liquor authority of an additional fee in the sum of one hundred ninety-two dollars in cities having a population of one hundred thousand or over and ninety-six dollars elsewhere, be granted authorization to sell from the licensed premises wine products in sealed containers at retail for consumption on or off such premises. Upon receipt of such additional fee, the liquor authority shall promptly issue a permit authorizing such sales by the licensee.

❷1-a. Any person licensed to sell beer at retail for consumption on the premises, pursuant to section fifty-five-a of this chapter, shall, by virtue of such license and upon payment to the liquor authority of an additional fee in the sum of one hundred ninety-two dollars in cities having a population of one hundred thousand or over and ninety-six dollars elsewhere, be granted authorization to sell from the licensed premises wine products in sealed containers at retail for consumption on such premises. Upon receipt of such additional fee, the liquor authority shall promptly issue a permit authorizing such sales by the licensee.
❷*(2002, chgd. by chap. 85(Z), eff. 8/1/2002.)*

2. Notwithstanding any other provisions of this chapter, any person receiving a permit pursuant to this section shall be subject to such provisions of this chapter as are applicable to persons licensed pursuant to section fifty-five of this chapter, and not to those provisions which are applicable only to persons licensed pursuant to sections sixty-four and eighty of this chapter.



**❸§80. Wine tasting.**

Any person licensed to sell wine pursuant to this article or section sixty-three of this chapter shall be permitted to conduct wine tastings. Wine tastings which are conducted under the auspices of an official agent of a farm winery, winery, wholesaler, or importer and where such agent is physically present at all times during the conduct of the tasting, then, in that event, any liability stemming from a right of action resulting from a wine tasting as authorized herein, and in accordance with the provisions of sections 11-100 and 11-101 of the general obligations law, shall accrue to the farm winery, winery, wholesaler, or importer. ❸*(1993, added by chap. 458, eff. 11/23/93.)*

**§81. License to sell wine at retail for consumption on the premises.**

1. The procedure set forth in section sixty-four hereof shall apply so far as applicable to applications for licenses to sell wine at retail for consumption on the premises, except as provided in subdivision two of this section.

❾1-a. Notwithstanding any other provision of this chapter, upon receipt in the city of New York of an application for a license under this section, an application for renewal under section one hundred nine of this chapter, or an application for an alteration to a premises licensed for consumption on the premises under section ninety-nine-d of this chapter, the applicant shall notify the community board established pursuant to section twenty-eight hundred of the New York city charter with jurisdiction over the area in which such licensed premises is to be located by certified mail, return receipt requested, wherein the prospective licensed premises is to be located or, in the case of an application for renewal, or alteration where it is presently located not less than thirty days prior to the submission of its application for a license under this section or for a renewal thereof pursuant to section one hundred nine of this chapter. Such community board may express an opinion for or against the granting of such license. Any such opinion shall be deemed part of the record upon which the liquor board makes its determination to grant or deny such license. ❾*(1999, added by chap. 582, eff. 9/1/99.)*

2. No such license shall be issued to any person for any premises other than premises for which a license may be issued under section sixty-four of this chapter or a hotel or premises which are kept, used, maintained, advertised or held out to the public to be a place where food is prepared and served for consumption on the premises in such quantities as to satisfy the liquor authority that the sale of wine intended is incidental to and not the prime source of revenue from the operation of such premises. Such license may also include such suitable space outside the licensed premises and adjoining it as may be approved by the liquor authority.

❷3. Such license shall in form and in substance be a license to the person specifically licensed to sell wine at retail, to be consumed upon the premises. Such license shall also be deemed to include a license to sell beer and soju at retail to be consumed under the same terms and conditions without the payment of any additional fee. For the purposes of this subdivision, "soju" shall mean an imported Korean alcoholic beverage that contains not more than twenty-four per centum alcohol, by volume, and is derived from agricultural products. ❷*(2002, chgd. by chap. 627, eff. 10/9/2002.)*

### §81-a. Special license to sell wine at retail for consumption on the premises.

1. On or after the effective date hereof, any person may make an application to the appropriate board for a special license to sell wine at retail to be consumed on the premises where sold.

2. Such special license shall in form and in substance be a license to the person specifically licensed to sell wine at retail to be consumed on the premises specifically licensed. Such license shall also be deemed to include a license to sell beer at retail to be consumed under the same terms and conditions, without the payment of any additional fee.

3. The provisions contained in subdivisions three, four, six, eight and nine of section sixty-four-a shall apply to applicants for licenses under this section.

4. a. No such license shall be issued to any person for any premises other than premises for which a license may be issued under section sixty-four of this chapter or a hotel or premises which are kept, used, maintained, advertised or held out to the public to be a place where food is prepared and served for consumption on the premises in such quantities as to satisfy the liquor authority that the sale of wine intended is incidental to and not the prime source of revenue from the operation of such premises. Such license may also include such suitable space outside the licensed premises and adjoining it as may be approved by the liquor authority.

b. Notwithstanding paragraph a of this subdivision, a special on-premises license for a premises in which the principal business shall be the operation of a legitimate theater by a corporation organized pursuant to the not-for-profit corporation law may be granted notwithstanding the proximity of such premises to any school, provided that the availability of alcoholic beverages on such premises shall not be advertised in any way at such premises in any manner visible from such street or avenue.

**❶§81-b. Temporary home vintner tasting permit.**

The liquor authority is hereby authorized to issue to a home vintner, for a period not to exceed three consecutive days, a temporary home vintner tasting permit for the purpose of allowing the wine that he or she produces to be tasted at outdoor or indoor gatherings, functions, occasions or events, within the hours fixed by or pursuant to subdivision five of section one hundred six of this chapter, during which alcoholic beverages may lawfully be sold or served upon premises licensed to sell alcoholic beverages at retail for on-premises consumption in the community in which is located the premises in which such gathering, function, occasion or event is held. The fee for such permit shall be twenty dollars. The liquor authority is authorized and directed to promulgate such rules and regulations as it deems necessary or appropriate to implement the provisions of this section and to protect the health, safety and welfare of the people of this state. ❶*(2001, added by chap. 32, eff. 5/14/2001; chgd. by chap. 138(1), (2), eff. 8/6/2001, expires and deemed repealed 5/14/2002.)*



**§82. Prohibited sales.**

The restrictions contained in section sixty-five hereof shall apply to persons licensed to sell wine at retail.

**❷§83. License fees.**

1. The annual fee for a winery license shall be six hundred twenty-five dollars.

1-a. The annual fee for a farm winery license shall be one hundred twenty-five dollars.

1-b. The fee for a temporary winery or farm winery permit shall be one hundred twenty-five dollars.

2. The annual fee for a license to sell wine at wholesale shall be eight hundred dollars.

3. The annual fee for a license to sell wine at retail, not to be consumed on the premises, shall be six hundred forty dollars for each such place where such business is carried on in cities having a population of one million or more; in cities having less than one million population and more than one hundred thousand, three hundred twenty dollars; and elsewhere, the sum of one hundred forty-five dollars.

4. The annual fee for selling wine at retail, to be consumed on the premises where sold, shall be as follows:

(a) In cities having a population of one hundred thousand or over the sum of four hundred eighty dollars per year; and

(b) Elsewhere, the sum of two hundred forty dollars per year.

4-a. The annual fee for a license to sell wine at retail to be consumed on the premises where sold where the premises to be licensed remain open only within the period commencing April first and ending October thirty-first of any one year or only within the period commencing October first and ending the following April thirtieth, the liquor authority, in its discretion, may grant a summer or winter license effective only for such appropriate period of time, for which an annual fee of one hundred twelve dollars shall be paid.

5. The annual fee for a special license to sell wine at retail, to be consumed on the premises where sold, shall be as follows:

(a) In cities having a population of one hundred thousand or over, the sum of five hundred seventy-six dollars per year; and

(b) Elsewhere, the sum of two hundred seventy dollars per year.

6. The annual fee for a special winery license shall be six hundred twenty-five dollars.

7. The annual fee for a special farm winery license shall be one hundred twenty-five dollars.

❷*(1993, chgd. by chaps. 332, 489; 1999, chgd. by chap. 540; 2001, chgd. by chaps. 32, 138; 2002, chgd. by chap. 85(Z), eff. 8/1/2002.)*

**§84. License fees; when due and payable; fee for part of year.**

The provisions contained in section sixty-seven shall apply to all licenses issued pursuant to this article.

**❸§85. Purchase from private collection.**

Notwithstanding any other provisions of this chapter any nonlicensed person owning bottled wine is authorized to sell that wine to a wholesale or retail licensee authorized to sell wine. The licensee involved in such sale shall ensure that each bottle of wine sold from a private collection has a permanently affixed label stating that the wine was acquired from a private collection. ❸*(1993, added by chap. 458, eff. 11/23/93.)*

## Article 7
## SPECIAL PERMITS

**§90. Kinds of permits.**

The following kinds of permits may be issued for carrying on the activities enumerated in this article with respect to alcoholic beverages, alcohol or spirits. No person shall engage in any of such activities without having obtained the appropriate permit required hereby therefor:

1. Industrial alcohol permit.
2. Alcohol permit.
2-a. Alcohol distributors' permits.
3. Solicitor's permit.
3-a. Broker's permit.
4. Trucking permit.
5. Drug store permit.
6. Warehouse permit.
7. Temporary outdoor permit.
8. Caterer's permit.
9. Special permit to remain open during certain hours of the morning.
10. Bottling permit.
11. Reconditioning permit.
12. Miscellaneous permits.

**§91. Industrial alcohol permit.**

1. An industrial alcohol permit may be issued by the liquor authority entitling the applicant to purchase alcohol intended for use in the manufacture and sale of any of the following, when they are unfit for beverage purposes, namely:

(a) Denatured alcohol purchased and used pursuant to acts of Congress and regulations promulgated thereunder.

(b) Patent, proprietary, medicinal, pharmaceutical, antiseptic and toilet preparations.

(c) Flavoring extracts, syrups and food products.

(d) Scientific, chemical, mechanical and industrial products.

2. Such permit shall be in such form as prescribed by the rules of the liquor authority and shall permit the purchaser to use said alcohol for the purpose named in such permit and in accordance with the terms and conditions of such permit and the rules of the liquor authority.

❷3. Such permit shall be issued for a calendar year, and the fee therefor shall be sixty-four dollars per year, or for any part thereof. ❷*(2002, chgd. by chap. 85(Z), eff. 8/1/2002.)*

4. Any person who shall knowingly sell any of the products enumerated in this section for beverage purposes, or who shall sell any of the same under circumstances from which he might reasonably deduce the intention of the purchaser to use them for such purposes, shall be subject to the penalties provided for in this chapter.

**§91-a. Industrial alcohol manufacturers' permits.**

1. An industrial alcohol manufacturer's permit may be issued by the liquor authority entitling the applicant to manufacture alcohol intended for use and/or used for the following purposes:

For scientific, chemical, mechanical, industrial, medicinal and culinary purposes.

For use by those authorized to procure alcohol tax-free, as provided by the acts of congress and regulations promulgated thereunder.

In the manufacture of denatured alcohol as provided by the acts of congress and regulations promulgated thereunder.

In the manufacture of patented, patent, proprietary, medicinal, pharmaceutical, antiseptic, toilet, scientific, chemical, mechanical and industrial preparations or products, unfit for beverage purposes.

In the manufacture of flavoring extracts and syrups, unfit for beverage purposes.

In the manufacture of ethanol from biomass feedstock for use as fuel (including but not limited to motor fuel, heating fuel or fuel for process heat).

2. Such permit shall be in such form as prescribed by the rules of the liquor authority and shall permit the manufacturer to manufacture and distribute said alcohol to holders of industrial alcohol permits, alcohol permits, distributors' alcohol permits class A, distributors' alcohol permits class B and distributors' alcohol permits class C but nothing contained herein shall authorize the manufacturing and distribution of said alcohol for beverage purposes.

3. ❷The annual fee for an industrial alcohol manufacturer's permit shall be eight hundred dollars, except that: ❷*(2002, chgd. by chap. 85(Z), eff. 8/1/2002.)*

(a) no holder of a class A distiller's license shall be required to obtain such permit or pay such fee;

(b) no fee shall be required from any applicant who certifies that he will manufacture, solely from biomass feedstock, ethanol for his own use as fuel;

(c) no fee shall be required from any applicant who certifies that he will manufacture, solely from biomass feedstock, less than one hundred thousand gallons of ethanol annually for use as a fuel;

(d) no fee shall be required from any applicant who certifies that he will manufacture, solely from biomass feedstock other than food crops, ethanol for use as fuel; and

(e) no fee shall be required from any applicant who certifies that he is the holder of an experimental distilled spirits plant permit, as provided by federal law and regulation, for the manufacture of ethanol for his own use as fuel.

Any permit issued pursuant to paragraph (b), (c), (d) or (e) of this subdivision shall clearly state the conditions upon which it is granted.

4. Such industrial alcohol manufacturer's permit shall be effective for a license year expiring on the thirty-first day of December following the date of issue, and the fee prescribed therefor by this section shall be the fee due and payable therefor, and shall be paid in advance at the time the application shall be made as provided by this section.

When application for any permit under this section is made, after the first day of January in any year, the fee therefor shall, for the balance of the year, be in proportion as the remainder of such year shall bear to the whole year, except, that it shall in no case be for less than one-half of such year.



**§92. Alcohol permit.**

1. The liquor authority is hereby authorized to issue special permits for the purchase of alcohol to the superintendent, or duly authorized officer, of a hospital, museum, laboratory, art, charitable, educational, or similar public institution, or to a drug store, or licensed physician, dentist, veterinarian, optometrist and chiropodist, or to a manufacturing establishment using alcohol in its processes of manufacture.

2. Such permit shall be issued in such form as prescribed by the liquor authority and shall permit the purchase and use of such alcohol for the purpose named in such permit and in accordance with the terms and conditions thereof and the rules of the liquor authority.

❷3. Such permit shall be issued for a calendar year, and the fee therefor shall be six dollars per year or for any part thereof. ❷*(2002, chgd. by chap. 85(Z), eff. 8/1/2002.)*

4. Any person who shall knowingly sell any alcohol for beverage purposes or who shall sell the same under circumstances from which he might reasonably deduce the intention of the purchaser to use it for such purposes, shall be subject to the penalties provided for in this chapter.

**§92-a. Alcohol distributors' permits.**

1. The following kinds of permits may be issued for the sale and distribution of alcohol.

(a) Distributor's alcohol permit-class a.

(b) Distributor's alcohol permit-class b.

(c) Distributor's alcohol permit-class c.

(d) Distributor's alcohol permit-class d.

2. (a) A class "a" permit shall authorize the holder thereof to sell and distribute to licensed rectifiers alcohol which is to be used for beverage purposes and to all holders of permits issued pursuant to this section

or sections ninety-one and ninety-two of this chapter. (b) A class "b" permit shall authorize the holder thereof to sell and distribute alcohol to holders of a class "c" alcohol distributor's permit or to holders of permits issued pursuant to section ninety-one and section ninety-two of this chapter. (c) A class "c" permit shall authorize the holder thereof to sell and distribute alcohol to holders of permits issued pursuant to section ninety-two of this chapter and to use alcohol in the preparation by him of any of the products enumerated in section ninety-one of this chapter. Such a permit may be applied for by and shall be issued only to a wholesale druggist. (d) A class "d" permit shall authorize the holder thereof to sell and distribute alcohol to the holder of winery licenses. Such permits shall be issued only to a person holding a winery license under this chapter.

Such permits shall be issued in such form as may be prescribed by the liquor authority, and the privileges granted thereby shall be exercised in accordance with the terms and conditions thereof and the rules of the liquor authority.

❷3. The annual fee for a distributor's alcohol permit, class "a," shall be sixteen hundred dollars.

❷4. The annual fee for a distributor's alcohol permit, class "b," shall be eight hundred dollars.

❷5. The annual fee for a distributor's alcohol permit, class "c," shall be one hundred sixty dollars.

❷6. The annual fee for a distributor's alcohol permit, class "d," shall be three hundred eighty-four dollars.

❷*(2002, chgd. by chap. 85(Z), eff. 8/1/2002.)*

7. Such distributors' alcohol permits shall be effective for a license year expiring on the thirty-first day of December following the date of issuance, and the fee prescribed therefor by this section shall be the fee due and payable therefor, and shall be paid in advance at the time the application shall be made as provided by this section.

When application for any permit under this section is made, after the first day of January in any year, the fee therefor shall, for the balance of the year, be in proportion as the remainder of such year shall bear to the whole year, except, that it shall in no case be for less than one-half of such year.

**§93. Solicitor's permit.**

1. No individual shall offer for sale or solicit any order in the state for the sale of any alcoholic beverage irrespective of whether such sale is to be made within or without the state, unless such person shall have a solicitor's permit.

2. Such a permit shall authorize the permittee to offer for sale or to solicit orders for the sale of any alcoholic beverages, and shall set forth the name, address and license number of the licensee whom the solicitor represents, and such solicitor shall not represent any licensee whose name does not appear upon such permit.

❷3. The license fee for such permit shall be twenty-six dollars per year, or for any part thereof, and the permit shall be issued for the calendar year.

❷4. Notwithstanding the foregoing provisions of this section, any duly licensed manufacturer or wholesaler may apply to the liquor authority for an annual temporary solicitor's employment permit. Such permit shall authorize such manufacturer or wholesaler to employ one or more persons as a solicitor for a period of not exceeding sixty consecutive working days provided that within thirty days after such employee has been employed as a solicitor such employee shall file his application for a solicitor's permit with the liquor authority. The license fee for such permit shall be thirty-eight dollars per year, or for any part thereof, and the permit shall be issued for the calendar year. Such permit and the exercise of the privileges hereby granted thereunder, shall be subject to such terms and conditions as may be prescribed by the liquor authority.

❷*(2002, chgd. by chap. 85(Z), eff. 8/1/2002.)*

❸5. Notwithstanding any provision of this chapter to the contrary, a licensed winery or licensed farm winery may obtain from the liquor authority a solicitor's permit authorizing the licensee to offer for sale or solicit any order for any New York state labelled wine. The authority shall not charge an application or permit fee for the issuance of a solicitor's permit to a licensed winery or farm winery. ❸*(1993, chgd. by chap. 490, eff. 1/1/94.)*

**§93-a. Broker's permit.**

1. No person shall engage as a broker in the purchase and sale of alcoholic beverages in this state unless such person shall have a broker's permit.

2. Such permit shall authorize the permittee to act as a broker in the purchase and sale of alcoholic beverages for a fee or commission, for or on behalf of a person authorized to manufacture or sell at wholesale alcoholic beverages within or without the state. Such permittee shall not buy or sell any alcoholic beverages for his own account, or take or deliver title to such alcoholic beverages, and shall not receive or store any alcoholic beverages in his own name in this state, or offer, agree to offer or sell any alcoholic beverages to any retailer within this state.

3. Such permit shall be issued either for one transaction or for a calendar year and the exercise of the privileges granted thereby shall be subject to such rules and conditions by the liquor authority as it deems necessary.

❷4. The fee for a broker's permit shall be fixed by the liquor authority, but shall not exceed twenty-six dollars for a permit valid for one transaction nor two hundred fifty-six dollars for a permit issued for a calendar year. ❷*(2002, chgd. by chap. 85(Z), eff. 8/1/2002.)*

**§94. Trucking permit.**

1. No vehicle shall be used in this state for the trucking or transportation of any alcoholic beverage unless such vehicle shall be registered with the liquor authority by a permit issued by it and shall have affixed thereto a sign to be approved by the liquor authority, containing the registration number of such vehicle. In lieu of such sign a vehicle may have in its cab a photostatic copy of its current permit issued by the Authority. This provision shall not apply to vehicles owned or hired and operated by a licensee.

❷2. Such permit shall be issued for the calendar year, and may cover one or more trucks and in cities having a population of one million or less to duly licensed taxicabs used to deliver only wine or liquor sold at retail and the fee therefor shall be at the rate of fifty-one dollars per truck or such duly licensed taxicab per year.

❷2-a. In lieu of such permits, the liquor authority may issue a fleet permit for an annual fee of sixty-four hundred dollars. Such fleet permit shall cover any and all vehicles owned or hired, and operated, by such permittee. In lieu of the sign required to be affixed to each vehicle pursuant to subdivision one of this section, the holder of a fleet permit may have in the cab of such vehicle a photostatic copy of its current fleet permit issued by the authority.

❷*(2002, chgd. by chap. 85(Z), eff. 8/1/2002.)*

3. If such application is made after July first in any one year, the fee shall be one-half of the annual fee herein provided for.

**§95. Drug store permit.**

The liquor authority may issue a drug store permit to sell liquor and/or wine for off-premises consumption pursuant to this section.

1. Application must be made upon a form to be provided by the liquor authority and shall be filed with the appropriate board. Section fifty-four shall control so far as applicable the procedure in connection with such application.

2. Such permit shall authorize the permittee to sell liquor or wine in the original sealed package only upon a written prescription of a regularly licensed physician in a quantity not exceeding one pint of liquor and one quart of wine; such prescription shall state the date thereof; the name of the person for whom prescribed and shall be preserved by the vendor and pasted in a book kept for the purpose and be but once filled. Such package shall not be opened after sale nor its contents consumed on the premises where sold.

3. No such permittee shall have, keep or offer for sale, or sell in the premises designated in the permit any liquor which is not of the strength, quality and purity prescribed in the latest United States Pharmacopoeia.

❷4. Such permit shall be issued for a calendar year and the fee therefor shall be at the rate of fifty-one dollars per year for each place where such traffic is carried on except that where application shall be filed after July first in any year the fee to be paid shall be the sum of twenty-six dollars for the balance of such year. ❷*(2002, chgd. by chap. 85(Z), eff. 8/1/2002.)*

**§96. Warehouse permit.**

❺1. (a) No alcoholic beverage shall be stored or kept in or upon any premises which shall not be duly licensed as provided for in this chapter, provided, however, that the liquor authority may issue a permit in such form as prescribed by its rules, for the storage of alcoholic beverages in other than licensed premises, except that no such permit shall be issued to any person licensed pursuant to the provisions of section fifty-four or fifty-four-a of this article, nor shall any such person licensed pursuant to the provisions of section fifty-four or fifty-four-a of this article store or cause to be stored any alcoholic beverages in other than its licensed premises.

(b) Notwithstanding the provisions of paragraph (a) of this subdivision, a person licensed pursuant to section fifty-four or fifty-four-a of this article may be issued a permit pursuant to this section for the storage of a private label brand or brands of beer for which the licensee is the registered owner or for a brand or brands of beer of which the licensee is the exclusive retail seller in the state.

❺*(1995, chgd. by chap. 545, eff. 1/1/96.)*

❺2. The authority is hereby empowered upon application therefor to issue a special retail warehouse permit for the storage of beer. Such permit may be issued to a person licensed pursuant to section fifty-four or section fifty-four-a of this article on an annual basis and shall be issued in such form as prescribed by the rules of the authority for the storage of beer in other than such licensee's licensed premises. No more than five such permits may be issued by the authority on a statewide basis at any time and such permits may only be issued to persons who own licensed premises having no more than twenty-five hundred square feet of retail space per each such premises and employing no more than five people on each premises during any period of operation. ❺*(1995, added by chap. 545, eff. 1/1/96.)*

❷3. Such permit shall be issued for the calendar year and the fee therefor shall be at the rate of two hundred fifty-six dollars per annum, except that where the application shall be filed after July first in any year the fee shall be one hundred twenty-eight dollars for the remainder of such period. ❷*(1995, renumbered by chap. 545; 2002, chgd. by chap. 85(Z), eff. 8/1/2002.)*

**§96-a. Bottling permit.**

1. No liquor or wine may be bottled in this state except by the manufacturer thereof or as hereinafter provided.

2. The liquor authority is hereby authorized to issue a bottling permit to a wholesale wine or liquor licensee to bottle, recask, filter or clarify wine or liquor, respectively, imported in bulk from a foreign country, on the premises of a United States customs bonded warehouse for which a warehouse permit has been issued under this chapter or in a foreign trade zone established pursuant to federal law. Such

permit and the exercise of the privileges granted thereunder shall be subject to the laws of the United States and the rules of the federal agency having jurisdiction thereunder, and such other rules as the state liquor authority deems necessary.

3. The liquor authority is hereby authorized to issue a bottling permit to a person to bottle, on the premises designated in the permit or in a United States customs bonded warehouse for which a warehouse permit has been issued under this chapter, liquor manufactured outside of the state of New York or wine produced in a foreign country and received in this state in bulk. Such bottling may be performed for or on behalf of wholesale liquor or wine licensees or for persons authorized to sell liquor or wine at wholesale pursuant to the laws and regulations of any other state, territorial possession of the United States or foreign country. Such permit shall also authorize the holder thereof to rebottle or recondition liquors and wines manufactured outside of the state of New York and received in this state, for or on behalf of wholesale liquor or wine licensees, or for persons authorized to sell liquor or wine at wholesale pursuant to the laws and regulations of any other state, territorial possession of the United States or foreign country. Such permit and the exercise of the privileges granted thereunder shall be subject to the laws of the United States and the rules of the federal agency having jurisdiction thereunder, and such other rules as the state liquor authority deems necessary.

❷4. Such permit shall be issued in the form prescribed by the liquor authority and shall be issued for the calendar year and the fee for a permit issued under subdivision two of this section shall be at the rate of four hundred eighty dollars per annum, except that where the application shall be filed after July first in any year the fee shall be two hundred forty dollars for the remainder of such period. The fee for a permit under subdivision three of this section shall be at the rate of sixteen hundred dollars per annum, except that where the application shall be filed after July first in any year the fee shall be eight hundred dollars for the remainder of such period. ❷*(2002, chgd. by chap. 85(Z), eff. 8/1/2002.)*

**§96-b. Reconditioning permit.**

1. The liquor authority may issue a reconditioning permit to a wholesale liquor licensee to recondition wines and liquors manufactured outside of the state of New York including filtering, clarifying, rebottling, labeling, relabeling or repacking such wines and liquors. Such permit may be issued to a wholesale wine licensee to recondition such wines under the same terms and conditions as provided herein. Only wines purchased in sealed containers not exceeding fifteen gallons in content or liquor in sealed containers not exceeding one quart in content may be so reconditioned. Such reconditioning shall be done on such premises and under such conditions as the liquor authority may prescribe.

2. Each such permit and the exercise of the privilege granted thereby shall be subject to the laws of the United States and the rules of the federal agency having jurisdiction thereunder and the rules and regulations to be promulgated by the liquor authority and operations conducted pursuant thereto shall be performed under such supervision as the liquor authority shall require.

❷3. Each such permit shall be issued in such form as shall be prescribed by the liquor authority and shall be valid for one day only. The fee for each such permit shall not exceed twenty-six dollars. ❷*(2002, chgd. by chap. 85(Z), eff. 8/1/2002.)*

**§97. Temporary beer and wine permit.**

❷1. The liquor authority is hereby authorized to issue temporary permits effective for a period not to exceed twenty-four consecutive hours to authorize the sale of beer and wine manufactured in New York state at outdoor or indoor gatherings, functions, occasions or events, within the hours fixed by or pursuant to subdivision five of section one hundred six of this chapter, during which alcoholic beverages may lawfully be sold or served upon premises licensed to sell alcoholic beverages at retail for on-premises consumption in the community in which is located the premises in which such gathering, function, occasion or event is held. The fee for such permit shall be twenty-six dollars. Such permit and the exercise of the privilege granted thereby shall be subject to such rules of the liquor authority as it deems necessary.

❷2. The liquor authority is hereby authorized to issue an annual permit to brewers and beer wholesalers authorizing such licensees to sell beer for consumption at outdoor or indoor gatherings, functions, occasions or events, provided that such gatherings are not open to admission to the general public nor is admission thereto made contingent upon the payment of an admission fee, donation or contribution, and further provided that such beer is not resold at such gatherings. Every brewer or beer wholesaler to whom a permit shall be issued hereunder shall require every person to whom beer shall be sold for use at such gatherings to make, execute and file with such brewer or beer wholesaler, upon a form to be prescribed by the liquor authority, a statement, that the beer purchased by such person will not be sold or offered for sale by such person. Such statement shall be accepted for all purposes as the equivalent of an affidavit, and if false, shall subject the person making and executing the same to the same penalties as if he had been duly sworn. Such permit shall be issued in the form prescribed by the liquor authority and shall run concurrently with the annual term of the brewer's license or of the wholesale beer license, and the fee for such permit shall be sixty-four dollars. Such a permit and the exercise of the privileges granted thereunder shall be subject to such rules by the liquor authority as it deems necessary. The provisions hereof shall not apply to the sale of beer for consumption in the home.
❷*(2002, chgd. by chap. 85(Z), eff. 8/1/2002.)*

**§97-a. Temporary retail permit.**

1. The liquor authority is hereby authorized to issue a temporary retail permit to the transferee of a retail license to continue the operation of a retail premises during the period a transfer application for the license from person to person at the same premises is pending and when all the following conditions exist:

(a) The premises shall have been operated under a retail license within thirty days of the date of filing the application for a temporary permit;

(b) The retail license for said premises shall have been surrendered into safekeeping pursuant to rules of the authority;

(c) The applicant for the temporary permit shall have filed with the authority an application for transfer of the retail license at such premises; and

❷(d) The application for the temporary permit shall be accompanied by a nonrefundable temporary permit filing fee of one hundred twenty-eight dollars for all retail beer licenses; all other temporary permit applications shall be accompanied by a filing fee of six hundred forty dollars. ❷*(2002, chgd. by chap. 85(Z), eff. 8/1/2002.)*

❷2. A temporary permit issued by the authority pursuant to this section shall be for a period not to exceed ninety days. A temporary permit may be extended at the discretion of the authority, for an additional thirty day period upon payment of an additional fee of sixty-four dollars for all retail beer licenses and ninety-six dollars for all other temporary permits and upon compliance with all conditions required herein. A temporary permit is a conditional permit and authorizes the holder thereof to purchase and sell such alcoholic beverages as would be permitted to be purchased and sold under the privileges of the retail license for which transfer application has been filed; to sell such alcoholic beverages to consumers only and not for resale; and to purchase such alcoholic beverages only by payment in currency or check for such alcoholic beverages on or before they are delivered to the premises. ❷*(1994, chgd. by chap. 361; 2002, chgd. by chap. 85(Z), eff. 8/1/2002.)*

3. Provided, however, that the holder of a temporary permit who also holds one or more retail licenses and is operating under such retail license or licenses in addition to the temporary permit, and who is not delinquent under the provisions of section one hundred one-a of this chapter as to any retail license under which he operates, may purchase alcoholic beverages on credit under the temporary permit.

4. Notwithstanding any other provision of law, a temporary permit may be summarily cancelled or suspended at any time if the authority determines that good cause for such cancellation or suspension exists. The authority shall promptly notify the holder of a temporary permit in writing of such cancellation or suspension and shall set forth the reasons for such action.

5. Application for a temporary permit shall be on such form as the authority shall prescribe.

Printed in the U.S.A. ab

6. Notwithstanding any inconsistent provision of law to the contrary, the authority may promulgate such rules and regulations as may be necessary to carry out the provisions of this section.

**§98. Caterer's permit.**

❷1. The liquor authority is hereby authorized to issue to caterers and other persons furnishing provisions and service for use at a particular function, occasion or event in a hotel, restaurant, club, ballroom or other premises a temporary indoor permit effective for a period not to exceed twenty-four consecutive hours, which shall authorize the service of alcoholic beverages at such function, occasion or event within the hours, fixed by or pursuant to subdivision five of section one hundred six of this chapter, during which alcoholic beverages may lawfully be sold or served upon premises licensed to sell alcoholic beverages at retail for on-premises consumption in the community in which is located the premises in which such function, occasion or event is held. The fee therefor shall be thirty-eight dollars. Such a permit and the exercise of the privilege granted thereby may be subjected to such rules by the liquor authority as it deems necessary and such rules as are in conformity with the provisions of subdivision two of this section. Such a permit may also be issued for functions, occasions or events at premises for which a summer license has been previously issued pursuant to this chapter. ❷*(2002, chgd. by chap. 85(Z), eff. 8/1/2002.)*

2. Except for good cause shown, the liquor authority shall issue upon proper application and payment of fee, an on-premises caterer's permit to a club licensed pursuant to the provisions of this chapter upon the club premises if it is shown:

a. That the club has not solicited the event, nor advertised such affair in any manner as open to the public and the alcoholic beverages shall be sold only to persons invited to and attending such function, occasion or event; and

b. That the particular function or event is to be held by a sodality, an auxiliary or other organization affiliated with the licensed club and also other organizations not affiliated with a licensed club, provided the function or event being held is in conjunction with the use of the primary athletic or sports facilities of the licensed club; and *(See other par. b below.)*

b. The particular function or event is to be held by a sodality or auxiliary affiliated with the club, or a particular charitable or non-profit function or event is to be held by a charitable or non-profit organization and such organization has one or more members who are also members of the club. *(See other par. b above.)*

3. The liquor authority may issue upon proper application and payment of fee, an on-premises caterer's permit to a club licensed pursuant to the provisions of this chapter if the facts set forth in the application establish to the satisfaction of the authority that no other suitably licensed premises authorized to sell alcoholic beverages to the public is available within a reasonable distance.

4. A caterer's permit will not be granted to a club licensed for a function to be held off the club premises except where such is exclusively for the use and benefit of the club members only and is so restricted.

### §99. Special permit to remain open during certain hours of the morning.

❷1. Any person licensed to sell alcoholic beverages for consumption on the premises pursuant to this chapter may apply to the liquor authority for a special permit to remain open on any week day between the hours of four o'clock a.m. or the closing hour prescribed by a rule adopted in a county on or before April first, nineteen hundred ninety-five or pursuant to subdivision eleven of section seventeen of this chapter, and eight o'clock a.m. The fee for such permit shall be fifty-one dollars per day. ❷*(1995, chgd. by chap. 83; 2002, chgd. by chap. 85(Z), eff. 8/1/2002.)*

❷2. The liquor authority may, in its discretion, issue to any such licensed person, whose premises are located within a trade area, a special permit to remain open during such hours of the morning on weekdays. The fee for such permit shall be at the rate of two hundred fifty-six dollars per annum. ❷*(2002, chgd. by chap. 85(Z), eff. 8/1/2002.)*

3. Such permits and the exercise of the privileges granted thereunder may be subjected by the liquor authority to such rules as it may deem necessary.

### ❶§99-a. Charitable permits.

1. The liquor authority is hereby authorized to issue a charitable permit to an organization to sell alcoholic beverages, at auction or otherwise, where the authority is satisfied: (a) that contributions made by an individual donor to such organization are deductible for Federal income tax purposes; (b) that the funds so raised will be used for the non-profit purposes of the organization; (c) that all such alcoholic beverages shall be in sealed containers; and (d) that not more than eighty cases shall be sold. Such permit shall be valid for a twenty-four hour period commencing at eight o'clock a.m. and only during the hours when such alcoholic beverages may lawfully be sold by retail licensees in the county in which the auction or sale is held. No alcoholic beverages sold pursuant to such permit shall be consumed on the premises at which they are sold.

2. The fee for a one-day charitable permit shall be twenty dollars. ❶*(2001, added by chap. 196, eff. 8/20/2001.)*

### §99-b. Miscellaneous permits.

1. The liquor authority is hereby authorized to issue a permit to:

a. A sheriff, marshal, assignee for the benefit of creditors, trustee or receiver in bankruptcy, executor or administrator of an estate, to sell the stock of alcoholic beverages which came into his possession pursuant to judicial process.

Printed in the U.S.A. ab

b. A steamship company or company operating aircraft, or its duly authorized agent, to purchase from a manufacturer or wholesaler in this state alcoholic beverages for ship's stores for consumption outside the territorial jurisdiction of the state, and not for purposes of resale in this state.

c. A person engaged in the manufacture of products which are unfit for beverage use and classified by the United States treasury department, as exempt from special and commodity taxes to purchase liquor, wine or beer from licensed wholesalers and manufacturers for use only in the process of manufacture of such products.

d. A fire insurance company or fire salvage company, under the supervision of the New York state department of insurance, to sell to licensees alcoholic beverages which came into its possession as a result of a fire on licensed premises.

e. A hospital, which shall mean a place for overnight care of the sick, conducted or licensed by the state or a political subdivision thereof or subject to visitation and inspection by the state board of social welfare to purchase liquor, wine or beer for medicinal use only in the treatment of bona fide patients of such hospital.

f. A licensee who is liquidating or selling his business, or a former licensee whose license was surrendered or expired, to sell his entire stock of alcoholic beverages to other licensees.

g. A warehouseman, railroad company, steamship company, or other person who has acquired a lien pursuant to law for the storage or carriage of alcoholic beverages, to sell such alcoholic beverages to a licensee.

h. *(Repealed.)*

i. A bank or trust company incorporated under articles three, seven or twelve of the banking law or a foreign banking corporation licensed by superintendent of insurance of this state or a banking corporation organized under the laws of the United States and doing business in this state, to sell warehouse receipts pertaining to alcoholic beverages which it has accepted as collateral security for a loan to a licensee and which it acquired through default in the payment of such loan.

j. A person duly licensed outside the state of New York to manufacture or sell alcoholic beverages at wholesale, or his duly authorized representative, to negotiate and consummate contracts or agreements with licensed wholesalers in this state for the establishment of operating agency relationships for the sale of its products in this state.

k. A person to purchase, receive or sell alcoholic beverages or receipts, certificates, contracts or other documents pertaining to alcoholic beverages, in cases not expressly provided for by this chapter, when in the judgment of the liquor authority it would be appropriate and consistent with the purpose of this chapter.

*l*. (1) Licensed wineries and licensed farm wineries to sell New York state labelled wine, by the bottle, at the state fair at recognized county fairs and at farmers markets operated on a not-for-profit basis.

(2) The permit shall be valid for the length of the event, but not for a period to exceed one year.

(3) No fee shall be charged for permits issued pursuant to this subdivision.

2. Each such permit and the exercise of the privilege granted thereby maybe subjected to such rules and conditions by the liquor authority as it deems necessary.

❷3. Each such permit shall be issued in such form as shall be prescribed by the liquor authority and shall be valid for one transaction only, except that a permit issued pursuant to paragraph b, c, e, or j of subdivision one of this section may be issued either for one transaction or for a calendar year. The liquor authority may, by rule, fix the quantity of alcoholic beverages to be involved in a single transaction under a permit issued pursuant to paragraph k of subdivision one of this section, but no single transaction so authorized shall involve more than twenty cases of alcoholic beverages. The fee for each such permit shall be fixed by the liquor authority, but shall not exceed ninety dollars for a permit valid for one transaction only nor two hundred fifty-six dollars for a permit issued for a calendar year. ❷*(2002, chgd. by chap. 85(Z), eff. 8/1/2002.)*

**§99-d. Miscellaneous fees.**

❾1. Before any substantial alteration to a licensed premises may be undertaken by or on the behalf of any licensee except a farm winery, the licensee shall make an application to the liquor authority for permission to effect such alteration. A substantial alteration shall include any enlargement or contraction of a licensed premises whether indoors or outdoors; any physical change that reduces the visibility that existed at the time of licensing; any other physical changes in the interior of a licensed premises that materially affect the character of the premises; and, in the case of establishments licensed for consumption on the premises, any material changes to the dining or kitchen facilities, or any change in the size or location of any bar within the contemplation of subdivision four of section one hundred of this chapter at which alcoholic beverages are dispensed. A minor alteration shall be deemed to be one costing and valued at less than ten thousand dollars, which does not materially affect the character of the premises or the physical structure that existed at the time of licensing. Before commencing work on the alteration, any licensee other than a farm winery licensee, shall request permission to effect such minor alteration and shall submit an affidavit to the liquor authority by filing the same in person or by certified mail return receipt requested on forms prescribed by the authority. A winery or farm winery licensee is not required to obtain permission from the authority to make a minor alteration to its premises. The affidavit shall include but not be limited to a description of the proposed alteration, the cost and value of the alteration, and the source of money making the alteration possible. Upon receipt of such affidavit, the authority shall have twenty days in which to review the proposed alteration and notify the licensee of any objection to the same by certified mail return receipt requested. If no such objection is made within such period permission shall be deemed to have been granted. Work may commence on such alteration if no objection is received by the twenty-fifth day after filing such affidavit. The cost of an alteration, for purposes of this subdivision, shall be equal to the total sum expended to complete the proposed alteration excluding professional fees. ❾*(1993, chgd. by chaps. 321, 490; 1994, chgd. by chap. 170; 1999, chgd. by chap. 372, eff. 7/27/99.)*

❼2. ❷Before any change in the members of a limited liability company or the transfer or assignment of a membership interest in a limited liability company or any corporate change in stockholders, stockholdings, alcoholic beverage officers, officers or directors, except officers and directors of a premises licensed as a club or a luncheon club under this chapter can be effectuated for the purposes of this chapter, there shall be filed with the liquor authority an application for permission to make such change and there shall be paid to the liquor authority in advance upon filing of the application a fee of one hundred twenty-eight dollars where the license fee is five hundred dollars or more and thirteen dollars in all other instances including changes relating solely to officers and directors of corporations and the alcoholic beverage officer of a club or luncheon club. ❷*(1998, chgd. by chap. 193; 2002, chgd. by chap. 85(Z), eff. 8/1/2002.)*

The foregoing provisions of this section shall not be applicable where there are ten or more stockholders and such change involves less than ten per centum of the stock of the corporation and the stock holdings of any stockholder are not increased thereby to ten per centum or more of the stock.

Where the same corporation operates two or more premises separately licensed under this chapter a separate corporate change shall be filed for each such licensed premises, except as otherwise provided for by rule of the liquor authority. The corporate change fee provided for herein shall not be applicable to more than one license held by the same corporation.

❼*(1997, chgd. by chap. 259, eff. 10/19/97.)*

❷3. Before any removal of a license to any premises other than the licensed premises or to any other part of the building containing the licensed premises, the licensee shall make an application to the liquor authority for permission to effect such removal and shall pay to the liquor authority in advance upon filing of the application a fee of one hundred ninety-two dollars where the base license fee is five hundred dollars or more and thirty-two dollars in all other instances. ❷*(2002, chgd. by chap. 85(Z), eff. 8/1/2002.)*

4. The liquor authority may make such rules as it deems necessary to carry out the provisions of this section.

**❖§99-e. Change in duration of permits.**

The liquor authority is authorized to change the periods during which permits authorized by sections ninety-one, ninety-one-a, ninety-two, ninety-two-a, ninety-three, ninety-three-a, ninety-four, ninety-five, ninety-six, ninety-six-a and ninety-nine-b of this article, shall be effective and to establish the commencement dates, duration and expiration dates thereof, provided that no such permit shall be effective for a period in excess of three years. When any change or changes are made in the duration of any such permit, the permit fee shall be equal to the annual permit fee specified in this article multiplied by the number of years for which such permit is issued. Any other provision of any other law to the contrary notwithstanding, an applicant, other than a not-for-profit organization as defined in section one hundred seventy-nine-q of the state finance law, shall not be issued a temporary permit pursuant to section ninety-seven of this article for events to take place upon any premise for which the authority has issued any license, or has issued a permit more than four times within any one year period, provided however that the authority may, in its sole discretion, issue additional single permits if it shall determine upon the issuance of each that (a) the application for such permit is not an attempt to circumvent licensing provisions of this chapter, and (b) the issuance of such permit would not be a detriment to the community or the surrounding neighborhood as such shall be determined by the authority after consultation with municipal authorities and police agencies and community boards for the purpose of reviewing community or neighborhood or police agency complaints, or violations of state or local laws. The liquor authority may make such rules as shall be appropriate to carry out the purpose of this section. ❖*(2000, chgd. by chap. 114, eff. 11/8/2000.)*

**❷§99-f. Special permits for minors to entertain.**

The liquor authority is hereby authorized to issue special permits to any person under the age of eighteen years for the purpose of enabling such person to appear as an entertainer on any premises licensed for retail sale hereunder. The provisions of this section shall apply to persons under the age of eighteen years who are not otherwise eligible to act as an entertainer pursuant to the provisions of subdivision two-b of section one hundred of this chapter. Such special permit shall be issued, in the discretion of the authority, upon the application of such minor. No such special permit shall be granted unless the written consent of both parents or the lawful guardian or guardians of such minor shall appear upon such application. The liquor authority may require the personal appearance at an office of the authority of such applicant and his parents or legal guardians at the time such application is made or at any other time prior to the consideration of such application by the authority upon written notice to the applicant and/or his parents or legal guardians. Such personal appearance, if requested, shall be for the purpose of enabling the authority to establish that the entertainment that the applicant is intending to perform is not contrary to the best interests of the minor. The liquor authority is hereby authorized and directed to promulgate rules and regulations for the orderly implementation and administration of the provisions of this section. Such rules and regulations shall provide for a reasonable limitation upon the types of entertainment for which an application for a special permit shall be granted and may provide for conditions or limitations which may be attached to the granting of such special permit. In addition to any conditions or limitations as may be so imposed, such rules or regulations shall impose as a condition for the granting of such special permit that a parent or legal guardian of the minor shall be present during such minor's appearance as an entertainer. Such special permit shall be subject to revocation, after a hearing upon a determination by the authority that the conditions or limitations attached upon such special permit have been violated. Such special permits shall be issued for limited periods not to exceed one year. The liquor authority may impose a fee for the issuance of such special permit. Such fee shall not exceed sixty-four dollars if issued for an annual period nor shall such fee exceed six dollars per month or any lesser period thereof for which a special permit has been issued. The liquor authority may waive such fee. The liquor authority shall revoke any special permit upon the written request of the parents or legal guardians of such minor. ❷*(2002, chgd. by chap. 85(Z), eff. 8/1/2002.)*



**§99-g. Sale of privately held wines.**

1. (a) Any nonlicensed person legally owning wine is authorized to sell that wine to a licensed person or through a licensed person to an individual or group of individuals by any lawful method of sale or by means of an auction by a licensed person conducted pursuant to this section. The licensee involved in such sale shall ensure that each bottle of wine sold from a private collection has a permanently affixed label stating that the wine was acquired from a private collection.

(b) For purposes of this section, "licensed person" means any person licensed under section sixty-three or seventy-nine of this chapter and who has been so licensed for a period of ten years or more.

2. (a) The liquor authority is hereby authorized to issue a wine auction permit to a licensed person to conduct auctions of wines. The wine auction permit shall be in addition to any permit requirements imposed by local law, ordinance or resolution by any municipality in which the auctioneer seeks to operate.

(b) A wine auction permit shall be issued for a calendar year. A wine auction permit shall allow the holder to conduct twelve auctions of wine during the period the wine auction permit shall be in effect.

❷(c) The fee therefor shall be thirty-two hundred dollars for each year or part thereof. ❷*(2002, chgd. by chap. 85(Z), eff. 8/1/2002.)*

(d) The permit shall be in the form prescribed by the authority.

3. A person owning, controlling or possessing wines may ship the wines from within or without New York state to a wine auction permittee or licensee; provided that such permittee or licensee shall ensure that each bottle is labelled in accordance with the provisions of paragraph (a) of subdivision one of this section. Although the wines to be offered at auction may not be owned by a wine auction permittee, upon receipt of the wines the permittee shall be responsible for the storage and warehousing of the wines, as well as be responsible for the delivery of the wines to the purchasers at auction and shall be responsible for the payment of all applicable state and local taxes.

4. Notwithstanding any other provision of this chapter, any person authorized to sell wine at wholesale or retail may purchase any wine offered at a wine auction conducted pursuant to this section and may resell any wine so purchased in accordance with the terms of his license; provided that such licensee shall ensure that each bottle is labelled in accordance with the provisions of paragraph (a) of subdivision one of this section.

5. A wine auction permittee shall be permitted to hold wine tastings on the premises of any location approved by the authority for conducting a wine auction.

6. A wine auction permittee shall be subject to all restrictions, regulations, and provisions heretofore set forth in the appropriate sections of this chapter governing the sale of wine for off-premises consumption, provided those provisions are not inconsistent with the provisions created pursuant to this section.

7. Wine tastings which are conducted under this* auspices of an official agent of a farm winery, winery, wholesaler or importer and where such agent is physically present at all times during the conduct of the tasting, then, in that event, any liability stemming from a right of action resulting from a wine tasting as authorized herein, and in accordance with the provisions of sections 11-100 and 11-101 of the general obligations law, shall accrue to the farm winery, winery, wholesaler, importer, or licensee.

**So in original. Probably should be "the".*

8. The authority shall adopt any rules consistent with and in furtherance of the implementation of this section.

*(1993, added by chap. 458, eff. 11/23/93.)*

## Article 8
## GENERAL PROVISIONS

## §100. Alcoholic beverages generally.

1. No person shall manufacture for sale or sell at wholesale or retail any alcoholic beverage within the state without obtaining the appropriate license therefor required by this chapter.

2. No manufacturer and no wholesaler shall sell, or agree to sell or deliver in this state any alcoholic beverage for the purposes of resale to any person who is not duly licensed pursuant to this chapter to sell such beverages, at wholesale or retail, as the case may be, at the time of such agreement and sale.

❷2-a. No retailer shall employ, or permit to be employed, or shall suffer to work, on any premises licensed for retail sale hereunder, any person under the age of eighteen years, as a hostess, waitress, waiter, or in any other capacity where the duties of such person require or permit such person to sell, dispense or handle alcoholic beverages; except that: (1) any person under the age of eighteen years and employed by any person holding a grocery or drug store beer license shall be permitted to handle and deliver beer and wine products for such licensee, (2) any person under the age of eighteen employed as a cashier by a person holding a grocery or drug store beer license shall be permitted to record and receive payment for beer and wine product sales when in the presence of and under the direct supervision of a person eighteen years of age or over, (2-a) any person under the age of eighteen years and employed by a person holding a grocery store or drug store beer license as either a cashier or in any other position to which handling of containers which may have held alcoholic beverages is necessary, shall be permitted to handle the containers if such have been presented for redemption in accordance with the provisions of title ten of article twenty-seven of the environmental conservation law, and (3) any person under the age of eighteen years employed as a dishwasher, busboy, or other such position as to which handling of containers which may have held alcoholic beverages is necessary shall be permitted to do so under the direct supervision of a person of legal age to purchase alcoholic beverages in the state. ❷*(2002, chgd. by chap. 249, eff. 7/30/2002.)*

2-b. Subject to the provisions of section ninety-nine-f of this chapter no retailer shall permit or suffer to appear as an entertainer, on any premises licensed for retail sale hereunder, any person under the age of eighteen years, except that a person under the age of eighteen years may appear as such entertainer, provided that:

(a) the parents or lawful guardian of such person expressly consent in writing to such appearance;

(b) the appearance is for a special function, occasion, or event;

(c) the appearance is approved by and made under the sponsorship of a primary or secondary school;

(d) the appearance takes place in the presence and under the direct supervision of a teacher of such school; and

(e) the appearance does not take place in a tavern. Failure to restrain such a person from so appearing shall be deemed to constitute permission.

3. Nothing contained in this chapter shall be construed to require that any food be sold or purchased with or in order to obtain any alcoholic beverage for consumption on the premises where sold.

4. Alcoholic beverages may be sold to be consumed on the premises at a bar, counter or similar contrivance. Only one such bar, counter or contrivance shall be permitted in any licensed premises, except that not more than two additional bars, counters or contrivances may be permitted by the liquor authority for good cause shown to it, and upon the payment to it of a fee, for each additional bar, equivalent to the

Printed in the U.S.A. ab

amount of the annual license fee paid by the licensee and except that if the licensed premises is a legitimate theatre or concert hall, or contiguous to and used in conjunction with a legitimate theatre or concert hall, additional bars, counters or contrivances may be permitted by the liquor authority upon payment to it of an annual fee of one hundred dollars for each such additional bar, counter or contrivance so permitted, in addition to the annual license fee paid by such licensee and except that if such licensed premises be located at a baseball park, race track, or either outdoor or indoor athletic field, facility, arena or stadium, additional bars, counters or contrivances where beer shall be sold at retail for consumption on the premises maybe* permitted by the liquor authority, upon payment to it of the annual fee of thirty dollars for each such additional bar, counter or contrivance so permitted, in addition to the amount of the annual license fee paid by the licensee, and except that temporary portable bars, counters or contrivances shall be permitted in a ballroom, meeting room or private dining-room on the licensed premises of a hotel, restaurant or club during such time as said ballroom, meeting room or private dining-room is used for a private dinner, entertainment, meeting or similar affair to which members of the general public are not admitted.

**So in original. Probably should be "may be".*

4-a. At race meetings, authorized by the state racing commission, notwithstanding any inconsistent provision of law, additional bars, counters or contrivances where alcoholic beverages shall be sold at retail for consumption on the premises may be permitted by the liquor authority, upon payment to it of a fee equivalent to the amount of the annual or summer license fee paid by the licensee for each such additional bar, counter or contrivance so permitted in addition to the amount of the annual or summer license fee paid by the licensee.

5. No retail licensee for off-premises consumption shall sell, deliver or give away, or cause, permit or procure to be sold, delivered or given away any alcoholic beverage, other than as provided herein, on credit: a retail licensee for off-premises consumption, except a winery licensee, may accept third party credit cards for the sale of an alcoholic beverage for which it is licensed; a winery licensee having the right to sell wine at retail for off-premises consumption may accept third party credit cards for the sale of said beverages at the winery premises only; and any person duly authorized to sell wine at retail for consumption off the premises may sell on credit to any regularly organized church, synagogue or religious organization, wines to be used for sacramental purposes only. For purposes of this subdivision, beer and wine products that are delivered and left at the residence of a consumer without payment of the balance due thereon shall not constitute a sale on credit.

6. No licensee shall sell or purchase any receipts, certificates, contracts or other documents issued for the storage of alcoholic beverages except as provided by the rules of the liquor authority. The liquor authority shall prescribe such rules for the purchase and sale of such

receipts, certificates, contracts or other documents issued for the storage of alcoholic beverages which, in its opinion, will best accomplish

(1) Elimination of fraudulent and deceptive transactions;

(2) Protection of purchasers against defaults by sellers;

(3) The delivery of the alcoholic beverages represented by such receipts or documents, and

(4) The payment of all taxes due thereon to the state.

7. Within ten days after filing a new application to sell liquor at retail under section sixty-three, sixty-four, sixty-four-a or sixty-four-b of this chapter, a notice thereof, in the form prescribed by the authority, shall be posted by the applicant in a conspicuous place at the entrance to the proposed premises. The applicant shall make reasonable efforts to insure such notice shall remain posted throughout the pendency of the application. The provisions hereof shall apply only where no retail liquor license has previously been granted for the proposed premise and shall, specifically, not be applicable to a proposed sale of an existing business engaged in the retail sale of liquor. The authority may adopt such rules it may deem necessary to carry out the purpose of this subdivision.



**§101. Manufacturers and wholesalers not to be interested in retail places.**

1. It shall be unlawful for a manufacturer or wholesaler licensed under this chapter to

❷(a) Be interested directly or indirectly in any premises where any alcoholic beverage is sold at retail; or in any business devoted wholly or partially to the sale of any alcoholic beverage at retail by stock ownership, interlocking directors, mortgage or lien or any personal or real property, or by any other means. The provisions of this paragraph shall not apply to (i) any such premises or business constituting the overnight lodging and resort facility located wholly within the boundaries of the town of North Elba, county of Essex, township eleven, Richard's survey, great lot numbers two hundred seventy-eight, two hundred seventy-nine, two hundred eighty, two hundred ninety-eight, two hundred ninety-nine, three hundred, three hundred eighteen, three hundred nineteen, three hundred twenty, three hundred thirty-five and three hundred thirty-six, and township twelve, Thorn's survey, great lot numbers one hundred six and one hundred thirteen, as shown on the Adirondack map, compiled by the conservation department of the state of New York—nineteen hundred sixty-four edition, in the Essex county atlas at page twenty-seven in the Essex county clerk's office, Elizabethtown, New York, provided that such facility maintains not less than two hundred fifty rooms and suites for overnight lodging, (ii) any such premises or business constituting the overnight lodging and resort facility located wholly within the boundaries of that tract or parcel of land situate in the city of Canandaigua, county of Ontario, beginning at a point in the northerly line of village lot nine where it meets with South Main Street, thence south sixty-nine degrees fifty-four minutes west a distance of nine hundred sixteen and twenty-three hundredths feet to an iron pin; thence in the same course a distance of fourteen feet to an iron pin; thence in the same course a distance of fourteen and four-tenths feet to a point; thence south fifteen degrees thirty-eight minutes and forty seconds east a distance of four hundred forty-six and eighty-seven hundredths feet to a point; thence south twenty-eight degrees thirty-seven minutes and fifty seconds east a distance of one hundred thirteen and eighty-four hundredths feet to a point; thence south eighty-five degrees and forty-seven minutes east a distance of forty-seven and sixty-one hundredths feet to an iron pin; thence on the same course a distance of three hundred and sixty-five feet to an iron pin; thence north seventeen degrees twenty-one minutes and ten seconds east a distance of four hundred fifty-seven and thirty-two hundredths feet to an iron pin; thence north nineteen degrees and thirty minutes west a distance of two hundred and forty-eight feet to a point; thence north sixty-nine degrees and fifty-four minutes east a distance of two hundred eighty-four and twenty-six hundredths feet to a point; thence north nineteen degrees and thirty minutes west a distance of sixty feet to the point and place of beginning, provided that such facility maintains not less than one hundred twenty rooms and suites for overnight lodging, (iii) any such premises or business constituting the overnight lodging facility located wholly within the boundaries of that tract or parcel of land situated in the borough of Manhattan, city and county of New York, beginning at a point on the northerly side of west fifty-fourth street at a point one hundred feet easterly from the intersection of the said northerly side of west fifty-fourth street and the easterly side of seventh avenue; running thence northerly and parallel with the easterly side of seventh avenue one hundred feet five inches to the center line of the block; running thence easterly and parallel with the northerly side of west fifty-fourth street and along the center line of the block fifty feet to a point; running thence northerly and parallel with the easterly side of seventh avenue one hundred feet five inches to the southerly side of west fifty-fifth street at a point distant one hundred fifty feet easterly from the intersection of the said southerly side of west fifty-fifth street and the easterly side of seventh avenue; running thence easterly along the southerly side of west fifty-fifth street thirty-one feet three inches to a point; running thence southerly and parallel with the easterly side of the seventh avenue one hundred feet five inches to the center line of the block; running thence easterly along the center line of the block and parallel with the southerly side of west fifty-fifth street, one hundred feet; running thence northerly and parallel with the easterly side of seventh avenue one hundred feet five inches to the southerly side of west fifty-fifth street; running thence easterly along the southerly side of west fifty-fifth street twenty-one feet ten and one-half inches to a point; running thence southerly and parallel with the easterly side of seventh avenue one hundred feet five inches to the center line of the block; running thence westerly along the center line of the block and parallel with the northerly side of west fifty-fourth street three feet one and one-half inches; running thence southerly and parallel with the easterly side of seventh avenue one hundred feet five inches to the northerly side of west fifty-fourth street at a point distant three hundred feet easterly from the intersection of the said northerly side of west fifty-fourth street and the easterly side of seventh avenue; running thence westerly and along the northerly side of west fifty-fourth street two hundred feet to the point or place of beginning, provided that such facility maintains not less than four hundred guest rooms and suites for overnight lodging, (iv) any such premises or business located on that tract or parcel of land, or any subdivision thereof, situate in the Village of Lake Placid, Town of North Elba, Essex County, New York; it being also a part of Lot No. 279, Township No. 11, Old Military Tract, Richard's Survey; it being also all of Lot No. 23 and part of Lot No. 22 as shown and designated on a certain map entitled "Map of Building Sites for Sale by B.R. Brewster" made by G.T. Chellis C.E. in 1892; also being PARCEL No. 1 on a certain map of lands of Robert J. Mahoney and wife made by G.C. Sylvester, P.E. & L.S. # 21300, dated August 4, 1964, and filed in the Essex County Clerk's Office on August 27, 1964, and more particularly bounded and described as follows; BEGINNING at the intersection of the northerly bounds of Shore Drive (formerly Mirror Street) with the westerly bounds of Park Place (formerly Rider Street) which point is also the northeast corner of Lot No. 23, from thence South 21° 50′ East in the westerly bounds of Park Place a distance of 119 feet, more or less, to a lead plug in the edge of the sidewalk marking the southeast corner of Lot No. 23 and the northeast corner of Lot No. 24; from thence South 68° 00′ 50″ West a distance of 50.05 feet to an iron pipe set in concrete at the corner of Lots 23 and 22; from thence South 65° 10′ 50″ West a distance of 7.94 feet along the south line of Lot No. 22 to an iron pipe for a corner; from thence North 23° 21′ 40″ West and at 17.84 feet along said line passing over a drill hole in a concrete sidewalk, and at 68.04 feet further along said line passing over an iron pipe at the southerly edge of another sidewalk, and at 1.22 feet further along said line passing over another drill hole in a sidewalk, a total distance of 119 feet, more or less, to the northerly line of Lot. No. 22; from thence easterly in the northerly line of Lot 22 and 23 to the northeast corner of Lot No. 23 and the point of beginning. Also including the lands to the center of Shore Drive included between the northerly straight line continuation of the side lines of the above described parcel, and to the center of Park Place, where they abut the above described premises SUBJECT to the use thereof for street purposes. Being the same premises conveyed by Morestuff, Inc. to Madeline Sellers by deed dated June 30, 1992, recorded in the Essex County Clerk's Office on July 10, 1992 in Book 1017 of Deeds at Page 318; (v) any such premises or business located on that certain piece or parcel of land, or any subdivision thereof, situate, lying and being in the Town of Plattsburgh, County of Clinton, State of New York and being more particularly bounded and described as follows: Starting at an iron pipe found in the easterly bounds of the highway known as the Old Military Turnpike, said iron pipe being located 910.39 feet southeasterly, as measured along the easterly bounds of said highway, from the southerly bounds of the roadway known as Industrial Parkway West, THENCE running S 31° 54′ 33″ E along the easterly bounds of said Old Military Turnpike Extension, 239.88 feet to a point marking the beginning of a curve concave to the west; thence southerly along said curve, having a radius of 987.99 feet, 248.12 feet to an iron pipe found marking the point of beginning for the parcel herein being described, said point also marked the southerly corner of lands of Larry Garrow, et al, as described in Book 938 of Deeds at page 224; thence N 07° 45′ 4″ E along the easterly bounds of said Garrow, 748.16 feet to a 3″x4″ concrete monument marking the northeasterly corner of said Garrow, the northwesterly corner of the parcel herein being described and said monument also marking the southerly bounds of lands of Salerno Plastic Corp. as described in Book 926 of Deeds at Page 186; thence S 81° 45′ 28″ E along a portion of the southerly bounds of said Salerno Plastic Corp., 441.32 feet to an iron pin found marking the northeasterly corner of the parcel herein being described and also marking the northwest corner of the remaining lands now or formerly owned by said Marx and Delaura; thence S 07° 45′ 40″ W along the Westerly bounds of lands now of formerly of said Marx and DeLaura and along the easterly bounds of the parcel herein being described, 560.49 feet to an iron pin; thence N 83° 43′ 21″ W along a portion of the remaining lands of said Marx and DeLaura, 41.51 feet to an iron pin; thence S 08° 31′ 30″ W, along a portion of the remaining lands of said Marx and Delaura, 75.01 feet to an iron pin marking northeasterly corner of lands currently owned by the Joint Council for Economic Opportunity of Plattsburgh and Clinton County, Inc. as described in Book 963 of Deeds at Page 313; thence N 82° 20′ 32″ W along a portion of the northerly bounds of said J.C.E.O., 173.50 feet to an iron pin; thence 61° 21′ 12″ W, continuing along a portion of the northerly bounds of said J.C.E.O., 134.14 feet to an iron pin; thence S 07° 45′ 42″ W along the westerly bounds of said J.C.E.O., 50 feet to an iron pin; thence S 66° 48′ 56″ W along a portion of the northerly bounds of remaining lands of said Marx and DeLaura, 100.00 feet to an iron pipe found on the easterly bounds of the aforesaid highway, said from pipe also being located on a curve concave to the west; thence running and running northerly along the easterly bounds of the aforesaid highway and being along said curve, with the curve having a radius of 987.93 feet, 60.00 feet to the point of beginning and containing 6.905 acres of land. Being the same premises as conveyed to Ronald Marx and Alice Marx by deed of CIT Small Business Lending Corp., as agent of the administrator, U.S. Small Business Administration, an agency of the United States Government dated

September 10, 2001 and recorded in the office of the Clinton County Clerk on September 21, 2001 as Instrument #135020; or (vi) any such premises or business located on the west side of New York state route 414 in military lots 64 and 75 located wholly within the boundaries of that tract or parcel of land situated in the town of Lodi, county of Seneca beginning at an iron pin on the assumed west line of New York State Route 414 on the apparent north line of lands reputedly of White (lib. 420, page 155); said iron pin also being northerly a distance of 1200 feet more or less from the centerline of South Miller Road; Thence leaving the point of beginning north 85-17′-44″ west along said lands of White a distance of 2915.90 feet to an iron pin Thence north 03-52′-48″ east along said lands of White, passing through an iron pin 338.36 feet distant, and continuing further along that same course a distance of 13.64 feet farther, the total distance being 352.00 feet to a point in the assumed centerline of Nellie Neal Creek; Thence in generally a north westerly direction the following courses and distances along the assumed centerline of Nellie Neal Creek; north 69-25′-11″ west a distance of 189.56 feet to a point; north 63-40′-00″ west a distance of 156.00 feet to a point; north 49-25′-00″ west a distance of 80.00 feet to a point; south 80-21′-00″ west a distance of 90.00 feet to a point; north 72-03′-00″ west a distance of 566.00 feet to a point; north 68-15′-00″ west a distance of 506.00 feet to a point; north 55-16′-00″ west a distance of 135.00 feet to a point; south 69-18′-00″ west a distance of 200.00 feet to a point; south 88-00′-00″ west a distance of 170.00 feet to a point on a tie line at or near the high water line of Seneca Lake; Thence north 25-17′-00″ east along said tie line a distance of 238.00 feet to an iron pipe; Thence south 82-04′-15″ east along lands reputedly of M. Wagner (lib. 464, page 133) a distance of 100.00 feet to an iron pin; Thence north 06-56′-47″ east along said lands of M. Wagner a distance of 100.00 feet to an iron pipe; Thence north 09-34′-28″ east along lands reputedly of Schneider (lib. 429, page 37) a distance of 50.10 feet to an iron pipe; Thence north 07-49′-11″ east along lands reputedly of Oney (lib. 484, page 24) a distance of 50.00 feet to an iron pipe; Thence north 82-29′-40″ west along said lands of Oney a distance of 95.30 feet to an iron pipe on a tie line at or near the highwater line of Seneca Lake; Thence north 08-15′-22″ east along said tie line a distance of 25.00 feet to an iron pin; Thence south 82-28′-00″ east along lands reputedly of Yu (lib. 405, page 420) a distance of 96.53 feet to an iron pipe; Thence north 34-36′-59″ east along said lands of Yu a distance of 95.00 feet to a point in the assumed centerline of Van Liew Creek; Thence in generally an easterly direction the following courses and distances along the assumed centerline of Van Liew Creek; north 72-46′-37″ east a distance of 159.98 feet to a point; north 87-53′-00″ east a distance of 94.00 feet to a point; south 71-12′-00″ east a distance of 52.00 feet to a point; south 84-10′-00″ east a distance of 158.00 feet to a point; south 59-51′-00″ east a distance of 160.00 feet to a point; south 83-29′-00″ east a distance of 187.00 feet to a point; Thence north 01-33′-40″ east along lands reputedly of Hansen (lib. 515, page 205) passing through an iron pipe 32.62 feet distant, and continuing further along that same course passing through an iron pin 205.38 feet farther, and continuing still further along that same course a distance of 21.45 feet farther, the total distance being 259.45 feet to the assumed remains of a White Oak stump; Thence north 69-16′-11″ east along lands reputedly of Schwartz (lib. 374, page 733) being tie lines along the top of the south bank of Campbell Creek a distance of 338.00 feet to a point; Thence south 57-17′32″* east along said tie line a distance of 136.60 feet to a point; Thence south 74-45′-00″ east along said tie line a distance of 100.00 feet to an iron pin; Thence north 04-46′-00″ east along said lands of Schwartz a distance of 100.00 feet to a point in the assumed centerline of Campbell Creek; Thence in generally an easterly direction the following courses and distances along the assumed centerline of Campbell Creek; south 71-34′-00″ east a distance of 330.00 feet to a point; north 76-53′-00″ east a distance of 180.00 feet to a point; north 83-05′00** east a distance of 230.00 feet to a point; south 66-44′-00″ east a distance of 90.00 feet to a point; south 81-10′-00″ east a distance of 240.00 feet to a point; south 45-29′-15″ east a distance of 73.18 feet to a point; Thence south 05-25′-50″ west along lands reputedly of Stanley Wagner (lib. 450, page 276) a distance of 135.00 feet to a point on the assumed north line of Military Lot 75; Thence south 84-34′-10″ east along said lands of Wagner and the assumed north line of Military Lot 75 a distance of 1195.06 feet to an iron pin; Thence south O6-57′52″*** west along said lands of M. Wagner (lib. 414, page 267) passing through an iron pin 215.58 feet distant, and continuing further along that same course a distance of 20.59 feet farther, the total distance being 236.17 feet to a point in the assumed centerline of Campbell Creek; Thence in generally a south easterly direction the following course and distances along the assumed centerline of Campbell Creek; north 78-23′-09″ east a distance of 29.99 feet to a point; south 46-09′-15″ east a distance of 65.24 feet to a point; north 85-55′-09″ east a distance of 60.10 feet to a point; south 61-59′-50″ east a distance of 206.91 feet to a point; north 63-58′-27″ east a distance of 43.12 feet to a point; south 28-51′-21″ east a distance of 47.72 feet to a point; south 15-14′-08″ west a distance of 33.42 feet to a point; south 79-16′-32″ east a distance of 255.15 feet to a point; south 62-19′-46″ east a distance of 75.82 feet to a point; north 76-10′-42″ east a distance of 99.60 feet to a point; north 82-12′55″**** east a distance of 86.00 feet to a point; south 44-13′53″***** east a distance of 64.08 feet to a point; north 67-52′-46″ east a distance of 73.98 feet to a point; north 88-13′-13″ east a distance of 34.64 feet to a point on the assumed west line of New York State Route 414; Thence south 20-13′-30″ east along the assumed west line of New York State Route 414 a distance of 248.04 feet to a concrete monument; Thence south 02-10′-30″ west along said road line a distance of 322.90 feet to an iron

pin; Thence 13-14′-50″ west along said road line a distance of 487.41 feet to an iron pin, said iron pin being the point and place of beginning;
**So in original. Probably should be "57-17′-32″".*
***So in original. Probably should be "83-05′-00″".*
****So in original. Probably should be "06-57′-52″".*
*****So in original. Probably should be "82-12′-55″".*
******So in original. Probably should be "44-13′-53″".*

Comprising an area of 126.807 acres of land according to a survey completed by Michael D. Karlsen entitled "Plan Owned by Stanley A. Wagner" known as Parcel A of Job number 98-505.

This survey is subject to all utility easements and easements and right-of-ways of record which may affect the parcel of land.

This survey is also subject to the rights of the public in and to lands herein referred to as New York State Route 414.

This survey intends to describe a portion of the premises as conveyed by Ruth V. Wagner to Stanley A. Wagner by deed recorded February 10, 1989 in Liber 450 of deeds, at Page 286.

This survey also intends to describe a portion of the premises as conveyed by Stanley W. VanVleet to Stanley A. Wagner by deed recorded April 30, 1980 in Liber 385 of Deeds, at Page 203.

ALSO ALL THAT OTHER TRACT OR PARCEL OF LAND SITUATE on the east side of New York State Route 414 in Military Lot 75 in the Town of Lodi, County of Seneca, State of New York bounded and described as follows:

Beginning at an iron pin on the assumed east line of New York State Route 414, said iron pin being north 50-44′-57″ east a distance of 274.92 feet from the south east corner of the parcel of land herein above described; Thence leaving the point of beginning north 00-26′01″* east along a mathematical tie line a distance of 504.91 feet to an iron pin; Thence south 37-00′-20″ east along lands reputedly of Tomberelli (lib. 419, page 243) passing through an iron pin 176.00 feet distant, and continuing further along that same course a distance of 2.01 feet farther, the total distance being 178.01 feet to a point; Thence south 09-03′-55″ west along lands reputedly of M. Wagner (lib. 491, page 181) a distance of 68.19 feet to an iron pipe; Thence south 15-36′-04″ west along said lands of M. Wagner a distance of 300.15 feet to an iron pipe; Thence south 72-04′-59″ west along said lands of M. Wagner a distance of 20.49 feet to an iron pin, said iron pin being the point and place of beginning.
**So in original. Probably should be "00-26′-01″".*

Comprising an area of 0.727 acre of lands according to a survey completed by Michael D. Karlsen entitled "Plan of Land Owned by Stanley A. Wagner" known as Parcel B of job number 98-505.

This survey is subject to all utility easements and easements and right-of-ways of record which may affect this parcel of land.

This survey is also subject to the rights of the public in and to lands herein referred to as New York State Route 414.

Printed in the U.S.A. ab

This survey intends to describe the same premises as conveyed by Henry W. Eighmey as executor of the Last Will and Testament of Mary C. Eighmey to Stanley A. Wagner by deed recorded July 2, 1996 in liber 542, page 92.

This survey also intends to describe a portion of the premises as conveyed by Ruth V. Wagner to Stanley A. Wagner by deed recorded February 10, 1989 in Liber 450 of deeds, at Page 286. The provisions of this paragraph shall not apply to any premises or business located wholly within the following described parcel: ALL THAT TRACT OR PARCEL OF LAND situate in the City of Corning, County of Steuben and State of New York bounded and described as follows: Beginning at an iron pin situate at the terminus of the westerly line of Townley Avenue at its intersection with the southwesterly line of New York State Route 17; thence S 00° 45′ 18″ E along the westerly line of Townley Avenue, a distance of 256.09 feet to a point; thence S 89° 02′ 07″ W through an iron pin placed at a distance of 200.00 feet, a total distance of 300.00 feet to an iron pin; thence N 00° 59′ 17″ W a distance of 47.13 feet to an iron pin; thence S 89° 02′ 07″ W a distance of 114.56 feet to a point situate in the southeast corner of Parcel A-2 as set forth on a survey map hereinafter described; thence N 14° 18′ 49″ E a distance of 124.40 feet to an iron pin situate at the southeast corner of lands now or formerly of Cicci (Liber 923, Page 771); thence N 14° 18′ 49″ E a distance of 76.46 feet to an iron pin; thence N 00° 57′ 53″ W a distance of 26.25 feet to an iron pin marking the southeast corner of parcel A-1 as set forth on the hereinafter described survey map; thence N 00° 58′ 01″ W a distance of 166.00 to an iron pin situate at the northeast corner of said Parcel A-1, which pin also marks the southeast corner of lands now or formerly of Becraft (Liber 1048, Page 1086); thence N 00° 57′ 53″ W a distance of 106.00 feet to an iron pin situate in the southerly line of lands now or formerly of the United States Postal Service; thence N 89° 02′ 07″ E along the southerly line of said United States Postal Service a distance of 81.47 feet to a point; thence N 14° 18′ 49″ E along the easterly line of said United States Postal Service a distance of 114.29 feet to an iron pin situate in the southwesterly line of New York State Route 17; thence S 32° 00′ 31″ E along the southwesterly line of New York State Route 17, a distance of 358.93 feet to an iron pin; thence continuing along the southwesterly line of New York state Route 17, S 38° 30′ 04″ E a distance of 108.18 feet to the iron pin marking the place of beginning. Said premises are set forth and shown as approximately 4.026 acres of land designated as Parcel A (excluding Parcels A-1 and A-2) on a survey map entitled "As-Built Survey of Lands of New York Inn, LLC, City of Corning, Steuben County, New York" by Weiler Associates, dated December 27, 2001, designated Job No. 12462. The provisions of this paragraph shall not apply to any premises licensed under section sixty-four of this chapter in which a manufacturer or wholesaler holds a direct or indirect interest, provided that: (I) said premises consist of an interactive entertainment facility which predominantly offers interactive computer and video entertainment attractions, and other games and also offers themed merchandise and food and beverages, (II) the sale of alcoholic beverages within the premises shall be restricted to an area consisting of not more than twenty-five percent of the total interior floor area of the premises, (III) the retail licenses* shall derive not less than sixty-five percent of the total revenue generated by the facility from interactive video entertainment activities and other games, including related attractions and sales of merchandise other than food and alcoholic beverages, (IV) the interested manufacturer or wholesaler, or its parent company, shall be listed on a national securities exchange and its direct or indirect equity interest in the retail licensee shall not exceed twenty-five percent, (V) no more than fifteen percent of said licensee's purchases of alcoholic beverages for sale in the premises shall be products produced or distributed by the manufacturer or wholesaler, (VI) neither the name of the manufacturer or wholesaler nor the name of any brand of alcoholic beverage produced or distributed by said manufacturer or wholesaler shall be part of the name of the premises, (VII) the name of the manufacturer or wholesaler or the name of products sold or distributed by such manufacturer or wholesaler shall not be identified on signage affixed to either the interior or the exterior of the premises in any fashion, (VIII) promotions involving alcoholic beverages produced or distributed by the manufacturer or wholesaler are not held in such premises and further, retail and consumer advertising specialties bearing the name of the manufacturer or wholesaler or the name of alcoholic beverages produced or distributed by the manufacturer or wholesaler are not utilized in any fashion, given away or sold in said premises, and (IX) except to the extent provided in this paragraph, the licensing of each premises covered by this exception is subject to all provisions of section sixty-four of this chapter, including but not limited to liquor authority approval of the specific location thereof. The provisions of this paragraph shall not prohibit (1) a manufacturer or wholesaler, if an individual, or a partner, of a partnership, or, if a corporation, an officer or director thereof, from being an officer or director of a duly licensed charitable organization which is the holder of a license for on-premises consumption under this chapter, nor (2) a manufacturer from acquiring any such premises if the liquor authority first consents thereto after determining, upon such proofs as it shall deem sufficient, that such premises is contiguous to the licensed premises of such manufacturer, and is reasonably necessary for the expansion of the facilities of such manufacturer. After any such acquisition, it shall be illegal for a manufacturer acquiring any such premises to sell or deliver alcoholic beverages manufactured by him to any licensee occupying such premises.

**So in original. Probably should be "licensees".*

❷*(1995, chgd. by chap. 502; 1996, chgd. by chap. 675; 1997, chgd. by chap. 550; 1998, chgd. by chap. 320; 2002, chgd. by chaps. 105, 407, eff. 6/28/2002, 8/13/2002, respectively.)*

(b) Make, or cause to be made, any loan to any person engaged in the manufacture or sale of any alcoholic beverage at wholesale or retail.

(c) Make any gift or render any service of any kind whatsoever, directly or indirectly, to any person licensed under this chapter which in the judgment of the liquor authority may tend to influence such licensee to purchase the product of such manufacturer or wholesaler. The provisions of this paragraph shall not be construed to prevent a manufacturer or wholesaler from entertaining a licensee at lunch or dinner.

(d) Enter into any contract with any retail licensee whereby such licensee agrees to confine his sales to alcoholic beverages manufactured or sold by one or more such manufacturers or wholesalers. Any such contract shall be void and subject the licenses of all parties concerned to revocation.



(e) The prohibitions and restrictions contained in paragraphs b, c and d above shall not apply to any contractual arrangements between a licensed manufacturer or wholesaler and a licensed retailer where such manufacturer or wholesaler has made a substantial investment, directly or through such retailer, in the construction, capitalization or furnishing of any exhibit, facility or installation in the area leased by the city of New York to New York World's Fair 1964-1965 Corporation, pursuant to chapter four hundred twenty-eight of the laws of nineteen hundred sixty, as amended, and such retailer is conducting his business as a part of such exhibit or installation or is responsible to such corporation for the construction, operation or maintenance of such exhibit, facility or installation. This modification to the prohibitions and restrictions contained in this paragraph shall continue until November first, nineteen hundred sixty-five.

2. Any lien, mortgage, or other interest or estate however, now held by a manufacturer or wholesaler on the real property of any licensee, which lien, mortgage, interest or estate was acquired on or before December thirty-first, nineteen hundred and thirty-two, shall not be included within the provisions of this section but the burden of establishing the time of the accrual of the interest comprehended by this subdivision shall be upon the person who claims to be entitled to the protection and exemption afforded hereby.

❸3. Any interest or estate mentioned in this section held by a manufacturer or wholesaler in an office building located in a city having a population of five hundred thousand or more and in which is located the licensed premises of such manufacturer or wholesaler shall not prohibit (1) the issuance of licenses pursuant to section sixty-four of this chapter for restaurant premises located in such building or (2) said manufacturer or wholesaler from being interested directly or indirectly in such restaurant premises, provided the building is not less than five stories in height, both the building and the interior of the restaurant premise have been granted landmark status in accordance with applicable state or local law and space within the building is also occupied by persons other than the manufacturer or wholesaler, and that the rental for the retail premises applied for shall be comparable to that for similar space in such building and similar buildings in the immediate neighborhood; and provided further that the provisions of this paragraph shall apply solely with respect to restaurant premises in a building located on a parcel of land wholly within the boundaries of the borough of Manhattan, city and county of New York, and bounded and described as follows: beginning at a corner formed by the intersection of the northerly side of East Fifty-second Street and the easterly side of Park Avenue; running northerly along the easterly side of Park Avenue, two hundred feet ten inches; thence easterly along the southerly side of East Fifty-third Street; three hundred two feet; thence southerly parallel with the easterly side of Park Avenue, one hundred feet five inches to the center line of the block; thence westerly along the center line of the block at right angles, seven feet; thence southerly parallel with the easterly side of Park Avenue, one hundred feet five inches to the northerly side of East Fifty-second Street; and thence westerly along the northerly side of East Fifty-second Street two hundred ninety-five feet to the corner of the point or place of beginning. The exemption herein provided shall apply to only one building and shall not be extended to any other building in which such manufacturer or wholesaler shall have any interest or estate. ❺*(1995, chgd. by chap. 185, eff. 7/19/95.)*

### §101-a. Terms of sale for alcoholic beverages sold or delivered to persons licensed to sell liquor and/or wine at retail for off-premises consumption.

1. The provisions of this section shall apply throughout the state, but shall apply to the sale and delivery of liquor and/or wine to persons licensed to sell liquor and/or wine at retail for off-premises consumption, and whenever the term "retail licensee" is used in this section, it shall mean and refer only to a person licensed to sell liquor and/or wine at retail for off-premises consumption.

2. No manufacturer or wholesaler licensed under this chapter shall sell or offer to sell or deliver any liquor or wine to any retail licensee except for cash to be paid at the time of delivery or on terms requiring payment by such retail licensee for such liquor or wine on or before the tenth day of the month following the month in which actual delivery is made.

3. Each such manufacturer and wholesaler is hereby required on or before the twelfth day of each month to give written notice of default, by registered or certified mail, to all retail licensees who have failed to make payment to him on or before the tenth day of such month for liquor or wine sold and delivered to such retail licensees during the previous month. Any such retail licensee receiving such notice shall not thereafter purchase liquor and/or wine except for cash until such time as it is determined that the name of such retail licensee shall not be published on the delinquent list as provided in subdivision four of this

section or until such time as the name of such retail licensee is removed or released in writing from the delinquent list as hereinafter provided in subdivision five of this section. Each such manufacturer and wholesaler is hereby required to file with the state liquor authority on or before the fifteenth day of each month, a written list setting forth the names and addresses of all retail licensees who have purchased liquor or wine from him and have failed on or before the tenth day of such month to pay for such liquor or wine delivered during the previous month, and each such manufacturer and wholesaler shall also file with the authority copies of the notices sent by him to such licensees as hereinabove required. The liquor authority, in its discretion, for good cause shown may extend for a period not exceeding three days the time of giving of written notice of default to retailers and extend for three days the filing with the liquor authority of the written list of defaults and copies of notices sent to licensees as heretofore required. The authority shall, as soon as practicable after the fifteenth day of each month, compile, publish and furnish to each manufacturer and wholesaler a list, to be designated "the delinquent list," of all retail licensees whose names and addresses have been reported by manufacturers and wholesalers as having failed to make payment as required by this section for liquor or wine sold and delivered to them, and no manufacturer or wholesaler, after the receipt of the delinquent list, shall knowingly, wilfully or intentionally sell any liquor or wine to any retail licensee whose name appears on such list, except for cash until such time as the name of such retail licensee is removed from such delinquent list, except as hereinafter stated. The receipt of the delinquent list by a manufacturer or wholesaler shall constitute knowledge of the names of the retail licensees who have failed to make payment for liquor or wine as required by this section. The failure of any manufacturer or wholesaler to comply with the foregoing provisions of this section shall subject the license of such manufacturer or wholesaler to suspension of not more than five days for the first offense and not more than thirty days for a subsequent offense.

4. In the event that any dispute shall exist between any manufacturer or wholesaler and the retail licensee to whom he shall have sold liquor or wine, either as to the fact of payment or as to the amount due for such liquor or wine or as to quantity of the liquor or wine sold and delivered, which dispute cannot be adjusted between the seller and purchaser, the authority is hereby authorized to receive statements from each of the parties to such dispute as to the facts and circumstances of such dispute and the reasons why the purchaser's name should not be published on the delinquent list and to determine whether or not such purchaser's name shall be published on such list.

5. The authority, in the case of a retail licensee who has actually made payment for liquor and/or wine, or on good cause shown to it, but only after investigation of the facts concerning the indebtedness of such licensee to manufacturers and wholesalers interested, and on notice to all such manufacturers and wholesalers interested, may permit

sales to persons named on any delinquent list, on terms other than for cash, but within the limitations of this section, prior to the publication of the next subsequent monthly delinquent list.

6. The license of any retail licensee who shall make purchase of or accept delivery of liquor or wine on any terms other than as stated in this section, may be suspended for not more than five days for the first offense and not more than thirty days for a subsequent offense. The failure of any retail licensee to make payment for any default before the expiration of the period of suspension shall be deemed and punishable as a subsequent offense until paid. In addition, such retail licensee may be required, after default in making payment in accordance with the provisions of this section, to make payment in cash for liquor or wine subsequently delivered.

7. The authority is hereby empowered to prescribe forms for notices of default, for lists of licensed persons to be filed by manufacturers and wholesalers, and for delinquent lists, and to promulgate regulations to govern the filing of such notices and lists and the place of the filing thereof, and the publication of such delinquent lists.

8. The authority is hereby empowered to promulgate and enforce rules and regulations requiring retail licensees to make payment to manufacturers and wholesalers of unpaid balances for liquor or wine sold and delivered before September first, nineteen hundred thirty-seven, provided that such rules and regulations may not require retail licensees to make payment in full of said balances prior to March thirty-first, nineteen hundred forty-one, if said licensees make equal monthly payments on account of such indebtedness in amounts sufficient to pay said balances in full on or before March thirty-first, nineteen hundred forty-one, nor impose any greater penalty than to require retail licensees in default of making such monthly payments to pay cash for all liquor or wine sold and delivered to such licensees after the time of such default, until such time as such default shall have been made good. The authority, shall not, however, because of such an indebtedness or failure to pay such, refuse to renew the license of any retail licensee.

9. All retail licensees shall make payments to manufacturers and wholesalers of unpaid balances for liquor and/or wine sold and delivered to retail licensees on and after September first, nineteen hundred thirty-seven; such retail licensees shall make payment in full of said balances prior to May thirty-first, nineteen hundred forty-two, which payment may be made in equal monthly payments on account of such indebtedness in amounts sufficient to pay said balances in full on or before May thirty-first, nineteen hundred forty-two. All retail licensees who shall fail to pay licensed manufacturers or wholesalers for liquor and/or wine sold and delivered to such retail licensees by such manufacturers or wholesalers subsequent to the enactment of this section, shall be required to liquidate and pay such unpaid balances to such manufacturers and wholesalers in equal monthly installments over a period of three months from the date upon which such unpaid

balances shall become due. The authority, shall not however, because of such an indebtedness or failure to pay such, refuse to renew the license of any retail licensee.

10. Nothing herein contained shall be construed to require any manufacturer or wholesaler to extend credit to any retail licensee nor to restrain any manufacturer or wholesaler from seeking to enforce by legal action or otherwise, payment of any sum or sums of money due or alleged to be due to any such manufacturer or wholesaler for liquor or wine sold and delivered to any such retail licensee prior to September first, nineteen hundred thirty-seven.

11. Whenever used in this section, "cash" means and includes currency and coin of the United States of America, certified check, money order, bank officer's check or draft, or a check drawn on the account of the retail licensee payable to the manufacturer or wholesaler and dated no later than the date of delivery of the alcoholic beverages and which is honored upon presentment for payment, provided however if any check or other instrument described herein tendered by a retail licensee on the delinquent list is not honored upon presentment for payment, the license of such retail licensee may be suspended for not more than fifteen days for the first offense and not more than sixty days for a subsequent offense which penalty shall be in addition to the penalty provided for by the provisions of subdivision six of this section; and provided further, that nothing herein contained shall require a manufacturer or wholesaler to accept a check tendered by or drawn on the account of a retail licensee on the delinquent list unless the same has been certified.



## §101-aa. Terms of sale

1. As used in this section:

a. "Credit period" means one of the following:

(1) A period beginning on the first Monday of a month and ending on the day preceding the first Monday of the following month.

(2) A period beginning on the second Monday of a month and ending on the day preceding the second Monday of the following month.

(3) A period beginning on the third Monday of a month and ending on the day preceding the third Monday of the following month.

(4) A period beginning on the fourth Monday of a month and ending on the day preceding the fourth Monday of the following month.

b. "Payment period" means the period ending on the thirteenth day of each month immediately following the end of the credit period for group one; the twentieth day of each month immediately following the end of the credit period for group two; the twenty-seventh day of each month immediately following the end of the credit period for group three; the fourth day of each month immediately following the end of the credit period for group four.

c. "Final payment date" means the last day of a payment period.

d. "Delinquent notice date" means the third business day immediately following a final payment date.

e. "Notification date" means the day immediately following a delinquent notice date.

f. "Retail licensee" means a person licensed to sell alcoholic beverages at retail (including a person holding a permit granted by the authority pursuant to subdivision six of section sixty-four of this chapter) except a person licensed to sell liquor and/or wine for off-premises consumption.

g. "Cash" means and includes currency and coin of the United States of America, certified check, money order, bank officer's check or draft, or a check drawn on the account of the retail licensee payable to the manufacturer or wholesaler and dated no later than the date of delivery of the alcoholic beverages and which is honored upon presentment for payment, provided, however, that if any check or other instrument described herein tendered by a retail licensee on the delinquent list is not honored upon presentment for payment, the license of such retail licensee may be suspended for not more than fifteen days for the first offense, and not more than sixty days for a subsequent offense, which penalty shall be in addition to the penalty provided for by the provisions of subdivision eight of this section, and provided further, that nothing herein contained shall require a manufacturer or wholesaler to accept a check tendered by or drawn on the account of a retail licensee on the delinquent list unless the same has been certified.

2. The authority shall, on or before October first, nineteen hundred sixty-five, in such manner as it may deem appropriate, divide all retail licensees into four appropriate groups, each of which shall be as nearly equal in the number of such licensees therein as practicable, and designated, respectively, as "Group 1", "Group 2", "Group 3" and "Group 4". Each such group shall be in a credit period designated by a number identical with the group number.

3. The first credit period for all retail licensees in group one shall begin on October first, nineteen hundred sixty-five, and a new credit period for all such licensees shall begin on the first day of each month thereafter. The first credit period for all retail licensees in groups two, three and four shall begin, respectively, on October eighth, fifteenth and twenty-second, nineteen hundred sixty-five, and a new credit period for all licensees in each such group shall begin, respectively, on the eighth, fifteenth and twenty-second of each month thereafter.

4. No manufacturer or wholesaler licensed under this chapter shall sell or deliver any alcoholic beverages to any retail licensee except for cash to be paid at the time of delivery or on terms requiring payment by such retail licensee for such alcoholic beverages on or before the final payment date of the credit period of the group to which such licensee has been assigned by the authority and within which delivery is made.

❼5. Each such manufacturer and wholesaler is hereby required, on or before the respective delinquent notice dates for each group of retail licensees, to give written notice of default, by registered or certified mail, to all such licensees therein who have failed to make payment to him on or before their final payment date for alcoholic beverages sold or delivered to them during their previous credit period. Any such retail licensee receiving such notice shall not thereafter purchase alcoholic beverages except for cash until such time as the authority determines that his name shall not be published on the delinquent list as provided in subdivision six of this section, or until such time as the authority permits sales or deliveries to him as provided in subdivision seven of this section. Each such manufacturer and wholesaler is hereby required to file with the authority, on or before each notification date, copies of the notices sent by him to all delinquent retail licensees as hereinabove required, and in addition, if the authority shall so require, a written list setting forth the names and addresses of all such delinquent licensees. The authority, in its discretion, may extend for a period not exceeding three days the date for giving written notice of default to delinquent retail licensees and extend for three days the date for filing with the authority the copies of notices sent to such licensees and/or the written list of delinquent retail licensees as hereinabove required. The authority shall, as soon as practicable after each notification date, compile and publish and furnish each manufacturer and wholesaler licensed under this chapter a list, to be designated "the delinquent list for group ... ," (the number of the appropriate group to be inserted by the authority) containing the names and addresses of all retail licensees in the appropriate group who have been reported by manufacturers and wholesalers pursuant to the provisions of this section or section one hundred one-aaa of this article as having failed to make payment as required by this section for alcoholic beverages sold or delivered to them, and no such manufacturer or wholesaler, on or after the fifth day after the receipt of such delinquent list, shall knowingly, wilfully or intentionally sell or deliver any alcoholic beverages to any such licensee whose name appears on such list, except for cash, until such time as the name of such licensee is removed therefrom, except as hereinafter permitted. The receipt of a delinquent list by a manufacturer or wholesaler shall constitute knowledge of the names of the retail licensees who have failed to make payment for alcoholic beverages as required by this section. The failure of any manufacturer or wholesaler to comply with the foregoing provisions of this section may, at the discretion of the authority, subject the license of such manufacturer or wholesaler to suspension for not more than five days for the first offense, and not more than thirty days for a subsequent offense. ❼*(1997, chgd. by chap. 389, eff. 12/1/98.)*

6. In the event that any dispute shall exist between any manufacturer or wholesaler and a retail licensee to whom he shall have sold alcoholic beverages, either as to the fact of payment or as to the amount due for such alcoholic beverages or as to the quantity of the alcoholic beverages sold or delivered, which dispute cannot be adjusted between them, the authority is hereby authorized to receive statements from

each of the parties to such dispute as to the facts and circumstances thereof and to determine whether or not such retail licensee's name should be published on the appropriate delinquent list.

7. The authority in the case of a retail licensee who has actually made payment for alcoholic beverages, or on good cause shown to it, may permit sales or deliveries to any retail licensee who has received notice of default or who is named on any delinquent list, on terms other than for cash, but within the limitations of this section, prior to the publication of the next appropriate delinquent list.

8. The license of any retail licensee who purchases or accepts delivery of alcoholic beverages on any terms, other than as provided in this section, may be suspended for not more than five days for the first offense and not more than thirty days for a subsequent offense. The failure of any such retail licensee to pay any amount in default before the expiration of the period of suspension shall be deemed and punishable as a subsequent offense until paid. In addition, the authority may require any such retail licensee, after default in making payment in accordance with the provisions of this section to make payment in cash for alcoholic beverages subsequently delivered.



9. a. All retail licensees who fail to pay manufacturers or wholesalers for alcoholic beverages sold or delivered to such retail licensees by such manufacturers or wholesalers subsequent to the effective date of this section, shall liquidate and pay such unpaid balances to such manufacturers or wholesalers in equal monthly installments over a period of three months from the date upon which such unpaid balances become due. The authority, shall not, however, because of such an indebtedness or failure to pay such refuse to renew the license of any such licensee.

b. All retail licensees shall, on or before October tenth, nineteen hundred sixty-five, make payment in full to manufacturers and wholesalers of all unpaid balances for alcoholic beverages sold and delivered to such licensees during the month of September, nineteen hundred sixty-five. All retail licensees in groups two, three, four and one shall, on or before November tenth, nineteen hundred sixty-five, make payment in full to manufacturers and wholesalers of all unpaid balances for alcoholic beverages sold and delivered between October first and October seventh, fourteenth, twenty-first and thirty-first, nineteen hundred sixty-five, respectively. The authority may impose any penalty or condition otherwise authorized by this section in the case of any such retail licensee who fails or refuses to liquidate and pay unpaid balance becoming due under this subdivision.

10. Nothing herein contained shall be construed to require any manufacturer or wholesaler to extend credit to any retail licensee nor to restrain any manufacturer or wholesaler from seeking to enforce by legal action or otherwise, payment of any sum or sums of money due or alleged to be due to any such manufacturer or wholesaler for alcoholic beverages sold or delivered to any such retail licensee.

11. The state liquor authority is hereby authorized to do such acts, prescribe such forms and make such rules, regulations and orders as it may deem necessary or proper fully to effectuate the provisions of this section, including but not limited to the changing of any date on which any act or function pursuant to this section is to be performed by any licensee or by the liquor authority.

12. For the purpose of raising the moneys necessary to defray the expenses incurred in the administration of this section, on or before the tenth day after this act becomes a law, there shall be paid to the liquor authority by each manufacturer and wholesaler licensed under this chapter to sell to retailers liquor and/or wines or beer, a sum equivalent to ten per centum of the annual license fee prescribed by this chapter for each such licensee. A like sum shall be paid by each person hereafter applying for any such license or the renewal of any such license, and such sum shall accompany the application and the license fee prescribed by this chapter for such license or renewal, as the case may be.



**❼§101-aaa. Terms of sale; beer or wine products.**

1. As used in this section:

a. "Credit period" means the following:

(1) A period beginning on the first day of each month and ending on the fifteenth day of such month; and

(2) A period beginning on the sixteenth day of each month and ending on the last day of such month.

b. "Payment period" means the period ending on the tenth day immediately following the last day of any credit period.

c. "Final payment date" means the last day of a payment period.

d. "Delinquent notice date" means the third business day immediately following a final payment date.

e. "Notification date" means the day immediately following a delinquent notice date.

f. "Retail licensee" means a person licensed pursuant to this chapter who purchases beer and/or wine products for resale for on or off premises consumption, except a person licensed to sell liquor and/or wine for off premises consumption.

g. "Cash" means and includes currency and coin of the United States of America, certified check, money order, bank officer's check or draft, or a check drawn on the account of the retail licensee payable to the manufacturer or wholesaler and dated no later than the date of delivery of the alcoholic beverages and which is honored upon presentment for payment; provided, however, that if any check or other instrument described in this paragraph tendered by a retail licensee on the delinquent list is not honored upon presentment for payment, the license of such retail licensee may be suspended for not more than fifteen days for the first offense, and not more than sixty days for a subsequent offense, which penalty shall be in addition to the penalty provided for by the provisions of sudivision* six of this section, and provided further, that nothing in this section shall require a manufacturer or wholesaler to accept a check tendered by or drawn on the account of a retail licensee on the delinquent list unless the same has been certified.

**So in original. Probably should be "subdivision".*

2. No manufacturer or wholesaler licensed under this chapter shall sell or deliver any beer or wine products to any retail licensee except for cash to be paid at the time of delivery or on terms requiring payment by such retail licensee for such beer or wine products on or before the final payment date of any credit period within which delivery is made.

3. Each such manufacturer and wholesaler shall, on or before the respective delinquent notice date, give written notice of default, by registered or certified mail, to all such licensees who have failed to make payment to the manufacturer or wholesaler on or before their final payment date for beer or wine products sold or delivered to such licensees during the previous credit period. Any such retail licensee receiving such notice shall not thereafter purchase beer or wine products except for cash until such time as the authority determines that its name shall not be published on the delinquent list as provided in this subdivision, or until such time as the authority permits sales or deliveries to such licensee as provided in subdivision five of this section. Each such manufacturer and wholesaler shall file with the authority, on or before each notification date, copies of the notices sent by it to all delinquent retail licensees, and in addition, if the authority shall so require, a written list setting forth the names and addresses of all such delinquent licensees. The authority, in its discretion, may extend for a period not exceeding three days the date for giving written notice of default to delinquent retail licensees and extend for three days the date for filing with the authority the copies of notices sent to such licensees and/or the written list of delinquent retail licensees. The authority shall, as soon as practicable after each notification date, compile, publish, and furnish each manufacturer and wholesaler licensed under this chapter a delinquent list containing the names and addresses of all retail licensees who have been reported by manufacturers and wholesalers pursuant to the provisions of this section or section one hundred one-aa of this article as having failed to make payment as required by this section or section one hundred one-aa of this article for beer or wine products sold or delivered to them, and no such manufacturer or wholesaler, on or after the fifth day after the receipt of such delinquent list, shall knowingly, wilfully or intentionally sell or deliver any beer or wine products to any such licensee whose name appears on such list, except for cash, until such time as the name of such licensee is removed therefrom, except as otherwise permitted by this section. The receipt of a delinquent list by a manufacturer or wholesaler shall constitute knowledge of the names of the retail licensees who have failed to make payment for beer or wine products as required by this section. The failure of any manufacturer or wholesaler to comply

with the provisions of this section may, at the discretion of the authority, subject the license of such manufacturer or wholesaler to suspension for not more than five days for the first offense, and not more than thirty days for a subsequent offense.

4. In the event that any dispute shall exist between any manufacturer or wholesaler and a retail licensee to whom such manufacturer or wholesaler shall have sold beer or wine products, either as to the fact of payment or as to the amount due for such beer or wine products or as to the quantity of the beer or wine products sold or delivered, which dispute cannot be adjusted between them, the authority is authorized to receive statements from each of the parties to such dispute as to the facts and circumstances thereof and to determine whether or not such retail licensee's name should be published on the delinquent list.

5. The authority in the case of a retail licensee who has actually made payment for beer or wine products, or on good cause shown to it, may permit sales or deliveries to any retial* licensee who has received notice of default or who is named on any delinquent list, on terms other than for cash, but within the limitations of this section, prior to the publication of the next delinquent list.

**So in original. Probably should be "retail".*

6. The license of any retail licensee who purchases or accepts delivery of beer or wine products on any terms, other than as provided in this section, may be suspended for not more than five days for the first offense and not more than thirty days for a subsequent offense. The failure of any such retail licensee to pay any amount in default before the expiration of the period of suspension shall be deemed and punishable as a subsequent offense until paid. In addition, the authority may require any such retail licensee, after default in making payment in accordance with the provisions of this section to make payment in cash for beer or wine products subsequently delivered.

7. Nothing contained in this section shall be construed to require any manufacturer or wholesaler to extend credit to any retail licensee nor to restrain any manufacturer or wholesaler from seeking to enforce by legal action or otherwise, payment of any sum or sums of money due or alleged to be due to any such manufacturer or wholesaler for beer or wine products sold or delivered to any such retail licensee.

8. There shall be paid to the liquor authority by each person applying after the effective date of this section for any license to sell beer or wine products to retailers or upon the renewal of such license, a sum equivalent to ten per centum of the annual license fee prescribed by this chapter for each such licensee. Such moneys shall be used by the authority to defray the expenses incurred in the administration of this section.

9. Notwithstanding the law in effect at the time of the sale, the final payment date for beer and/or wine products sold prior to the effective date of this section for which payment has not been made shall be the first final payment date as determined by the provisions of this section.

*❼(1997, added by chap. 389, eff. 12/1/98.)*

**§101-b. Unlawful discriminations prohibited; filing of schedules; schedule listing fund.**

1. It is the declared policy of the state that it is necessary to regulate and control the manufacture, sale, and distribution within the state of alcoholic beverages for the purpose of fostering and promoting temperance in their consumption and respect for and obedience to the law. In order to eliminate the undue stimulation of sales of alcoholic beverages and the practice of manufacturers and wholesalers in granting discounts, rebates, allowances, free goods, and other inducements to selected licensees, which contribute to a disorderly distribution of alcoholic beverages, and which are detrimental to the proper regulation of the liquor industry and contrary to the interests of temperance, it is hereby further declared as the policy of the state that the sale of alcoholic beverages should be subjected to certain restrictions, prohibitions and regulations. The necessity for the enactment of the provisions of this section is, therefore, declared as a matter of legislative determination.

2. It shall be unlawful for any person who sells liquors or wines to wholesalers or retailers

(a) to discriminate, directly or indirectly, in price, in discounts for time of payment or in discounts on quantity of merchandise sold, between one wholesaler and another wholesaler, or between one retailer and another retailer purchasing liquor or wine bearing the same brand or trade name and of like age and quality; (b) to grant, directly or indirectly, any discount, rebate, free goods, allowance or other inducement of any kind whatsoever, except a discount or discounts for quantity of liquor or for quantity of wine and a discount not in excess of one per centum for payment on or before ten days from date of shipment.

3. ❽(a) No brand of liquor or wine shall be sold to or purchased by a wholesaler, irrespective of the place of sale or delivery, unless a schedule, as provided by this section, is filed with the liquor authority, and is then in effect. Such schedule shall be in writing duly verified, and filed in the number of copies and form as required by the authority, and shall contain, with respect to each item, the exact brand or trade name, capacity of package, nature of contents, age and proof where stated on the label, the number of bottles contained in each case, the bottle and case price to wholesalers, the net bottle and case price paid by the seller, which prices, in each instance, shall be individual for each item and not in "combination" with any other item, the discounts for quantity, if any, and the discounts for time of payment, if any. Such brand of liquor or wine shall not be sold to wholesalers except at the price and discounts then in effect unless prior written permission of the authority is granted for good cause shown and for reasons not inconsistent with the purpose of this chapter. Such schedule shall be filed by (1) the owner of such brand, or (2) a wholesaler selling such brand and who is designated as agent for the purpose of filing such schedule if the owner of the brand is not licensed by the authority, or

(3) with the approval of the authority, by a wholesaler, in the event that the owner of the brand is unable to file a schedule or designate an agent for such purpose. As used in this subdivision the term "item" shall be deemed to include a sealed, pre-wrapped package consisting of a sealed container of liquor, wine or wine product and other merchandise reasonably used in connection with the preparation, storage or service of liquor, wine or wine products provided that such other merchandise shall not be potable or edible. ❽*(1995, chgd. by chaps. 357, 358; 1998, chgd. by chap. 237, eff. 9/1/98.)*

(b) No brand of liquor or wine shall be sold to or purchased by a retailer unless a schedule, as provided by this section, is filed with the liquor authority, and is then in effect. Such schedule shall be in writing duly verified, and filed in the number of copies and form as required by the authority, and shall contain, with respect to each item, the exact brand or trade name, capacity of package, nature of contents, age and proof where stated on the label, the number of bottles contained in each case, the bottle and case price to retailers, the net bottle and case price paid by the seller, which prices, in each instance, shall be individual for each item and not in "combination" with any other item, the discounts for quantity, if any, and the discounts for time of payment, if any. Such brand of liquor or wine shall not be sold to retailers except at the price and discounts then in effect unless prior written permission of the authority is granted for good cause shown and for reasons not inconsistent with the purpose of this chapter. Such schedule shall be filed by each manufacturer selling such brand to retailers and by each wholesaler selling such brand to retailers.

(c) Provided however, nothing contained in this section shall require any manufacturer or wholesaler to list in any schedule to be filed pursuant to this section any item offered for sale to a retailer under a brand which is owned exclusively by one retailer and sold at retail within the state exclusively by such retailer.

(d)—(i) *(Repealed.)*

4. Each such schedule required by paragraph (a) of subdivision three of this section shall be filed on or before the twenty-fifth day of each month and the prices and discounts set forth therein shall become effective on the first day of the second succeeding calendar month and shall be in effect for such second succeeding calendar month. Each such schedule required by paragraph (b) of subdivision three of this section shall be filed on or before the fifth day of each month, and the prices and discounts set forth therein shall become effective on the first day of the calendar month following the filing thereof, and shall be in effect for such calendar month. Within ten days after the filing of such schedule the authority shall make them or a composite thereof available for inspection by licensees. Within three business days after such inspection is provided for, a wholesaler may amend his filed schedule for sales to retailers in order to meet lower competing prices and discounts for liquor or wine of the same brand or trade name, and of like age and quality, filed pursuant to this section

by any licensee selling such brand, provided such amended prices are not lower and discounts are not greater than those to be met. Any amended schedule so filed shall become effective on the first day of the calendar month following the filing thereof and shall be in effect for such calendar month. All schedules filed shall be subject to public inspection, from the time that they are required to be made available for inspection by licensees, and shall not be considered confidential. Each manufacturer and wholesaler shall retain in his licensed premises for inspection by licensees a copy of his filed schedules as then in effect. The liquor authority may make such rules as shall be appropriate to carry out the purpose of this section.

4-a. No licensee shall refuse to sell any brand of liquor or wine to any licensee authorized to purchase such brand of liquor or wine from such licensee at the price listed in the schedule of prices of such brand of liquor or wine required to be filed by such licensee with the authority pursuant to this section, provided the purchaser pays cash therefor, and except as herein provided.

(a) A schedule of prices to wholesalers filed by the brand owner or its agent with the authority, pursuant to this section, may limit the distribution or resale of a brand to wholesalers by the filing by the brand owner or its agent with the authority of the names, addresses and license numbers of such wholesalers. Such list shall be filed each month together with the schedule of prices, and no name shall be added thereto or removed therefrom after filing except with permission of the authority.

(b) Only those wholesalers listed, pursuant to paragraph (a) of this subdivision, may schedule the price to retailers for such brand, except that when not inconsistent with the purpose of this section, the authority may authorize any other wholesaler to schedule a price after furnishing the quantity, source of purchase and any other information the authority may require.

(c) When distribution or resale of a brand has been restricted, pursuant to paragraph (a) of this subdivision, such brand shall not be sold or purchased by any wholesalers who are not listed in accordance with paragraph (a) of this subdivision.

(d) For good cause shown to the satisfaction of the authority, permission may be granted for the filing of schedules limiting the distribution or resale of a brand to retailers.

(e) Manufacturers and wholesalers may not require or compel retailers to purchase other brands in order to be able to buy a particular brand.

(f) Nothing contained in this subdivision shall be construed as authority for permitting any conduct or activity by any brand owner or its agent or any wholesaler of liquor or wine proscribed by the antitrust laws of this state or the United States.

(g) If any provision of any paragraph of this subdivision or any subdivision of this section or the application thereof to any person or circumstance shall be adjudged invalid by a court of competent jurisdiction, such order or judgment shall be confined in its operation to the controversy in which it was rendered and shall not affect or invalidate the remainder of any provision of this subdivision or any subdivision of this section or the application of any part thereof to any other person or circumstance and to this end the provisions of each paragraph of this subdivision and each subdivision of this section are hereby declared to be severable.

5. ❾(a) (i) Notwithstanding any other provision of law, each such schedule required by paragraph (a) of subdivision three of this section which is filed by a winery or farm winery, shall be filed annually on or before the twenty-fifth day of November. The prices and discounts set forth therein shall become effective on the first day of the second succeeding calendar month and shall remain in effect for such twelve succeeding calendar months, unless a price change filing is made pursuant to subparagraph (ii) of this paragraph.

(ii) A winery or farm winery licensee may file a price schedule change at any time between the required annual filings. Each such price schedule change shall be filed on or before the twenty-fifth day of each month for a change in prices to become effective on the first day of the second succeeding calendar month and shall remain in effect until the effective date of the next filing.

❾(b) (i) Notwithstanding any other provision of law, each such schedule required by paragraph (b) of subdivision three of this section which is filed by a winery or farm winery licensee shall be filed annually on or before the fifth day of December. The prices and discounts set forth therein shall become effective on the first day of the calendar month following the filing thereof, and shall remain in effect for such twelve succeeding calendar months, unless a price change filing is made pursuant to subparagraph (ii) of this paragraph.

(ii) A winery or farm winery licensee may file a price schedule change at any time between the required annual filings. Each such price schedule change shall be filed on or before the fifth day of each month for a change in prices to become effective on the first day of the calendar month following the filing thereof and shall remain in effect until the effective date of the next filing.

*❾(1999, chgd. by chap. 539, eff. 11/4/99.)*

(c) Within ten days after the filing of such schedules the authority shall make them or a composite thereof available for inspection by licensees. Within three business days after such inspection is provided for, a wholesaler may amend his filed schedule for sales to retailers in order to meet lower competing prices and discounts for wine of the same brand or trade name, and of like age and quality, filed pursuant to this section by any licensee selling such brand, provided such amended prices are not lower and discounts are not greater than those to be set. Any amended schedule so filed shall become effective on the first day of the calendar month following the filing thereof and shall be in effect until the effective date of the next filing.

(d) All schedules filed shall be subject to public inspection, from the time that they are required to be made available for inspection by licensees, and shall not be considered confidential. Each manufacturer and wholesaler shall retain in his licensed premises for inspection by licensees a copy of his filed schedules as then in effect. The liquor authority may make such rules as shall be appropriate to carry out the purpose of this subdivision.

6. For the purpose of raising the moneys necessary to defray the expenses incurred in the administration of this section, on or before the tenth day after this act becomes a law, there shall be paid to the liquor authority by each manufacturer and wholesaler licensed under this chapter to sell to retailers liquors and/or wines, a sum equivalent to fifteen per centum of the annual license fee prescribed by this chapter for each such licensee. A like sum shall be paid by each person hereafter applying for any such license or the renewal of any such license, and such sum shall accompany the application and the license fee prescribed by this chapter for such license or renewal as the case may be. In the event that any other law requires the payment of a fee by any such licensee or applicant as set forth in this section for schedule listing, then and in such event the total fee imposed by this section and such other law or laws on each such licensee shall not exceed in the aggregate a sum equivalent to fifteen per centum of the annual license fee prescribed by this chapter for such license.

7. The authority may revoke, cancel or suspend any license issued pursuant to this chapter, and may recover (as provided in section one hundred twelve of this chapter) the penal sum of the bond filed by a licensee, or both, for any sale or purchase in violation of any of the provisions of this section or for making a false statement in any schedule filed pursuant to this section or for failing or refusing in any manner to comply with any of the provisions of this section.

**§§101-bb, 101-bbb.** *(Repealed.)*

**§102. General prohibitions and restrictions.**

1. (a) No person shall send or cause to be sent into the state any letter, postcard, circular, newspaper, pamphlet, order kit, order form, invitation to order, price list, or publication of any kind containing an advertisement or a solicitation of any order for any alcoholic beverages, irrespective of whether the purchase is made or to be made within or without the state, or whether intended for commercial or personal use or otherwise, unless such person shall be duly licensed hereunder to traffic in alcoholic beverages.

(b) No person shall issue or publish or cause to be issued or published in the state any letter, postcard, circular, newspaper, pamphlet, order kit, order form, invitation to order, price list, or publication of any kind containing an advertisement or a solicitation of any, order for any alcoholic beverages, irrespective of whether the purchase is made or to be made within or without the state, or whether intended for commercial or personal use or otherwise, unless such person shall be duly licensed hereunder to traffic in alcoholic beverages.

(c) No alcoholic beverages shall be shipped into the state unless the same shall be consigned to a person duly licensed hereunder to traffic in alcoholic beverages. This prohibition shall apply to all shipments of alcoholic beverages into New York state and includes importation or distribution for commercial purposes, for personal use, or otherwise, and irrespective of whether such alcoholic beverages were purchased within or without the state, provided, however, this prohibition shall not apply to any shipment consigned to a New York resident who has personally purchased alcoholic beverages for his personal use while outside the United States for a minimum period of forty-eight consecutive hours and which he has shipped as consignor to himself as consignee. Purchases made outside the United States by persons other than the purchaser himself, regardless whether made as his agent, or by his authorization or on his behalf, are deemed not to have been personally purchased within the meaning of this paragraph.



(d) No common carrier or other person shall bring or carry into the state any alcoholic beverages, unless the same shall be consigned to a person duly licensed hereunder to traffic in alcoholic beverages, provided, however, that alcoholic beverages may be delivered by a trucking permittee from a steamship or railroad station or terminal to a New York resident who has personally purchased alcoholic beverages for his personal use while outside the United States for a minimum period of forty-eight consecutive hours, and which he has shipped as consignor to himself as consignee, and except as so stated, no trucking permittee shall accept for delivery, deliver or transport from a steamship or railroad station or terminal any shipment of alcoholic beverages consigned to a non-licensed person having his home or business in New York state. Purchases of alcoholic beverages made outside the United States by persons other than the purchaser himself, regardless whether made as his agent, or by his authorization or on his behalf, are deemed not to have been personally purchased within the meaning of this paragraph.

(e) Subdivisions (c) and (d) hereof shall apply to alcoholic beverages, either in the original package or otherwise, whether intended for commercial or personal use, as well as otherwise, and to foreign, interstate, as well as intrastate, shipments or carriage, irrespective of whether such alcoholic beverages were purchased within or without the state.

(f) Nothing in this chapter shall be deemed to exempt from taxation the sale or use of any alcoholic beverages subject to any tax imposed under or pursuant to the authority of the tax law or to grant any other exemption from the provisions of such law.

2. No person holding any license hereunder, other than a license to sell an alcoholic beverage at retail for off-premises consumption, shall knowingly employ in connection with his business in any capacity whatsoever, any person, who has been convicted of a felony, or any of

the following offenses, who has not subsequent to such conviction received an executive pardon therefor removing any civil disabilities incurred thereby, a certificate of good conduct or other relief from disabilities provided by law, or the written approval of the state liquor authority permitting such employment, to wit:

(a) Illegally using, carrying or possessing a pistol or other dangerous weapon;

(b) Making or possessing burglar's instruments;

(c) Buying or receiving or criminally possessing stolen property;

(d) Unlawful entry of a building;

(e) Aiding escape from prison;

(f) Unlawfully possessing or distributing habit forming narcotic drugs;

(g) Violating subdivisions six, eight, ten or eleven of section seven hundred twenty-two of the former penal law as in force and effect immediately prior to September first, nineteen hundred sixty-seven, or violating sections 165.25, 165.30 or subdivision three of section 240.35 of the penal law;

(h) Vagrancy or prostitution; or

(i) Ownership, operation, possession, custody or control of a still subsequent to July first, nineteen hundred fifty-four.

If, as hereinabove provided, the state liquor authority issues its written approval for the employment by a licensee, in a specified capacity, of a person previously convicted of a felony or any of the offenses above enumerated, such person, may, unless he is subsequently convicted of a felony or any of such offenses, thereafter be employed in the same capacity by any other licensee without the further written approval of the authority unless the prior approval given by the authority is terminated.

The liquor authority may make such rules as it deems necessary to carry out the purpose and intent of this subdivision.

3. *(Renumbered to subd. 3-a.)*

3-a. No licensee or permittee shall purchase or agree to purchase any alcoholic beverages from any person within the state who is not duly licensed to sell such alcoholic beverage as the case may be, at the time of such agreement and sale nor give any order for any alcoholic beverage to any individual who is not the holder of a solicitor's permit, except as provided for in section eighty-five or ninety-nine-g of this chapter.

❸3-b. No retail licensee shall purchase, agree to purchase or receive any alcoholic beverage except from a person duly licensed within the state by the liquor authority to sell such alcoholic beverage at the time of such agreement and sale to such retail licensee, except as provided for in section eighty-five or ninety-nine-g of this chapter.
❸*(1993, chgd. by chap. 458, eff. 11/23/93.)*

4. No licensee or any of his or its agents, servants or employees shall peddle any liquor and/or wine from house to house by means of a truck or otherwise, where the sale is consummated and delivery made

concurrently at the residence or place of business of a consumer. This subdivision shall not prohibit the delivery by a licensee to consumers, pursuant to sales made at the place of business of said licensee.

5. No licensee shall employ any canvasser or solicitor for the purpose of receiving an order from a consumer for any liquor and/or wine at the residence or place of business of such consumer, nor shall any licensee receive or accept any order, for the sale of any liquor and/or wine, which shall be solicited at the residence or place of business of a consumer. This subdivision shall not prohibit the solicitation by a wholesaler of an order from any licensee at the licensed premises of such licensee.

6. No alcoholic beverage shall be released for delivery from any warehouse located within the state, except upon a permit having first been obtained as provided by this chapter. Applications for such permits may be filed at the office of the liquor authority in New York, Albany or Buffalo, whichever is nearest to the location of the warehouse, and shall be upon a form to be prepared by the liquor authority. This provision shall not apply to alcoholic beverages, which are to be released for shipment outside of the state.

7. Each person owning or operating any warehouse located within the state shall keep and maintain as part of his permanent records, treasury department forms fifty-two and fifty-two-a as heretofore required by the United States government.



### §103. Provisions governing manufacturers.

1. No manufacturer shall sell, or agree to sell or deliver in the state any liquors and/or wines, as the case may be, in any cask, barrel, keg, hogshead or other container, except in sealed containers containing quantities in accordance with federal size standards adopted pursuant to the federal alcohol administration act, as amended (27 U.S.C. 201 et seq.); and provided further, that (a) Class A distillers may sell or deliver liquor in bulk to the holder of a Class A or B distiller's license or to a permittee engaged in the manufacture of products which are unfit for beverage use; (b) Class C distillers may sell or deliver fruit brandy in bulk to the holder of a winery license, a holder of a Class B distiller's license or to a permittee engaged in the manufacture of products which are unfit for beverage use; and (c) a winery licensee may sell or deliver wine in bulk to a holder of a winery license, the holder of a distiller's license of any class, or to a permittee engaged in the manufacture of products which are unfit for beverage use. Such containers shall have affixed thereto such labels as may be required by the rules of the liquor authority, together with all necessary federal revenue and New York state excise tax stamps, as required by law.

2. No manufacturer shall transport alcoholic beverages in any vehicle owned and operated or hired and operated by such manufacturer, unless there shall be attached to or inscribed upon both sides of such vehicle a sign, showing the name and address of the licensee, together with the following inscription: "New York State Distiller (or Brewer or

Winery) License No. .........," in uniform letters not less than three and one-half inches in height. In lieu of such sign a manufacturer may have in the cab of such vehicle a photostatic copy of its current license issued by the authority, and such copy duly authenticated by the authority.

3. No manufacturer shall deliver any alcoholic beverages, except in vehicles owned and operated by such manufacturer, or hired and operated by such manufacturer from a trucking or transportation company registered with the liquor authority, and shall only make deliveries at the licensed premises of the purchaser.

4—6. *(Repealed.)*

7. Each manufacturer shall keep and maintain upon the licensed premises, adequate books and records of all transactions involving the manufacture and sale of his or its products, which shall show the ingredients but not the formula or recipe used in the manufacture of such alcoholic beverages together with the quantity of alcoholic beverages manufactured by such manufacturer; the names, addresses, and the license numbers of the purchasers of such alcoholic beverages, together with the quantities involved in such purchases, whether the same shall be sold within or without the state. Each sale shall be recorded separately on a numbered invoice, which shall have printed thereon the number, the name of the licensee, the address of the licensed premises, and the current license number. Such manufacturer shall deliver to the purchaser a true duplicate invoice stating the name and address of the purchaser, the quantity of alcoholic beverages, description by brands and the price of such alcoholic beverages, and a true, accurate and complete statement of the terms and conditions on which such sale is made. Any terms and conditions of a sale not stated on said invoice shall constitute a service within the meaning of section one hundred and one, subdivision one (c) of this chapter. Such books, records and invoices shall be kept for a period of two years and shall be available for inspection by any authorized representative of the liquor authority.

8. No manufacturer shall furnish or cause to be furnished to any licensee, any exterior or interior sign, printed, painted, electric or otherwise, except as authorized by the liquor authority.

9. Nothing contained in this chapter shall prohibit a brewer from manufacturing, bottling or storing non-alcoholic carbonated beverages on the licensed premises provided such business was conducted by the licensee prior to July first, nineteen hundred thirty-nine.

**§104. Provisions governing wholesalers.**

1. ❷(a) No wholesaler shall be engaged in any other business on the premises to be licensed; except that nothing contained in this chapter shall (1) prohibit a beer wholesaler from (i) acquiring, storing or selling non-alcoholic snack foods, as defined in paragraph (b) of this subdivision, (ii) manufacturing, bottling, storing, or selling non-alcoholic carbonated beverages, (iii) manufacturing, storing or selling

non-alcoholic non-carbonated soft drinks, mineral waters, spring waters, drinking water, non-taxable malt or cereal beverages, juice drinks, fruit or vegetable juices, ice, liquid beverage mixes and dry or frozen beverage mixes, (iv) acquiring, storing or selling wine products, (v) the sale of promotional items on such premises, or (vi) the sale of tobacco products at retail by wholesalers who are licensed to sell beer and other products at retail, (2) prohibit a wholesaler authorized to sell wine from manufacturing, acquiring or selling wine merchandise, as defined in paragraph (d) of this subdivision, or (3) prohibit a licensed winery or licensed farm winery from engaging in the business of a wine wholesaler for New York state labeled wines produced by any licensed winery or licensed farm winery or prohibit such wine wholesaler from exercising any of its rights pursuant to sections seventy-six and seventy-six-a of this chapter provided that the operation of such beer and wine wholesalers business shall be subject to such rules and regulations as the liquor authority may prescribe. ❷*(2002, chgd. by chap. 223, eff. 7/30/2002.)*



(b) "Non-alcoholic snack foods" as used in paragraph (a) of this subdivision shall include ready to eat finger foods ordinarily intended to be served cold or at room temperature, such as nut and seed meats, cooked pork rinds, pretzels, popped corn and a variety of other similar finger foods which are prepared from high-starch and/or cellulosic edible materials.

(c) "Promotional items" are items which bear advertising information, are of nominal value, are obtained by a licensee through a supplier of alcoholic beverages and are designated and designed for unconditional sale or distribution to the public. The sale or distribution of promotional items shall be incidental to the licensee's sale of alcoholic beverages. All promotional items shall be properly invoiced.

❷(d) "Wine merchandise" as used in paragraph (a) of this subdivision shall include corkscrews, ice, the sale of publications, including prerecorded video and/or audio cassette tapes, designed to help educate consumers in their knowledge and appreciation of wine and wine products, as defined in section three of this chapter, or the sale of glasses designed for the consumption of wine, racks designed for the storage of wine, and devices designed to minimize oxidation in bottles of wine which have been uncorked. ❷*(2002, added by chap. 223, eff. 7/30/2002.)*

2. No wholesaler shall sell, or agree to sell or deliver in the state any liquors and/or wines, as the case may be, in any cask, barrel, keg, hogshead or other container, except in a sealed package containing quantities in accordance with federal size standards adopted pursuant to the federal alcohol administration act, as amended (27 U.S.C. 201 et seq.); provided, however, that wholesalers may store, warehouse or keep off the licensed premises any liquors and/or wines in bulk for sale to a rectifier or to a permittee engaged in the manufacture of products which are unfit for beverage use. Such containers shall have affixed thereto such labels as may be required by the rules of the liquor authority,

together with all necessary federal revenue and New York state excise tax stamps, as required by law.

3. Each wholesaler shall have painted on the front window of the licensed premises, or if there be no window, on a sign affixed to the front of the building containing said licensed premises, the name of the licensee together with the inscription, "New York State wholesale beer, liquor or wine license number ..........,"; as the case may be, in uniform letters not less than three and one-half inches in height.

4. *(Repealed.)*

5. No wholesaler shall transport alcoholic beverages in any vehicle owned and operated or hired and operated by such wholesaler, unless there shall be attached to or inscribed upon both sides of such vehicle a sign, showing the name and address of the licensee, together with the following inscription: "New York State wholesale beer, liquor or wine license number .........," as the case may be, in uniform letters not less than three and one-half inches in height. In lieu of such sign, a wholesaler may have in the cab of such vehicle a photostatic copy of its current license issued by the authority, and such copy duly authenticated by the authority.

6. No wholesaler shall deliver any alcoholic beverages, except in vehicles owned and operated by such wholesaler, or hired and operated by such wholesaler from a trucking or transportation company registered with the liquor authority, and shall only make deliveries at the licensed premises of the purchaser.

7—9. *(Repealed.)*

10. Each wholesaler shall keep and maintain upon the licensed premises, adequate books and records of all transactions involving the business transacted by such wholesaler, which shall show the amount of alcoholic beverages in gallons, purchased by such wholesaler together with the names, license numbers and places of business of the persons from whom the same was purchased and the amount involved in such purchases, as well as the amount of alcoholic beverages, in gallons, sold by such wholesaler together with the names, addresses, and license numbers of such purchasers whether the same shall be purchased or sold within or without the state. Each sale shall be recorded separately on a numbered invoice, which shall have printed thereon the number, the name of the licensee, the address of the licensed premises, and the current license number. Such wholesaler shall deliver to the purchaser a true duplicate invoice stating the name and address of the purchaser, the quantity of alcoholic beverages, description by brands and the price of such alcoholic beverages, and a true, accurate and complete statement of the terms and conditions on which such sale is made. Any terms and conditions of a sale not stated on said invoice shall constitute a service within the meaning of section one hundred and one, subdivision one (c) of this chapter. Such books, records and invoices shall be kept for a period of two years and shall be available for inspection by any authorized representative of the liquor authority.

11. No wholesaler shall furnish or cause to be furnished to any licensee, any exterior or interior sign, printed, painted, electric or otherwise, unless authorized by the liquor authority.

**§104-a. Provisions governing vendors.**

1. No sign, of any kind, printed, painted, or electric, advertising any brand of beer shall be permitted on the exterior or interior of such premises, except by permission of the liquor authority.

2. No vendor shall transport beer in any vehicle owned and operated or hired and operated by such vendor, for off-premises consumption, unless there shall be attached to or inscribed upon both sides of such vehicle a sign, showing the name and address of the licensee together with the following inscription, "New York State Beer Vendor's License No. ..........," as the case may be, in uniform letters not less than three and one-half inches in height. In lieu of such sign, a vendor may have in the cab of such vehicle a photostatic copy of its current license issued by the authority, and such copy duly authenticated by the authority.



3. No vendor for off-premises consumption shall sell or deliver to any person beer in excess of five gallons at one and at the same time.

4. Each vendor for off-premises consumption shall keep and maintain upon the licensed premises, adequate books and records of all transactions involving the business transacted by such vendor, which shall show the amount of beer purchased by such licensee together with the names, license numbers and places of business of the persons from whom the same was purchased, and the amount involved in such purchases, as well as the amount of beer sold by such vendor, and the amount involved in each sale. Such books and records shall be available for inspection by any authorized representative of the liquor authority.

**§105. Provisions governing licensees to sell at retail for consumption off the premises.**

1. No retail license to sell liquors and/or wines for consumption off the premises shall be granted for any premises, unless the applicant shall be the owner thereof, or shall be in possession of said premises under a lease, in writing, for a term not less than the license period except, however, that such license may thereafter be renewed without the requirement of a lease as herein provided. This subdivision shall not apply to premises leased from government agencies, as defined under subdivision twelve-b of section three of this chapter; provided, however, that the appropriate administrator of such government agency provides some form of written documentation regarding the terms of occupancy under which the applicant is leasing said premises from the government agency for presentation to the state liquor authority at the time of the license application. Such documentation shall include the terms of occupancy between the applicant and the government agency, including, but not limited to, any short-term leasing agreements or written occupancy agreements.

2. No premises shall be licensed to sell liquors and/or wines at retail for off-premises consumption, unless said premises shall be located in a store, the principal entrance to which shall be from the street level and located on a public thoroughfare in premises which may be occupied, operated or conducted for business, trade or industry or on an arcade or subsurface thoroughfare leading to a railroad terminal. There may be not more than one additional entrance which shall be from the street level and located on and giving access to and from a public or private parking lot or parking area having space for not less than five automobiles.

3. No retail license to sell liquor and/or wine for off-premises consumption shall be granted for any premises which shall be located on the same street or avenue, and within two hundred feet of a building occupied exclusively as a school, church, synagogue or other place of worship; the measurements to be taken in a straight line from the center of the nearest entrance to the building used for such school, church, synagogue or other place of worship to the center of the nearest entrance of the premises to be licensed; except, however, that no license shall be denied to any premises at which a license under this chapter has been in existence continuously from a date prior to the date when a building on the same street or avenue and within two hundred feet of said premises has been occupied exclusively as a school, church, synagogue or other place of worship.

Within the context of this subdivision, the word "entrance" shall mean a door of a school, of a house of worship, or of the premises sought to be licensed, regularly used to give ingress to students of the school, to the general public attending the place of worship, and to patrons or guests of the premises proposed to be licensed, except that where a school or house of worship is set back from a public thoroughfare, the walkway or stairs leading to any such door shall be deemed an entrance; and the measurement shall be taken to the center of the walkway or stairs at the point where it meets the building line or public thoroughfare. A door which has no exterior hardware, or which is used solely as an emergency or fire exit, or for maintenance purposes, or which leads directly to a part of a building not regularly used by the general public or patrons, is not deemed an "entrance".

4. *(Repealed.)*

5. No retail licensee of liquor and/or wine for off-premises consumption shall keep upon the licensed premises any liquors and/or wines in any cask, barrel, keg, hogshead or other container, except in the original sealed package, as received from the manufacturer or wholesaler. Such containers shall have affixed thereto such labels as may be required by the rules of the liquor authority, together with all necessary federal revenue and New York state excise tax stamps, as required by law. Such containers shall not be opened nor its contents consumed on the premises where sold, except for the purpose of wine tasting or sampling by any person pursuant to authorization to conduct such a sampling or tasting pursuant to subdivision two of section

seventy-six of this chapter except those to whom sales are prohibited in section sixty-five of this chapter.

6. Each person licensed to sell liquor and/or wine for off-premises consumption shall have painted on the front window of the licensed premises, the name of the licensee together with the inscription, "New York State Retail Liquor or Wine Store License No. ...........," as the case may be, in uniform letters not less than three and one-half inches in height.

7. No sign of any kind printed, painted or electric, advertising any brand of liquors or wines shall be permitted on the exterior or interior of such premises, except by permission of the liquor authority.

8. No retail licensee, for off-premises consumption, shall transport liquors or wines in any vehicle owned and operated or hired and operated by such retail licensee, for off-premises consumption, except liquors and wines transported to the home of a purchaser not to be resold by the purchaser, unless there shall be attached to or inscribed upon both sides of such vehicle a sign, showing the name and address of the licensee together with the following inscription, "New York State Retail Liquor or Wine Store License No. ..........," as the case may be, in uniform letters not less than three and one-half inches in height, except deliveries may be made in passenger type vehicles owned by the licensee and operated by the licensee or his agent, or hired by the licensee and operated by the licensee or his agent, provided the person making the delivery shall have upon his person while so delivering a photostatic copy of the current license issued by the authority. In lieu of such sign, a retail licensee may have in the cab of such vehicle a photostatic copy of its current license issued by the authority, and such copy duly authenticated by the authority.

9. No retail licensee for off-premises consumption shall deliver any liquors or wines except in vehicles owned and operated by such licensee, or hired and operated by such licensee from a trucking or transportation company registered with the liquor authority, and shall only make such deliveries at the premises of the purchaser.

10. (a) Each retail licensee of liquor and/or wine for off-premises consumption shall have conspicuously displayed within the interior of the licensed premises where sales are made and where it can be readily inspected by consumers a printed price list of the liquors and/or wines offered for sale therein; and no liquor and/or wine shall be sold except at the price set forth in such list;

(b) No screen, blind, curtain, partition, article or thing shall be permitted in the windows or upon the doors of such licensed premises, which shall prevent a clear view into the interior of such licensed premises from the sidewalk, at all times; and

(c) No booth, screen, partition or other obstruction shall be permitted in the interior of said licensed premises.

11. No retail licensee of liquor and/or wine for off-premises consumption shall keep or permit to be kept upon the licensed premises, any liquors and/or wines in any unsealed bottle or other unsealed

container, except for the purpose of wine tasting or sampling by any person pursuant to authorization to conduct such a sampling or tasting pursuant to subdivision two of section seventy-six of this chapter except those to whom sales are prohibited in section sixty-five of this chapter.

12. No retail licensee of liquor and/or wine for off-premises consumption shall sell or deliver any liquors and/or wines to any person with knowledge of, or with reasonable cause to believe, that the person to whom such liquors and/or wines are so sold or delivered, has acquired the same for the purpose of peddling them from place to place, or of selling or giving them away in violation of the provisions of this chapter or in violation of the rules and regulations of the liquor authority.

13. *(Repealed.)*

14. No premises licensed to sell liquor and/or wine for off-premises consumption shall be permitted to remain open:

(a) On Sunday.

(b) On any other day between midnight and eight o'clock antemeridian.

(c) On the twenty-fifth day of December, known as Christmas day, and if any such day is Sunday, the next day thereafter.

In any community where daylight saving time is in effect, such time shall be deemed the standard time for the purpose of this law.

15. Each retail licensee for off-premises consumption shall keep and maintain upon the licensed premises, adequate books and records of all transactions involving the business transacted by such licensee, which shall show the amount of liquors and wines, purchased by such licensee together with the names, license numbers and places of business of the persons from whom the same were purchased, and the amount involved in such purchases, as well as the amount of liquors or wines, sold by such licensee, and the amount involved in each sale. Such books and records shall be available for inspection by any authorized representative of the liquor authority.

16. No retail licensee to sell liquors and/or wines for off-premises consumption shall be interested, directly or indirectly, in any premises where liquors, wines or beer are manufactured or sold at wholesale or any other premises where liquor or wine is sold at retail for off-premises consumption, by stock ownership, interlocking directors, mortgage or lien on any personal or real property or by any other means. Any lien, mortgage or other interest or estate, however, now held by such retailer on or in the personal or real property of such manufacturer or wholesaler, which mortgage, lien, interest or estate was acquired on or before December thirty-first, nineteen hundred thirty-two, shall not be included within the provisions of this subdivision; provided, however, the burden of establishing the time of the accrual of the interest comprehended by this subdivision, shall be upon the person who claims to be entitled to the protection and exemption afforded hereby.

17. No retail licensee for off-premises consumption shall make or cause to be made any loan to any person engaged in the manufacture or sale of liquors, wines or beer at wholesale. No retail licensee to sell liquors and/or wines for off-premises consumption shall make or cause to be made any loan to any person engaged in the manufacture or sale of liquors, wines or beer at wholesale or to any person engaged in the sale of liquors and/or wines at retail for off-premises consumption.

18. A drug store holding a permit to sell liquors and/or wines for off-premises consumption pursuant to this chapter shall be subject to the following conditions:

(a) Liquors and/or wines sold by it shall not be consumed on the premises where sold or in any outbuilding, yard, booth or garden appertaining thereto or connected therewith.

(b) Such permittee shall keep and maintain upon the licensed premises, adequate books and records, which shall show the amount of liquors and wines, in gallons, purchased by such permittee together with the names, license numbers and places of business, of the persons from whom the same were purchased and the amount involved in such purchases, which books and records shall be available for inspection by any authorized representative of the liquor authority.

(c) No liquor or wine shall be displayed in any window of the premises designated in the drug store permit.

(d) No drug store permittee shall use any placard or card advertising the sale of any liquor or wine unless such card, placard or advertisement shall conspicuously state that the sale of liquor or wine in the said premises designated in the drug store permit is limited to medicinal liquor to be sold by prescription only.

19. *(Repealed.)*

20. Each retail licensee of liquor and/or wine shall designate the price of each item of liquor or wine by attaching to or otherwise displaying immediately adjacent to each such item displayed in the interior of the licensed premises where sales are made a price tag, sign or placard setting forth the bottle price at which each such item is offered for sale therein.

21. No retail license to sell liquor and/or wine for consumption off the premises shall be granted for any public billiard or pocket billiard room, or for establishments of any description in which billiards is played or which maintains any apparatus or paraphernalia for the playing of billiards or pocket billiards and is conducted as a public place of business for profit. Notwithstanding any prohibition to the contrary, a license may be issued to an establishment wherein billiards or pocket billiards are played or may be played on a table which measures not more than three feet by six feet provided that not more than two such tables are in the establishment at any one time and further provided that the cue sticks used, and available for use, are made of light plexiglass or some similar light material.

❶22. No person licensed to sell alcoholic beverages at retail for off-premises consumption, shall suffer or permit any gambling, or offer any gambling on the licensed premises, or suffer or permit illicit drug activity on the licensed premises. The use of the licensed premises or any part thereof for the sale of lottery tickets, when duly authorized and lawfully conducted thereon, shall not constitute gambling within the meaning of this subdivision. ❶*(1994, added by chap. 491, eff. 10/24/94.)*

❷23. All premises licensed under sections fifty-four, fifty-four-a, sixty-three and seventy-nine of this chapter shall be subject to inspection by any peace officer described in subdivision four of section 2.10 of the criminal procedure law acting pursuant to his special duties, or police officer or any duly authorized representative of the state liquor authority, during the hours when the said premises are open for the transaction of business. ❷*(2002, added by chap. 85(F), eff. 5/29/2002.)*



**§105-a. Sale of beer at retail on Sunday.**

No person, firm or corporation holding any license or permit issued under this chapter shall sell, offer for sale or give away beer at retail on Sunday between three antemeridian and twelve noon. Persons, firms or corporations holding licenses and/or permits issued under the provisions of the alcoholic beverage control law permitting the sale of beer at retail, may sell such beverages at retail on Sunday before three antemeridian and after twelve noon for off-premises consumption to persons making purchases at the licensed premises to be taken by them from the licensed premises.

**§105-b. Posting of certain signs.**

1. The authority shall prepare, have printed and distribute across the state to all persons with a license to sell any alcoholic beverage for consumption on the premises or a license to sell any alcoholic beverage for consumption off the premises, a sign or poster with conspicuous lettering that states: "Government Warning: According to the Surgeon General, women should not drink alcoholic beverages during pregnancy because of the risk of birth defects". Such sign or poster must have conspicuous lettering in at least seventy-two point bold face type that states the warning set forth in this subdivision, except that such sign or poster shall be captioned with the word "warning" in at least two inch lettering.

2. All persons with a license to sell any alcoholic beverage for consumption on the premises or a license to sell any alcoholic beverage for consumption off the premises shall display in a conspicuous place the sign or poster upon receiving it from the authority. Such sign shall be placed as close as possible to the place where alcoholic beverages are sold.

3. Any person with such license who violates the provisions of this section shall be subject to a civil penalty, not to exceed one hundred dollars for each day of violation.

4. Compliance with the provisions of any local law requiring the posting of signs containing warnings regarding alcoholic beverages enacted on or before the date on which the provisions of this section shall have become a law, shall be deemed to be in compliance with the provisions of this section. Nothing contained herein, however, shall be deemed to exempt any licensee not otherwise subject to the provisions of any such local law from complying with the provisions of this section.

**§106. Provisions governing licensees to sell at retail for consumption on the premises.**

1. No retail license for on-premises consumption shall be granted for any premises, unless the applicant shall be the owner thereof, or shall be in possession of said premises under a lease, in writing, for a term not less than the license period except, however, that such license may thereafter be renewed without the requirement of a lease as herein provided. This subdivision shall not apply to premises leased from government agencies, as defined under subdivision twelve-b of section three of this chapter; provided, however, that the appropriate administrator of such government agency provides some form of written documentation regarding the terms of occupancy under which the applicant is leasing said premises from the government agency for presentation to the state liquor authority at the time of the license application. Such documentation shall include the terms of occupancy between the applicant and the government agency, including, but not limited to, any short-term leasing agreements or written occupancy agreements.



❖2. (a) No retail licensee for on-premises consumption, except corporations operating railroad cars or aircraft being operated on regularly scheduled flights by a United States certificated airline or persons or corporations operating a hotel, as defined in subdivision fourteen of section three of this chapter, for exclusive use in the furnishing of room service in the manner prescribed by rule or regulation of the state liquor authority, shall keep upon the licensed premises any liquors and/or wines in any cask, barrel, keg, hogshead or other container, except in the original sealed package as received from the manufacturer or wholesaler. Such containers shall have affixed thereto such labels as may be required by the rules of the liquor authority, together with all necessary federal revenue and New York state excise stamps as required by law. No retail licensee for on-premises consumption shall reuse, refill, tamper with, adulterate, dilute or fortify the contents of any container of alcoholic beverages as received from the manufacturer or wholesaler.

(b) Notwithstanding the provisions of paragraph (a) of this subdivision, a retail licensee for on-premises consumption may prepare and keep drinks containing alcoholic beverages in dispensing machines, having capacities of not less than a gallon, which continually mix such drinks.

❖*(1998, chgd. by chap. 40; 2000, chgd. by chap. 512, eff. 11/3/2000.)*

3. No retail licensee for on-premises consumption shall sell, deliver or give away, or cause or permit or procure to be sold, delivered or given away any liquors and/or wines for consumption off the premises where sold.

4. (a) No liquors and/or wines shall be sold or served in premises licensed under section sixty-four or clause (a) of subdivision six of section sixty-four-a of this chapter, except at tables where food may be served and except as provided by subdivision four of section one hundred.

(b) No liquors and/or wines shall be sold or served in premises licensed under clause (b) of subdivision six of section sixty-four-a of this chapter, except at such times and upon such conditions and by the use of such facilities as the liquor authority, by regulation, may prescribe with due regard to the convenience of the public and the strict avoidance of sales prohibited by this chapter.

4-a. No beer shall be sold or served at a bar, counter or other similar contrivance unless a card, sign or plate, visible to the customer, upon which the name of the brewer is conspicuously and legibly displayed, is annexed or affixed to the tap or faucet from which the beer is drawn.

❺5. No alcoholic beverages shall be sold, offered for sale or given away upon any premises licensed to sell alcoholic beverages at retail for on-premises consumption, during the following hours:

(a) Sunday, from four ante meridiem to twelve noon.

(b) On any other day between four ante meridiem and eight ante meridiem.

Unless otherwise approved by the authority pursuant to subdivision eleven of section seventeen of this chapter, where any rule has been adopted in a county on or before April first, nineteen hundred ninety-five, further restricting the hours of sale for alcoholic beverages, such restricted hours shall be the hours, during which the sale of alcoholic beverages at retail for on-premises consumption shall not be permitted within such county.

Nor shall any person be permitted to consume any alcoholic beverages upon any such premises later than one-half hour after the start of the prohibited hours of sale provided for in this section.
❺*(1995, chgd. by chap. 83, eff. 6/20/95.)*

6. No person licensed to sell alcoholic beverages shall suffer or permit any gambling on the licensed premises, or suffer or permit such premises to become disorderly. The use of the licensed premises, or any part thereof, for the sale of lottery tickets, playing of bingo or games of chance, or as a simulcast facility or simulcast theater pursuant to the racing, pari-mutuel wagering and breeding law, when duly authorized and lawfully conducted thereon, shall not constitute gambling within the meaning of this subdivision.

6-a. No retail licensee for on-premises consumption shall suffer or permit any person to appear on licensed premises in such manner or attire as to expose to view any portion of the pubic area, anus, vulva or genitals, or any simulation thereof, nor shall suffer or permit any female to appear on licensed premises in such manner or attire as to expose to view any portion of the breast below the top of the areola, or any simulation thereof.

6-b. No retail licensee for on-premises consumption shall suffer or permit any contest or promotion which endangers the health, safety, and welfare of any person with dwarfism. Any retail licensee in violation of this section shall be subject to the suspension or revocation of said licensee's license to sell alcoholic beverages for on-premises consumption. For the purposes of this section, the term "dwarfism" means a condition of being abnormally small which is caused by heredity, endocrine dysfunction, renal insufficiency or deficiency or skeletal diseases that result in disproportionate short stature and adult height of less than four feet ten inches.

❶6-c. (a) No retail licensee for on-premises consumption shall suffer, permit or promote an event on its premises wherein the contestants deliver, or are not forbidden by the applicable rules thereof from delivering kicks, punches or blows of any kind to the body of an opponent or opponents, whether or not the event consists of a professional match or exhibition, and whether or not the event or any such act, or both, is done for compensation.

(b) The prohibition contained in paragraph (a) of this subdivision, however, shall not be applied to any professional match or exhibition which consists of boxing, sparring, wrestling, or martial arts and which is excepted from the definition of the term "combative sport" contained in subdivision one of section five-a of chapter nine hundred twelve of the laws of nineteen hundred twenty, as added by chapter fourteen of the laws of nineteen hundred ninety-seven.

(c) In addition to any other penalty provided by law, a violation of this subdivision shall constitute an adequate ground for instituting a proceeding to suspend, cancel or revoke the license of the violator in accordance with the applicable procedures specified in section one hundred nineteen of this article.

❶*(2001, added by chap. 254, eff. 9/5/2001.)*

❸7. ❸*(1998, repealed by chap. 40, eff. 4/14/98.)*

8. A club or a luncheon club licensed to sell alcoholic beverages for on-premises consumption shall be permitted to sell such beverages only to its members and to their guests accompanying them.

❸9. No restaurant and no premises licensed to sell liquors and/or wines for on-premises consumption under clause (a) of subdivision six of section sixty-four-a of this chapter shall be permitted to have any opening or means of entrance or passageway for persons or things between the licensed premises and any other room or place in the building containing the licensed premises, or any adjoining or abutting premises, unless such licensed premises are in a building used as a hotel and serves as a dining room for guests of such hotel, or unless such premises are a bona fide restaurant with such access for patrons and guests from any part of such building or adjoining or abutting premises as shall serve public convenience in a reasonable and suitable manner; or unless such licensed premises are in a building owned or operated by any county, town, city, village or public authority or agency, in a park or other similar place of public accommodation. All glass in any window or door on said licensed premises shall be clear and shall not be opaque, colored, stained or frosted. ❸*(1998, chgd. by chap. 40, eff. 4/14/98.)*

10. A vessel licensed to sell liquors and/or wines for on-premises consumption shall not be permitted to sell any liquors and/or wines, while said vessel is moored to a pier or dock, except that vessels sailing on established schedules shall be permitted to sell liquors and/or wines for a period of three hours prior to the regular advertised sailing time.

11. A railroad car or aircraft being operated on regularly scheduled flights by a United States certificated airline licensed to sell liquors and/or wines for on-premises consumption shall be permitted to sell liquors and/or wines only to passengers and while in actual transit, except that a railroad operating licensed cars shall be allowed to sell liquors and/or wines from portable carts located on station platforms located at Penn Station, Grand Central Station, Jamaica, Hunterspoint Avenue or Flatbush from which such licensed railroad cars depart.

❸12. Each retail licensee for on-premises consumption shall keep and maintain upon the licensed premises, adequate records of all transactions involving the business transacted by such licensee which shall show the amount of alcoholic beverages, in gallons, purchased by such licensee together with the names, license numbers and places of business of the persons from whom the same were purchased, the amount involved in such purchases, as well as the sales of alcoholic beverages made by such licensee. The liquor authority is hereby authorized to promulgate rules and regulations permitting an on-premises licensee operating two or more premises separately licensed to sell alcoholic beverages for on-premises consumption to inaugurate or retain in this state methods or practices of centralized accounting, bookkeeping, control records, reporting, billing, invoicing or payment respecting purchases, sales or deliveries of alcoholic beverages, or methods and practices of centralized receipt or storage of alcoholic beverages within this state without segregation or earmarking for any such separately licensed premises, wherever such methods and practices assure the availability, at such licensee's central or main office in this state, of data reasonably needed for the enforcement of this chapter. Such records shall be available for inspection by any authorized representative of the liquor authority. ❸*(1998, chgd. by chap. 40, eff. 4/14/98.)*

❷13. No retail licensee for on-premises consumption shall be interested, directly or indirectly, in any premises where liquors, wines or beer are manufactured or sold at wholesale, by stock ownership, interlocking directors, mortgage or lien on any personal or real property or by any other means, except that liquors, wines or beer may be manufactured or sold wholesale by the person licensed as a manufacturer or wholesaler thereof on real property owned by an interstate railroad corporation or a United States certificated airline with a retail license for on-premises consumption, or on premises or with respect to a business constituting an overnight lodging and resort facility located wholly within the boundaries of the town of North Elba, county of Essex, township eleven, Richard's survey, great lot numbers two hundred seventy-eight, two hundred seventy-nine, two hundred eighty, two hundred ninety-eight, two hundred ninety-nine, three hundred, three hundred eighteen, three hundred nineteen, three hundred twenty, three hundred thirty-five and three hundred thirty-six, and township twelve, Thorn's survey, great lot numbers one hundred six and one hundred thirteen, as shown on the Adirondack map, compiled by the conservation department of the state of New York - nineteen hundred sixty-four edition, in the Essex county atlas at page twenty-seven in the Essex county clerk's office, Elizabethtown, New York, provided that such facility maintains not less than two hundred fifty rooms and suites for overnight lodging, or on premises or with respect to the operation of a restaurant in an office building located in a city having a population of five hundred thousand or more and in which is located the licensed premises of such manufacturer or wholesaler, provided that the building, the interior of the retail premise and the rental therefor fully comply with the criteria set forth in paragraph two of subdivision three of section one hundred one of this article, any such premises or business located on that tract or parcel of land, or any subdivision thereof, situate in the Village of Lake Placid, Town of North Elba, Essex County, New York; it being also a part of Lot No. 279, Township No. 11, Old Military Tract, Richard's Survey; it being also all of Lot No. 23 and part of Lot No. 22 as shown and designated on a certain map entitled "Map of Building Sites for Sale by B.R. Brewster" made by G.T. Chellis C.E. in 1892; also being PARCEL No. 1 on a certain map of lands of Robert J. Mahoney and wife made by G.C. Sylvester, P.E. & L.S. # 21300, dated August 4, 1964, and filed in the Essex County Clerk's Office on August 27, 1964, and more particularly bounded and described as follows; BEGINNING at the intersection of the northerly bounds of Shore Drive (formerly Mirror Street) with the westerly bounds of Park Place (formerly Rider Street) which point is also the northeast corner of Lot No. 23, from thence South 21°50′ East in the westerly bounds of Park Place a distance of 119 feet, more or less, to a lead plug in the edge of the sidewalk marking the southeast corner of Lot No. 23 and the northeast corner of Lot No. 24; from thence South 68°00′50″ West a distance of 50.05 feet to an iron pipe set in concrete at the corner of Lots 23 and 22; from thence South 65°10′50″ West a distance of 7.94 feet along the south line of Lot No. 22 to an iron pipe for a corner; from thence North 23°21′40″ West and at 17.84 feet along said line passing over a drill hole in a concrete sidewalk, and at 68.04 feet further along said line passing over an iron pipe at the southerly edge of another sidewalk, and at

1.22 feet further along said line passing over another drill hole in a sidewalk, a total distance of 119 feet, more or less, to the northerly line of Lot No. 22; from thence easterly in the northerly line of Lot 22 and 23 to the northeast corner of Lot No. 23 and the point of beginning. Also including the lands to the center of Shore Drive included between the northerly straight line continuation of the side lines of the above described parcel, and to the center of Park Place, where they abut the above described premises SUBJECT to the use thereof for street purposes. Being the same premises conveyed by Morestuff, Inc. to Madeline Sellers by deed dated June 30, 1992, recorded in the Essex County Clerk's Office on July 10, 1992 in Book 1017 of Deeds at Page 318, or any such premises or business located on that certain piece or parcel of land, or any subdivision thereof, situate, lying and being in the Town of Plattsburgh, County of Clinton, State of New York and being more particularly bounded and described as follows: Starting at an iron pipe found in the easterly bounds of the highway known as the Old Military Turnpike, said iron pipe being located 910.39 feet southeasterly, as measured along the easterly bounds of said highway, from the southerly bounds of the roadway known as Industrial Parkway West, THENCE running S 31° 54′ 33″ E along the easterly bounds of said Old Military Turnpike Extension, 239.88 feet to a point marking the beginning of a curve concave to the west; thence southerly along said curve, having a radius of 987.99 feet, 248.12 feet to an iron pipe found marking the point of beginning for the parcel herein being described, said point also marked the southerly corner of lands of Larry Garrow, et al, as described in Book 938 of Deeds at page 224; thence N 07° 45′ 4″ E along the easterly bounds of said Garrow, 748.16 feet to a 3″x4″ concrete monument marking the northeasterly corner of said Garrow, the northwesterly corner of the parcel herein being described and said monument also marking the southerly bounds of lands of Salerno Plastic Corp. as described in Book 926 of Deeds at Page 186; thence S 81° 45′ 28″ E along a portion of the southerly bounds of said Salerno Plastic Corp., 441.32 feet to an iron pin found marking the northeasterly corner of the parcel herein being described and also marking the northwest corner of the remaining lands now or formerly owned by said Marx and Delaura; thence S 07° 45′ 40″ W along the Westerly bounds of lands now of formerly of said Marx and DeLaura and along the easterly bounds of the parcel herein being described, 560.49 feet to an iron pin; thence N 83° 43′ 21″ W along a portion of the remaining lands of said Marx and DeLaura, 41.51 feet to an iron pin; thence S 08° 31′ 30″ W, along a portion of the remaining lands of said Marx and Delaura, 75.01 feet to an iron pin marking northeasterly corner of lands currently owned by the Joint Council for Economic Opportunity of Plattsburgh and Clinton County, Inc. as described in Book 963 of Deeds at Page 313; thence N 82° 20′ 32″ W along a portion of the northerly bounds of said J.C.E.O., 173.50 feet to an iron pin; thence 61° 21′ 12″ W, continuing along a portion of the northerly bounds

Printed in the U.S.A. ab

of said J.C.E.O., 134.14 feet to an iron pin; thence S 07° 45′ 42″ W along the westerly bounds of said J.C.E.O., 50 feet to an iron pin; thence S 66° 48′ 56″ W along a portion of the northerly bounds of remaining lands of said Marx and DeLaura, 100.00 feet to an iron pipe found on the easterly bounds of the aforesaid highway, said from pipe also being located on a curve concave to the west; thence running and running northerly along the easterly bounds of the aforesaid highway and being along said curve, with the curve having a radius of 987.93 feet, 60.00 feet to the point of beginning and containing 6.905 acres of land. Being the same premises as conveyed to Ronald Marx and Alice Marx by deed of CIT Small Business Lending Corp., as agent of the administrator, U.S. Small Business Administration, an agency of the United States Government dated September 10, 2001 and recorded in the office of the Clinton County Clerk on September 21, 2001 as Instrument #135020, or on premises or with respect to a business constituting the overnight lodging facility located wholly within the boundaries of that tract or parcel of land situated in the borough of Manhattan, city and county of New York, beginning at a point on the northerly side of west fifty-fourth street at a point one hundred feet easterly from the intersection of the said northerly side of west fifty-fourth street and the easterly side of seventh avenue; running thence northerly and parallel with the easterly side of seventh avenue one hundred feet five inches to the center line of the block; running thence easterly and parallel with the northerly side of west fifty-fourth street and along the center line of the block fifty feet to a point; running thence northerly and parallel with the easterly side of seventh avenue one hundred feet five inches to the southerly side of west fifty-fifth street at a point distant one hundred fifty feet easterly from the intersection of the said southerly side of west fifty-fifth street and the easterly side of seventh avenue; running thence easterly along the southerly side of west fifty-fifth street thirty-one feet three inches to a point; running thence southerly and parallel with the easterly side of the seventh avenue one hundred feet five inches to the center line of the block; running thence easterly along the center line of the block and parallel with the southerly side of west fifty-fifth street, one hundred feet; running thence northerly and parallel with the easterly side of seventh avenue one hundred feet five inches to the southerly side of west fifty-fifth street; running thence easterly along the southerly side of west fifty-fifth street twenty-one feet ten and one-half inches to a point; running thence southerly and parallel with the easterly side of seventh avenue one hundred feet five inches to the center line of the block; running thence westerly along the center line of the block and parallel with the northerly side of west fifty-fourth street three feet one and one-half inches; running thence southerly and parallel with the easterly side of seventh avenue one hundred feet five inches to the northerly side of west fifty-fourth street at a point distant three hundred feet easterly from the intersection of the said northerly side of west fifty-fourth street and the easterly side of seventh avenue; running thence westerly and along the northerly side of west fifty-fourth street two hundred feet to the point or place of beginning, provided that such facility maintains not less than four hundred guest rooms and suites for overnight lodging. Any lien, mortgage or other interest or estate now held by said retail licensee on or in the personal or real property of such manufacturer or wholesaler, which mortgage, lien, interest or estate was acquired on or before December thirty-first, nineteen hundred thirty-two, shall not be included within the provisions of this subdivision; provided, however, the burden of establishing the time of the accrual of the interest, comprehended by this subdivision shall be upon the person who claims to be entitled to the protection and exemption afforded hereby. ❷*(1995, chgd. by chap. 185; 1996, chgd. by chap. 675; 2002, chgd. by chap. 105, eff. 6/28/2002.)*

14. No retail licensee for on-premises consumption shall make or cause to be made any loan to any person engaged in the manufacture or sale of liquors, wines or beer at wholesale.

❺15. All retail licensed premises shall be subject to inspection by any peace officer, acting pursuant to his or her special duties, or police officer and by the duly authorized representatives of the liquor authority, during the hours when the said premises are open for the transaction of business. ❺*(1995, chgd. by chap. 83, eff. 6/20/95.)*

❽16. ❽*(1998, repealed by chap. 40, eff. 4/14/98.)*

17. Notwithstanding any other provision of law, a retail licensee for on-premises consumption that is a person or corporation operating a hotel shall be permitted to sell liquors, beer, and/or wines through a mechanical device or vending machine placed in the lodger's rooms and to which access to such device or machine is restricted by means of a locking device which requires the use of a key, magnetic card or similar device provided, however, that no such key, card or similar device shall be provided to any person under the age of twenty-one or to any person who is visibly intoxicated.

**§106-a. Notice of arrest and convictions.**

❼1. When an arrest for gambling activity, illicit drug activity, prostitution activity, or for a breach of the peace or for a crime of a violent nature, or for a crime of weapons possession occurs or where the activity or crime has taken place in a licensed premises, the arresting agency shall notify in writing, the authority and the district attorney of the county in which the licensed premises are located within two weeks of the arrest and set forth therein the name of the arrestee, the date of the arrest, the time of the arrest, the exact place of the arrest, the name of the licensee, the name and address of the licensed premises, the offense or offenses allegedly committed by the arrestee, the factual circumstances of the arrest, the name or names of the arresting officer, and such other information as may reasonably be required by the authority. ❼*(1997, chgd. by chap. 420, eff. 11/18/97.)*

❶2. Such district attorney shall maintain a written record of all notices forwarded as required by subdivision one of this section and where the arrestee named in said notice is convicted of either the offense charged or a lesser included offense as defined by the penal law, the district attorney shall so notify the authority in writing. In addition, where a person is convicted of a violation of paragraph (b) of subdivision one of section sixty-five-b of this chapter or of a violation of subdivision one of section sixty-five of this chapter, the district attorney shall promptly notify the authority of such conviction in writing and shall include in such notification the information required to be provided pursuant to subdivision one of this section. ❶*(1998, chgd. by chaps. 383, 652; 2001, chgd. by chap. 549, eff. 12/12/2001.)*

**§106-b.** *(Expired 7/1/93.)*



**§107. Advertising and forms of notices of the issuance of licenses.**

Every person procuring a license hereunder must publish a notice thereof as herein provided:

1. Where the licensed premises are located in any county other than New York, Kings, Queens or Bronx, notice shall be published once a week for two successive weeks in a daily or weekly newspaper published in the city, town or village in which the licensed premises are located, except that if there shall be no daily or weekly newspaper published in the city, town or village in which the licensed premises are located, then such notice shall be published in a daily or weekly newspaper published in the county in which the licensed premises are located, once a week for two successive weeks. The provisions of this section shall only be applicable to the original license issued to the licensee for the premises.

2. Where the licensed premises are located in the counties of New York, Kings, Queens or Bronx, such notice shall be published once a week for two successive weeks in one daily and one weekly newspaper published in the county in which the licensed premises are located. This provision is only applicable to the original license issued to the licensee for the premises.

3. The notice to be so published shall be printed in English, in substantially the following forms:

(a) Form of notice for manufacturer's license. Notice is hereby given that manufacturer's license (fill in beer, liquor or wine manufacturer or rectifier and number) has been issued to the undersigned to manufacture (beer, liquor or wine, as the case may be) under the alcoholic beverage control law in the premises located at (fill in street address, city, town or village and county in which licensed premises are located).

(Name of licensee)
(Address of licensee)

(b) Form of notice for wholesaler's license. Notice is hereby given that wholesaler's license (fill in beer, liquor or wine wholesaler and license number) has been issued to the undersigned to sell (beer, liquor or wine, as the case may be) at wholesale under the alcoholic beverage control law in the premises located at (fill in street address, city, town or village and county in which licensed premises are located).

(Name of licensee)
(Address of licensee)

(c) Form of notice for off-premises license. Notice is hereby given that license (fill in beer, liquor or wine store and license number) has been issued to the undersigned to sell (beer, liquor or wine, as the case may be) at retail under the alcoholic beverage control law at (fill in street address, city, town or village and county in which licensed premises are located) for off-premises consumption.

(Name of licensee)
(Address of licensee)

(d) Form of notice for on-premises license. Notice is hereby given that license (fill in beer, liquor or wine as the case may be, and license number) has been issued to the undersigned to sell (beer, liquor or wine, as the case may be) at retail in a (hotel, club, restaurant, vessel, car, or other type of establishment, as the case may be) under the alcoholic beverage control law at (fill in street address, city, town or village and county in which licensed premises are located) for on-premises consumption.

(Name of licensee)
(Address of licensee)

4. The first publication of said notice shall be made within fifteen days after the date of issuance of said license and proof of such publication, in the form hereinafter set forth, shall be obtained by the licensee and retained by him during the license year. The form of proof of such publication shall be as follows:

STATE OF NEW YORK ) ss:
County of ............... )

.................... of ................., being duly sworn, says that he is .......................... of the publishers of the ............................, a (daily) or (weekly) newspaper (printed and) published in the (city, town, or village and county) ............... and that the notice of which the annexed is a true copy, has been published in said newspaper for two successive weeks commencing on the ........ day of ............ 195..... .

.................................

Sworn to before me this
.........................,
195.....

**§107-a. Labeling containers of alcoholic beverages.**

1. The liquor authority is hereby authorized to promulgate rules and regulations governing the labeling and offering of alcoholic beverages bottled, packaged, sold or possessed for sale within this state.

2. Such regulations shall be calculated to prohibit deception of the consumer; to afford him adequate information as to quality and identity; and to achieve national uniformity in this field in so far as possible.

3. The bottling, packaging, sale or possession by any licensee of any alcoholic beverage not labelled or offered in conformity with this section shall be ground for suspension, revocation or cancellation of the license.

4. (a) No liquor, wine or beer shall be labelled, offered or advertised for sale unless in accordance with this section and unless the brand or trade name label affixed to or imprinted upon the container of such alcoholic beverage shall have been registered with and approved by the authority and the appropriate fee paid as provided for in this section.

(b) An application for registration of a brand or trade name label shall be filed by (1) the owner of the brand or trade name if such owner is licensed by the authority, or (2) a wholesaler selling such brand who is appointed as exclusive agent, in writing, by the owner of the brand or trade name for the purpose of filing such application, if the owner of the brand or trade name is not licensed by the authority, or (3) any wholesaler, with the approval of the authority, in the event that the owner of the brand or trade name does not file or is unable to file such application or designate an agent for such purposes, or (4) any wholesaler, with the approval of the authority, in the event that the owner of the brand or trade name is a retailer who does not file such application, provided that the retailer shall consent to such filing by such wholesaler. Such retailer may revoke his consent at any time, upon written notice to the authority and to such wholesaler.



Unless otherwise permitted or required by the authority, the application for registration of a liquor or wine brand or trade name label filed pursuant to this section shall be filed by the same licensee filing schedules pursuant to section one hundred one-b of this chapter.

Cordials and wines which differ only as to fluid content, age, or vintage year, as defined by such regulations, shall be considered the same brand; and those that differ as to type or class may be considered the same brand by the authority where consistent with the purposes of this section.

(c)(1) The application for registration of a brand or trade name label shall be filed by registered mail, return receipt requested, on a form prescribed by the authority, and shall contain such information as the authority shall require. Such application shall be accompanied by the appropriate fee prescribed by paragraph (d) of this subdivision.

(2) Provided, however, where a brand or trade name label has been approved by the federal bureau of alcohol, tobacco and firearms, it shall be deemed registered and approved by the authority if:

(i) the applicant submits on a form prescribed by the authority, by registered mail, return receipt requested, a true copy of the brand or trade name label approval issued by the federal bureau of alcohol, tobacco and firearms along with the appropriate fee as established in paragraph (d) of this subdivision; and

(ii) the authority does not deny such application within thirty days after receipt.

(3) Provided, however, that where a brand or trade name label for wine has been approved by the federal bureau of alcohol, tobacco and firearms, it shall be deemed registered and approved by the authority and no application, application fee, or annual registration fee shall be submitted to the authority.

➊(d) The annual fee for registration of any brand or trade name label for liquor shall be two hundred fifty dollars; the annual fee for registration of any brand or trade name label for beer shall be one hundred fifty dollars; the annual fee for registration of any brand or trade name label for wine shall be fifty dollars. Such fee shall be in the form of a check or draft. No annual fee for registration of any brand or trade name label for wine shall be required if it has been approved by the federal bureau of alcohol, tobacco and firearms pursuant to this section.

Each brand or trade name label registration approved pursuant to this section shall be valid for a term which shall run concurrently with the term of the license of the person registering such brand or trade name label.

Each brand or trade name label registration approved pursuant to this section shall be valid only for the licensee to whom issued and shall not be transferable.

➊*(1994, chgd. by chap. 361, eff. 7/20/94.)*

(e) If the authority shall deny the application for registration of a brand or trade name label pursuant to this section, it shall return the registration fee to the applicant, less twenty-five per centum of such fee and shall notify the applicant, in writing with the specific reasons for its denial.

(f) When not inconsistent with the purposes of this subdivision and whenever necessary to avoid practical difficulties or unnecessary hardship to any licensee affected by this section, the authority may, until October first, nineteen hundred sixty-three, exempt any brand from the fee provisions of this subdivision upon satisfactory showing by the licensee that such brand is being discontinued. The authority may at any time exempt any discontinued brand from such fee provisions where a manufacturer or wholesaler has an inventory of one hundred cases or less of liquor or wine and five hundred cases or less of beer, and certifies to the authority in writing that such brand is being discontinued. The authority may also at any time exempt any discontinued brand from such fee provisions where a retailer discontinuing a brand owned by him has a balance of an order yet to be delivered of fifty cases or less of liquor or wine, or two hundred fifty cases or less of beer.

❖(g) The authority shall exempt from such fee provisions the registration of each brand label used for beer that is produced in small size batches on the licensed premises in batches totalling fifteen hundred barrels of beer or less annually and that is dispensed or served exclusively through a vat to tap system for consumption on such premises

or sold or offered for sale to retail customers or used for the purpose of sampling. ❖*(2000, added by chap. 561, eff. 11/21/2000.)*
*(1993, chgd. by chap. 490, eff. 1/1/94.)*

**§108. Restrictions upon licensees.**

No licensee except the holder of a brewer's or distiller's license or a winery license shall keep or permit to be kept or consumed on the licensed premises any alcoholic beverage except the alcoholic beverages which he is permitted to sell under the terms of the license issued to him.

**§109. Renewals of licenses and permits.**

❺1. Each license and permit, except a temporary permit effective for one day only, issued pursuant to this chapter may be renewed upon application therefor by the licensee or permittee and the payment of the annual fee for such license or permit as prescribed by this chapter. In the case of applications for renewals, the liquor authority may dispense with the requirements of such statements as it deems unnecessary in view of those contained in the application made for the original license or permit, but in any event the submission of photographs of the licensed premises shall be dispensed with provided the applicant for such renewal shall file a statement with such authority to the effect that there has been no alteration of such premises since the original license was issued. An applicant for a retail license for on-premises consumption shall also submit to the authority a copy of the valid certificate of occupancy or such other document issued by the local code enforcement agency for the premises for which the original license was issued. The liquor authority may make such rules as may be necessary not inconsistent with this chapter regarding applications for renewals of licenses and permits and the time for making the same. ❺*(1995, chgd. by chap. 396, eff. 8/2/95.)*

❺1-a. The authority shall provide an application for renewal of a license issued under section sixty-four or sixty-four-a of this chapter not less than sixty days prior to the expiration of the current license. ❺*(1995, added by chap. 83, eff. 6/20/95.)*

❻2. In the case of any application for renewal of a license under sections fifty-five, fifty-five-a, sixty-four, sixty-four-a, sixty-four-b, eighty-one, and eighty-one-a of this chapter, the liquor authority shall require the applicant to notify the clerk of the village, town or city wherein the licensed premises is located, in the same manner and under the same requirements as set forth in subdivision two-a of section sixty-four of this chapter. ❻*(1996, chgd. by chap. 512, eff. 10/7/96.)*

**❖§110. Information to be requested in applications for licenses or permits.**

1. The following shall be the information required on an application for a license or permit:

(a) A statement of identity as follows:

(i) If the applicant is an individual, his name, date and place of birth, citizenship, permanent home address, telephone number and social security number, as well as any other names by which he has conducted a business at any time.

(ii) If the applicant is a corporation, the corporate name of the applicant, its place of incorporation, its main business address (and if such main business address is not within the state, the address of its main place of business within the state), other names by which it has been known or has conducted business at any time, its telephone number, its federal employer identification number, and the names, ages, citizenship, and permanent home addresses of its directors, officers and its shareholders (except that if there be more than ten shareholders then those shareholders holding ten percent or more of any class of its shares).

(iii) If the applicant is a partnership, its name, its main business address (and if such main business address is not within the state, the address of its main place of business within the state), other names by which it has been known or has conducted business at any time, its telephone number, its federal employer identification number, and the names, ages, citizenship, and permanent home addresses of each of its partners.

(b) A statement identifying the street and number of the premises to be licensed, if the premises have a street and number, and otherwise such description as will reasonably indicate the locality thereof; photographs, drawings or other items related to the appearance of the interior or exterior of such premises, and a floor plan of the interior, shall be required. The applicant shall also state the nature of his interest in the premises; and the name of any other person interested as a partner, joint venturer, investor or lender with the applicant either in the premises or in the business to be licensed.

(c) A description of any other alcohol beverage license or permit under this chapter or any other alcoholic beverage control law which, within the past ten years, the applicant (including any officers, directors, shareholders or partners listed in the statement of identity under paragraph (a) of this subdivision or the spouse of any such person) or the applicant's spouse held or applied for.

(d) A statement that such applicant or the applicant's spouse has not been convicted of a crime addressed by the provisions of section one hundred twenty-six of this article which would forbid the applicant (including any officers, directors, shareholders or partners listed in the statement of identity under paragraph (a) of this subdivision or the spouse of such person) or the applicant's spouse to traffic in alcoholic beverages, a statement whether or not the applicant (including any officers, directors, shareholders or partners listed in the statement of identity under paragraph (a) of this subdivision or the spouse of any such person) or the applicant's spouse is an official described in section one hundred twenty-eight of this article, and a description of any crime that the applicant (including any officers, directors, shareholders or partners listed under paragraph (a) of this subdivision or the spouse of any such person) or the applicant's spouse has been convicted of and whether such person has received a pardon, certificate of good conduct or certificate of relief from disabilities; provided, however, that no person shall be denied any license solely on the grounds that such person is the spouse of a person otherwise disqualified from holding a license under this chapter.

(e) A statement that the location and layout of the premises to be licensed does not violate any requirement of this chapter relating to location and layout of licensed premises, with a copy of the certificate of occupancy for the premises.

(f) A statement that the applicant has control of the premises to be licensed by ownership of a fee interest or a leasehold with a term at least as long as the license for which the application is being made, or by a binding contract to acquire the same and a statement of identity under paragraph (a) of this subdivision for the lessor of any leasehold with a copy of the lease, contract or deed evidencing fee ownership of the premises.



(g) A financial statement adequate to show all persons who, directly or indirectly have an economic interest in the establishment or acquisition of the business for which the license or permit application is being made, to identify the sources of funds to be applied in such establishment or acquisition, and to describe the terms and conditions governing such establishment with copies of such financial documents as the authority may reasonably require.

(h) The fingerprints of the applicants.

2. All license or permit applications shall be signed by the applicant (if an individual), by an officer (if a corporation), or by all partners (if a partnership). Each person signing such application shall verify it or affirm it as true under the penalties of perjury.

◉3. All license or permit applications shall be accompanied by a check, draft or other forms of payment as the authority may require or authorize in the amount required by this chapter for such license or permit. ◉*(1999, chgd. by chap. 411, eff. 4/1/2000.)*

4. If there be any change, after the filing of the application or the granting of a license, in any of the facts required to be set forth in such application, a supplemental statement giving notice of such change, cost and source of money involved in the change, duly verified, shall be filed with the authority within ten days after such change. Failure to do so shall, if willful and deliberate, be cause for revocation of the license.

5. In giving any notice, or taking any action in reference to a licensee of a licensed premises, the authority may rely upon the information furnished in such application and in any supplemental statement connected therewith, and such information may be presumed to be correct, and shall be binding upon a licensee or licensed premises as if correct. All information required to be furnished in such application or supplemental statements shall be deemed material in

any prosecution for perjury, any proceeding to revoke, cancel or suspend any license, and in the authority's determination to approve or deny the license.

6. The authority may in its discretion waive the submission of any category of information described in this section for any category of license or permit, provided that it shall not be permitted to waive the requirement for submission of any such category of information solely for an individual applicant or applicants.

7. The authority may, by rule, adopt additional categories of information which may be reasonably necessary to carry out the provisions of this section.

*❖(1999, repealed and added by chap. 403; 2000, chgd. by chap. 114, eff. 11/8/2000.)*



**⊕§110-a. Notice of application for certain licenses to be published by applicant.**

1. Every person applying for a license to sell alcoholic beverages pursuant to subdivision four of section fifty-one, or section fifty-five, sixty-four, sixty-four-a, sixty-four-c, eighty-one or eighty-one-a of this chapter shall publish notice thereof pursuant to subdivision two of this section.

2. All applicants required to publish notice of an application for a license pursuant to subdivision one of this section shall, in such form as prescribed by subdivision three of this section, publish such notice as follows:

(a) Where the prospective licensed premises are located in any county other than New York, Kings, Queens or Bronx, notice shall be published once a week for two successive weeks in a daily or weekly newspaper, to be designated by the county clerk, published in the city, town or village in which the prospective licensed premises are located, except that if there shall be no daily or weekly newspaper published in the city, town or village in which the prospective licensed premises are located, then such notice shall be published in a daily or weekly newspaper, to be designated by the county clerk, published in the county in which the prospective licensed premises are located, once a week for two successive weeks.

(b) Where the prospective licensed premises are located in the counties of New York, Kings, Queens or Bronx, such notice shall be published once a week for two successive weeks in one daily and one weekly newspaper, to be designated by the county clerk, published in the county in which the prospective licensed premises are located.

3. Such notice shall be printed in English, in substantially the following form:

Form of notice for on-premises license. Notice is hereby given that license (fill in beer, liquor or wine as the case may be, and license number) has been applied for by the undersigned to sell (beer, liquor or wine, as the case may be) at retail in a (hotel, club, restaurant, vessel, car, or other type of establishment, as the case may be) under the alcoholic beverage control law at (fill in street address, city, town or village and county in which licensed premises are located) for on-premises consumption.

(Name of licensee)
(Address of licensee)

4. The provisions of this section shall apply only to the application for the original license issued to the licensee for the premises.

5. Except for good cause shown, the first publication of such notice shall be made within ten days after the date of the submission of the application for such license to the authority. Two original copies of proof of such publication, in the form set forth in this subdivision shall be obtained by the applicant for such license, who shall within fifteen days of receipt of such original copies of such proof, submit one original copy to the authority, and the second original copy of such proof shall be retained by the applicant for such license. Except for good cause shown, the authority shall not issue the license sought by the applicant unless such proof is submitted within such fifteen-day period. The form of proof of such publication shall be as follows:



STATE OF NEW YORK)
________________) SS:
County of .......)

............ of .................... being duly sworn, says that he is .......... of the publishers of the ..................... (daily) or (weekly) newspaper (printed and) published in the (city, town, or village and county) ....................., and that the notice of which the annexed is a true copy, has been published in said newspaper for two successive weeks commencing on the ............ day of .................... 199....

............................

Sworn to before me this ............ day of ..................
⑨*(1999, added by chap. 77, eff. 8/21/99.)*

**⑧§111. License to be confined to premises licensed.**

A license issued to any person, pursuant to chapter one hundred eighty of the laws of nineteen hundred thirty-three or this chapter, for any licensed premises shall not be transferable to any other person or to any other premises or to any other part of the building containing the licensed premises except in the discretion of the authority. It shall be available only to the person therein specified, and only for the premises licensed and no other except if authorized by the authority. Provided, however, that the provisions of this section shall not be deemed to prohibit the issuance of a license under section seventy-six-b or seventy-six-c of this chapter. For the purposes of this section each railroad car and each vessel shall be deemed premises separately to be licensed. ⑧*(1993, chgd. by chap. 489, eff. 10/24/93.)*

### §112. Bonds of licensees and permittees.

The liquor authority may require the licensees and permittees of one or more of the kinds or classes described in this chapter to file with it a bond to the people of the state of New York issued by a surety company, approved by the superintendent of insurance as to solvency and responsibility and authorized to transact business in this state, in such penal sum as the liquor authority may heretofore have prescribed or hereafter shall prescribe, conditioned that such licensee or permittee will not suffer or permit any violation of the provisions of this chapter and that all fines and penalties which shall accrue, during the time the license or permit shall be in effect, will be paid, together with all costs taxed or allowed in any action or proceeding brought or instituted for a violation of any of the provisions of this chapter. A suit to recover on any bond filed pursuant to chapter one hundred eighty of the laws of nineteen hundred thirty-three or this chapter may be brought by the liquor authority or on relation of any party aggrieved, in a court of competent jurisdiction and in the event that the obligor named in such bond has violated any of the conditions of such bond, recovery for the penal sum of such bond may be had in favor of the people of the state.



### ⓢ§113. Premises for which no license shall be granted.

1. Where a license for any premises licensed has been revoked, the liquor authority in its discretion may refuse to issue a license under this chapter, for a period of two years after such revocation, for such licensed premises or for any part of the building containing such licensed premises and connected therewith.

2. In determining whether to issue such a license for such two year period, in addition to any other factors deemed relevant, the liquor authority shall, in the case of a license revoked due to the illegal sale of alcohol to a minor, determine whether the proposed subsequent licensee has obtained such premises through an arm's length transaction, and, if such transaction is not found to be an arm's length transaction, the liquor authority shall deny the issuance of such license.

3. For purposes of this section, "arm's length transaction" shall mean a sale of a fee or all undivided interests in real property, or lease of any part thereof, in the open market, between an informed and willing buyer and seller where neither is under any compulsion to participate in the transaction, unaffected by any unusual conditions indicating a reasonable possibility that the sale was made for the purpose of permitting the original licensee to avoid the effect of the revocation. The following sales shall be presumed not to be arm's length transactions unless adequate documentation is provided demonstrating that the sale or lease was not conducted, in whole or in part, for the purpose of permitting the original licensee to avoid the effect of the revocation:

(a) a sale between relatives;

(b) a sale between related companies or partners in a business; or

(c) a sale or lease affected by other facts or circumstances that would indicate that the sale or lease is not entered into for the primary purpose of permitting the original licensee to avoid the effect of the revocation.

*(1996, chgd. by chap. 572, eff. 12/6/96.)*

**§114. Licenses, publication, general provisions.**

1. All licenses issued pursuant to this chapter shall be distinctive in color and design so as to be readily distinguishable from each other.

2. No license shall be transferable or assignable except that notwithstanding any other provision of law, the license of a sole proprietor converting to corporate form, where such proprietor becomes the sole stockholder and only officer and director of such new corporation, may be transferred to the subject corporation if all requirements of this chapter remain the same with respect to such license as transferred and, further, the licensee shall transmit to the authority, within ten days of the transfer of license allowable under this subdivision, on a form prescribed by the authority, notification of the transfer of such license.

3. No license shall be pledged or deposited as collateral security for any loan or upon any other condition; and any such pledge or deposit, and any contract providing therefor, shall be void.

4. Licenses issued under this chapter shall contain, in addition to any further information or material to be prescribed by the rules of the liquor authority, the following information: (a) Name of person to whom license is issued; (b) kind of license and what kind of traffic in alcoholic beverages is thereby permitted; (c) description by street and number, or otherwise, of licensed premises; (d) a statement in substance that such license shall not be deemed a property or vested right, and that it may be revoked at any time pursuant to law.

5. There shall be printed and furnished by the liquor authority to each licensee a statement of the causes for which licenses may be revoked. Such statement shall be prepared by the liquor authority and delivered to the licensee with his license or as soon thereafter as may be practicable. Any amendments thereto shall also be sent by the liquor authority to all licensees as soon as may be practicable after such amendments. Failure to send such statements or changes therein, or failure to receive the same, or any misstatement or error contained in such statements or amendments shall, however, not be an excuse or justification for any violation of law, or prevent, or remit, or decrease any penalty or forfeiture therefor.

6. Before commencing or doing any business for the time for which a license has been issued said license shall be enclosed in a suitable wood or metal frame having a clear glass space and a substantial wood or metal back so that the whole of said license may be seen therein, and shall be posted up and at all times displayed in a conspicuous place in the room where such business is carried on, so that all persons visiting such place may readily see the same. It shall be unlawful for any person

holding a license to post such license or to permit such license to be posted upon premises other than the premises licensed, or upon premises where traffic in alcoholic beverages is being carried on by any person other than the licensee, or knowingly to deface, destroy or alter any such license in any respect. Whenever a license shall be lost or destroyed without fault on the part of the licensee or his agents or employees, a duplicate license in lieu thereof may be issued by the liquor authority in its discretion and in accordance with such rules and regulations and the payment of such fees, not exceeding five dollars, as it may prescribe.

**➊§114-a. License or permit issuance and registration approval.**

No license or permit shall be issued and no registration approved pursuant to this chapter until such time as any check or draft submitted for payment of the required fee has been honored by the payor financial institution, provided, however, that this provision shall not apply in the case of a certified check, bank officers' check or money order. ➊*(1994, added by chap. 361, eff. 7/20/94.)*

**§115. Rules need not be uniform.**

Whenever in this chapter the liquor authority is authorized to adopt rules in respect to a particular subject or matter, such rules need not be uniform in their application to the various localities within the jurisdiction of such authority, but may vary in accordance with a reasonable classification of such localities.

**§116. Deliveries of alcoholic beverages.**

No alcoholic beverage shall be transported within this state by any vehicle unless such vehicle is owned and operated, or hired and operated by a licensee and unless there shall be attached to or inscribed upon both sides of such vehicle so as to be visible from a reasonable distance, a sign setting forth the name and address of such licensee in such form and with such additional information as the liquor authority may prescribe; provided, however, (a) that alcoholic beverages may be transported by a retail licensee to the home of a purchaser not to be resold by the purchaser; (b) that alcoholic beverages owned by a person may be transported from place to place not for purposes of sale; (c) that alcoholic beverages may be delivered from a licensee to a steamship or railroad station or terminal for purposes of transportation, and may be delivered from a steamship or railroad station or terminal to a purchaser for purposes of consumption, or to a licensee by any bona fide trucking agency holding a permit under this chapter. In lieu of such sign, a licensee may have in the cab of such vehicle a photostatic copy of its current license issued by the authority, and such copy duly authenticated by the authority.

**§117. Transportation of alcoholic beverages.**

No common carrier or person operating a transportation facility in this state, other than the United States government, shall receive for transportation or delivery within the state any alcoholic beverages

Printed in the U.S.A. ab

unless the shipment is accompanied by copy of a bill of lading, or other document, showing the name and address of the consignor, the name and address of the consignee, the date of the shipment, and the quantity and kind of alcoholic beverage contained therein.

**❾§117-a. Unlimited drink offerings prohibited.**

❷1. No licensee, acting individually or in conjunction with one or more licensees, shall:

(a) offer, sell, serve, or deliver to any person or persons an unlimited number of drinks during any set period of time for a fixed price.

(b) allow a person, agent, party organizer, or promoter, as such terms shall be defined by the authority in rule and regulation, to offer, sell, serve, or deliver to any person or persons an unlimited number of drinks during any set period of time for a fixed price.

(c) advertise, promote, or charge a price for drinks that in the judgment of the authority creates an offering of alcoholic beverages in violation of the purposes and intent of this section, or which in the judgment of the authority is an attempt to circumvent the intent and purposes of this section, such as, but not limited to, offerings of free drinks, or multiple drinks for free or for the price of a single drink, or for a low initial price followed by a price increment per hour or other period of time, or for such a minor amount that in the judgment of the authority the pricing would constitute an attempt to circumvent the intent and purposes of this section.
❷*(2002, chgd. by chap. 289, eff. 12/4/2002.)*

2. As used in this section, licensee means and includes the licensee, and any employees, or agents of such licensee.

❖3. With respect to an individual licensee, this section shall not apply to private functions not opened to the public, such as weddings, banquets, or receptions, or other similar functions, or to a package of food and beverages where the service of alcoholic beverages is incidental to the event or function. ❖*(2000, chgd. by chap. 114, eff. 11/8/2000.)*

4. The authority shall investigate any documented allegation of a violation of this section upon a complaint by any person.

5. The authority shall promulgate rules and regulations necessary to implement the provisions of this section.
❾*(1999, added by chap. 403, eff. 11/24/99.)*

**❻§118. Revocation of licenses for cause.**

1. Any license or permit issued pursuant to this chapter may be revoked, cancelled, suspended and/or subjected to the imposition of a civil penalty for cause, and must be revoked for the following causes:

(a) Conviction of the licensee, permittee or his agent or employee for selling any illegal alcoholic beverages on the premises licensed.

(b) For transferring, assigning or hypothecating a license or permit.

2. Notwithstanding the issuance of a license or permit by way of renewal, the liquor authority may revoke, cancel or suspend such license or permit and/or may impose a civil penalty against any holder of such

license or permit, as prescribed by this section and section one hundred nineteen of this chapter, for causes or violations occurring during the license period immediately preceding the issuance of such license or permit, and may recover, as provided in section one hundred twelve of this chapter, the penal sum of the bond on file during said period.

3. As used in this section, the term "for cause" shall also include the existence of a sustained and continuing pattern of noise, disturbance, misconduct, or disorder on or about the licensed premises, related to the operation of the premises or the conduct of its patrons, which adversely affects the health, welfare or safety of the inhabitants of the area in which such licensed premises are located.
❻*(1996, chgd. by chap. 536, eff. 8/8/96.)*

## §119. Procedure for revocation or cancellation.

1. Any license or permit issued by the liquor authority pursuant to chapter one hundred eighty of the laws of nineteen hundred thirty-three or this chapter may be revoked, cancelled or suspended and/or be subjected to the imposition of a monetary penalty in the manner prescribed by this section.

❺2. The liquor authority may on its own initiative or on complaint of any person institute proceedings to revoke, cancel or suspend any retail license and may impose a civil penalty against the licensee after a hearing at which the licensee shall be given an opportunity to be heard. Such hearing shall be held in such manner and upon such notice as may be prescribed by the rules of the liquor authority. ❺*(1995, chgd. by chap. 83, eff. 6/20/95.)*

3. All other licenses or permits issued under this chapter may be revoked, cancelled, suspended and/or made subject to the imposition of a civil penalty by the liquor authority after a hearing to be held in the manner to be determined by the rules of the liquor authority.

❺4. ❼(a) The provisions of this subdivision shall apply in all cases of licensee or permittee failure after receiving appropriate notice, to comply with a summons, subpoena or warrant relating to a paternity or child support proceeding and arrears in payment of child support or combined child and spousal support referred to the authority by a court pursuant to the requirements of section two hundred forty-four-c of the domestic relations law or pursuant to section four hundred fifty-eight-b or five hundred forty-eight-b of the family court act.

❼(b) Upon receipt of an order from the court based on arrears in payment of child support or combined child and spousal support pursuant to one of the foregoing provisions of law, the authority, if it finds such person to have been issued a license or permit, shall within thirty days of receipt of such order from the court, provide notice to the licensee or permittee of, and initiate, a hearing which shall be held at least twenty days and no more than thirty days after the sending of such notice to the licensee or permittee. The hearing shall be solely held for the purpose of determining whether there exists as of the date of the hearing proof that full payment of all arrears of support established by the order of the court to be due from the licensee or permittee have been paid. Proof of such payment shall be a certified check showing full payment of established arrears or a notice issued by the court or the support collection unit, where the order is payable to the support collection unit designated by the appropriate social services district. Such notice shall state that full payment of all arrears of support established by the order of the court to be due have been paid. The licensee or permittee shall be given full opportunity to present such proof of payment at the hearing in person or by counsel. The only issue to be determined by the authority as a result of the hearing is whether the arrears have been paid. No evidence with respect to the appropriateness of the court order or ability of the respondent party in arrears to comply with such order shall be received or considered by the authority.

❼*(1997, chgd. by chap. 398, eff. 1/1/98.)*

(c) Notwithstanding any inconsistent provision of this article or of any other provision of law to the contrary, such license or permit shall be suspended if at the hearing, provided for by paragraph (b) of this subdivision, the licensee or permittee fails to present proof of payment as required by such subdivision. Such suspension shall not be lifted unless the court or the support collection unit, where the court order is payable to the support collection unit designated by the appropriate social services district, issues notice to the authority that full payment of all arrears of support established by the order of the court to be due have been paid.

❼(d) Upon receipt of an order from the court based on failure to comply with a summons, subpoena, or warrant relating to a paternity or child support proceeding, the authority, if it finds such person has been issued a license or permit, shall within thirty days of receipt of such order from the court, provide notice to the licensee or permittee that his or her license shall be suspended in sixty days unless the conditions in paragraph (e) of this subdivision are met.

❼(e) Notwithstanding any inconsistent provision of this article or of any other provision of law to the contrary, such license or permit shall be suspended in accordance with the provisions of paragraph (c) of this subdivision unless the court terminates its order to commence suspension proceedings. Such suspension shall not be lifted unless the court issues an order to the authority terminating its order to commence suspension proceedings.

❼*(1997, added by chap. 398, eff. 1/1/98.)*

❼(f) The authority shall inform the court of all actions taken hereunder as required by law.

❼(g) This subdivision applies to support obligations paid pursuant to any order of child support or child and spousal support issued under provisions of article three-A or section two hundred thirty-six or two hundred forty of the domestic relations law, or article four, five or five-A of the family court act.

❼(h) Notwithstanding any inconsistent provision of this article or of any other provision of law to the contrary, the provisions of this subdivision shall apply to the exclusion of any other requirements of this article and to the exclusion of any other requirement of law to the contrary.

❼*(1997, relettered by chap. 398, eff. 1/1/98.)*
❺*(1995, added by chap. 81, eff. 7/1/95.)*

❶5. Where a licensee is convicted of two or more qualifying offenses within a five year period, the authority, upon receipt of notification of such second or subsequent conviction pursuant to the provisions of subdivision two of section one hundred six-a of this article, shall, in addition to any other sanction or civil or criminal penalty imposed pursuant to this chapter, impose on such licensee a civil penalty not to exceed five hundred dollars. For purposes of this subdivision, a qualifying offense shall mean (a) the offense defined in subdivision one of section sixty-five of this chapter; or (b) the offense defined in paragraph (b) of subdivision one of section sixty-five-b of this chapter. For purposes of this subdivision, a conviction of a licensee or an employee or agent of such licensee shall constitute a conviction of such licensee. ❶*(1998, added by chap. 383; chgd. by chap. 652; 2001, chgd. by chap. 549, eff. 12/12/2001.)*

### ❹§120. Decisions by liquor authority.

❖A decision upon any [application or] hearing [submitted to or held] *conducted* by the liquor authority shall be rendered within thirty days after such [submission or] hearing, *and a decision on any application submitted to the authority shall be rendered within sixty days, provided however that:*

❖*1. On or before such sixtieth business day after the receipt of an application for a permit or license, the authority shall mail written notice to the applicant specifying:*

*(a) That the permit or license is granted conditioned on satisfactory completion of appropriate checks on fingerprints that reveal no information that would require denial of application;*

*(b) That the application is denied, in which case the authority shall include a statement of the reasons for denial; or*

*(c) That the application is not complete, in which case the authority shall include a concise statement of the respects in which the application is incomplete, and shall further state that a decision to grant or deny the application will be made on or before the seventy-fifth business day after the original receipt of such application based upon the information then in possession of the authority. Computation of such seventy-five day requirement shall not include the time between the dates of mailing such notice of incompleteness to the applicant and receipt of any additional information from the applicant in response.*

❖*(2000, chgd. by chap. 114, eff. 9/9/2000, expires and deemed repealed 12/31/2001. Matter in italics expires and deemed repealed 12/31/2001. Matter in brackets eff. 12/31/2001.)*

*2. If the authority shall fail to mail a decision on an application for a license or a permit within the time periods required by this section, the applicant may cause notice of such failure to be given to the authority by means of registered or certified mail, return receipt requested addressed to the chairman of the authority. If within five business days after receipt of such notice, the authority fails to mail a decision, the applicant shall be entitled to interest payments as provided herein. Interest shall be calculated on the full amount of the fee required to be paid for the specific license or permit from the day of the receipt of the registered or certified letter sent to the chairman until the date the authority mails a decision. Interest shall be calculated at a rate equal to the rate set by the commissioner of taxation and finance for corporate taxes pursuant to paragraph one of subsection (e) of section one thousand ninety-six of the tax law, except that such rates shall be applied per week rather than per annum. Any such interest payments made pursuant to this subdivision shall be made from appropriations for state operations that are available for the administrative programs of the authority.*

*3. Notwithstanding any inconsistent provisions of this chapter or any rule or regulation of the authority, the procedures provided in this section shall govern the review by the authority of all applications for a permit or license made pursuant to this chapter.*



➒➒4. The authority shall provide a report on the effect of this section to the governor and the legislature not later than May first, two thousand one. Such report shall include, but not be limited to, the success of the authority in meeting the time frames described in this section, the number of applications dealt with by the authority which have both complied with and failed to comply with the time frames set forth herein, and the amount of interest paid. The report shall also include any recommendations the authority deems necessary to improve compliance with the time-frames set forth in this section. In preparing such report, the authority shall consult with licensees and their appropriate representatives, trade groups, and associations, and such other groups, including the division of the budget, as shall be appropriate, to determine the effectiveness of this section in enforcing adherence to the time-frames described in this section. ➒➒*(1999, added by chap. 411(F), eff. 11/24/99.)*

➒*(1995, chgd. by chaps. 83; 1999, chgd. by chaps. 403, 411(F), eff. 11/24/99, 8/9/99, expires and deemed repealed 12/31/2001. Matter in italics expires and deemed repealed 12/31/2001. Matter in brackets eff. 12/31/2001.)*

### ➎§120-a. Corporate change; hearing on application.

Upon the disapproval by the authority of an application for a corporate change in the stockholders, stockholdings, officers or directors the liquor authority shall provide for a hearing at which the applicant may produce any evidence it shall desire with reference to such disapproval by the authority. ➎*(1995, chgd. by chap. 83, eff. 6/20/95.)*

**❺§121. Review by courts.**

The following actions by the liquor authority shall be subject to review by the supreme court in the manner provided in article seventy-eight of the civil practice law and rules provided that no stay shall be granted pending the determination of the matter except on notice to the liquor authority and for a period not exceeding thirty days:

1. Refusal by the liquor authority to issue a license or a permit.
2. The revocation, cancellation or suspension of a license or permit by the liquor authority.
3. The failure or refusal by the liquor authority to render a decision within the time required by section one hundred twenty of this article.
4. The transfer by the liquor authority of a license or permit to any other premises, or the failure or refusal by the liquor authority to approve such a transfer.
5. The issuance of an order of warning by the liquor authority.
6. Refusal to approve alteration of premises.
7. Refusal to approve a corporate change in stockholders, stock-holdings, officers or directors.
8. Refusal by the liquor authority to grant permission for an additional bar pursuant to subdivision four of section one hundred of this chapter.

❺*(1995, chgd. by chap. 83, eff. 6/20/95.)*

**❼§122. Continuance of business by receiver or other representative.**

If a corporation or copartnership holding any license or holding a permit for which an annual fee of one hundred dollars or more is prescribed by this chapter shall be dissolved, or if a receiver or assignee for the benefit of creditors be appointed therefor, or if a receiver, assignee for the benefit of creditors or a committee or conservator of the property of an individual holding any license or holding a permit for which an annual fee of one hundred dollars or more is prescribed by this chapter be appointed, during the time for which such license or permit was granted, or if a person, including a member of a copartnership, holding any license or holding a permit for which an annual fee of one hundred dollars or more is prescribed by this chapter shall die during the term for which such license or permit was given, such corporation, copartnership, receiver or assignee, or the administrator or executor of the estate of such individual, or of such deceased member of a copartnership, or a committee of the property of a person adjudged to be incompetent, or a conservator of the property of an individual, or a petition under title eleven of the United States code shall have been filed and a trustee has been appointed or the holder of the license of* permit has been permitted to remain in possession without the appointment of a trustee, may continue to carry on such business upon such premises for the balance of the term for which such license or permit was effective, with the same rights and subject to the same restrictions and liabilities as if he had been the original applicant for and the original holder, or one of either of them, of such license or permit, providing the approval of the liquor authority shall be first obtained. Before continuing such business, such receiver, assignee, individual, committee, or conservator, debtor in possession, or trustee in bankruptcy shall file a statement setting forth in such form and substance as the liquor authority may prescribe the facts and circumstances by which he has succeeded to the rights of the original licensee or permittee. The liquor authority may, in its discretion, permit the continuance of such business or may refuse to do so. In the event that the authority determines to permit the continuance of the business, the license or permit shall be submitted to the authority and shall have affixed thereto a certificate in the form prescribed by the authority. For each such certificate a fee shall be paid to the liquor authority of fifty dollars by the applicant, except in the case of an off-premise beer license, such fee shall be ten dollars which shall be paid into the same fund as other license fees herein provided for. ❼*(1997, chgd. by chap. 408, eff. 11/18/97.)*

**So in original. Probably should be "or".*



**§123. Injunction for unlawful manufacturing, sale or consumption of liquor, wine or beer.**

1. (a) If any person shall engage or participate or be about to engage or participate in the manufacturing or sale of liquor, wine or beer in this state without obtaining the appropriate license therefor, or shall traffic in liquor, wine or beer contrary to any provision of this chapter, or otherwise unlawfully, or shall traffic in illegal liquor, wine or beer, or, operating a place for profit or pecuniary gain, with a capacity for the assemblage of twenty or more persons, shall permit a person or persons to come to such place of assembly for the purpose of consuming alcoholic beverages without having the appropriate license therefor pursuant to section sixty-four-b of this chapter, the liquor authority or any taxpayer residing in the city, village or town in which such activity is or is about to be engaged or participated in or such traffic is being conducted, or the city, town or village, may present a verified petition or complaint to a justice of the supreme court at a special term of the supreme court of the judicial district in which such city, village or town is situated, for an order enjoining such person engaging or participating in such activity or from carrying on such business. Such petition or complaint shall state the facts upon which such application is based. Upon the presentation of the petition or complaint, the justice or court shall grant an order requiring such person to appear before such justice or court at or before a special term of the supreme court in such judicial district on the day specified therein, not more than ten days after the granting thereof, to show cause why such person should not be permanently enjoined from engaging or participating in such activity or from carrying on such business, or why such person should not be enjoined from carrying on such business contrary to the provisions of this chapter. A copy of such petition or complaint and order shall be

served upon the person, in the manner directed by such order, not less than three days before the return day thereof. On the day specified in such order, the justice or court before whom the same is returnable shall hear the proofs of the parties and may, if deemed necessary or proper, take testimony in relation to the allegations of the petition or complaint. If the justice or court is satisfied that such person is about to engage or participate in the unlawful traffic in alcoholic beverages or has unlawfully manufactured or sold liquor, wine or beer without having obtained a license or contrary to the provisions of this chapter, or has trafficked in illegal liquor, wine or beer, or, is operating or is about to operate such place for profit or pecuniary gain, with such capacity, and has permitted or is about to permit a person or persons to come to such place of assembly for the purpose of consuming alcoholic beverages without having such appropriate license, an order shall be granted enjoining such person from thereafter engaging or participating in or carrying on such activity or business. If, after the entry of such an order in the county clerk's office of the county in which the principal place of business of the corporation or copartnership is located, or in which the individual so enjoined resides or conducts such business, and the service of a copy thereof upon such person, or such substituted service as the court may direct, such person, copartnership or corporation shall, in violation of such order, manufacture or sell liquor, wine or beer, or illegal liquor, wine, or beer, or permit a person or persons to come to such place of assembly for the purpose of consuming alcoholic beverages, such activity shall be deemed a contempt of court and be punishable in the manner provided by the judiciary law, and, in addition to any such punishment, the justice or court before whom or which the petition or complaint is heard, may, in his or its discretion, order the seizure and forfeiture of any liquor, wine or beer and any fixtures, equipment and supplies used in the operation or promotion of such illegal activity, including any bar, bar or refrigeration equipment, vending machines, gaming machines and jukeboxes, and such property shall be subject to forfeiture pursuant to the provisions of subdivision two of this section. Costs upon the application for such injunction may be awarded in favor of and against the parties thereto in such sums as in the discretion of the justice or court before whom or which the petition or complaint is heard may seem proper.

(b) The owner, lessor or lessee of a building, erection or place where alcoholic beverages are unlawfully manufactured, sold, consumed or permitted to be unlawfully manufactured, sold or consumed may be made respondents or defendants in the proceeding or action.

2. (a) This seized property shall be delivered by the peace officer, acting pursuant to his special duties or police officer having made the seizure to the custody of the authority or the district attorney of the county wherein the seizure was made as may be directed by the court, except that in the cities of New York and Buffalo, the seized property shall be delivered to the custody of the authority or of the police department of

Printed in the U.S.A. ab

such cities, together with a report of all the facts and circumstances of the seizure.

(b) It shall be the duty of the authority or such district attorney or, if the seizure was made in the cities of New York or Buffalo, of the authority or corporation counsel of such city, as the case may be, to inquire into the facts of the seizure so reported and if it appears probable that a forfeiture has been incurred, for the determination of which the institution of proceedings in the supreme court is necessary, to cause the proper proceedings to be commenced and prosecuted, at any time after thirty days from the date of seizure, to declare such forfeiture, unless, upon inquiry and examination the authority or such person, as the case may be, decides that such proceedings can not probably be sustained or that the ends of public justice do not require that they should be instituted or prosecuted, in which case, the authority or such person shall cause such seized property to be returned to the owner thereof.

(c) Notice of the institution of the forfeiture proceeding shall be served either (i) personally on the owners of the seized property or (ii) by registered mail to the owners' last known address and by publication of the notice once a week for two successive weeks in a newspaper published or circulated in the county wherein the seizure was made.

(d) Forfeiture shall not be adjudged where the owners established by preponderance of the evidence that (i) the use of such seized property was not intentional on the part of any owner, or (ii) said seized property was used by any person other than an owner thereof, while such seized property was unlawfully in the possession of a person who acquired possession thereof in violation of the criminal laws of the United States, or of any state.

(e) The authority or such person having custody of the seized property, after such judicial determination of forfeiture, shall, by a public notice of at least five days, sell such forfeited property at public sale. The net proceeds of any such sale, after deduction of the lawful expenses incurred, shall be paid into the general fund of the county wherein the seizure was made except that the net proceeds of the sale of property seized in the cities of New York and Buffalo shall be paid into the respective general funds of such cities.

(f) Whenever any person interested in any property which is seized and declared forfeited under the provisions of this section files with a justice of the supreme court a petition for the recovery of such forfeited property, the justice of the supreme court may restore said forfeited property upon such terms and conditions as he deems reasonable and just, if the petitioner establishes either of the affirmative defenses set forth in paragraph (d) of subdivision two of this section and that the petitioner was without personal or actual knowledge of the forfeiture proceeding. If the petition be filed after the sale of the forfeited property, any judgment in favor of the petitioner shall be limited to the net proceeds of such sale, after deduction of the lawful expenses and costs incurred by the seizing party.

(g) No suit or action under this section for wrongful seizure shall be instituted unless such suit or action is commenced within two years after the time when the property was seized.

**§124. Liquor authority to be necessary party to certain proceedings.**

The state liquor authority shall be made a party to all actions and proceedings affecting in any manner the submission of the local option questions provided for in this chapter, or the result of any vote thereupon; to all actions and proceedings relative to issuance or revocation of licenses or permits; to all injunction proceedings, and to all other civil actions or proceedings which in any manner affect the enjoyment of the privileges or the operation of the restrictions provided for in this chapter.

**§125. Disposition of moneys received for license fees.**

The moneys received for license fees provided for in this chapter shall be turned over by the liquor authority to the state comptroller. It shall be placed by the state comptroller in the fund derived from the proceeds of the taxes on liquor, wine and beer provided for in article eighteen of the tax law and become a part thereof and be subject to all of the provisions of law relating to such fund.

**§126. Persons forbidden to traffic in alcoholic beverages.**

The following are forbidden to traffic in alcoholic beverages:

1. Except as provided in subdivision one-a of this section, a person who has been convicted of a felony or any of the misdemeanors mentioned in section eleven hundred forty-six of the former penal law as in force and effect immediately prior to September first, nineteen hundred sixty-seven, or of an offense defined in section 230.20 or 230.40 of the penal law, unless subsequent to such conviction such person shall have received an executive pardon therefor removing this disability, a certificate of good conduct granted by the board of parole, or a certificate of relief from disabilities granted by the board of parole or a court of this state pursuant to the provisions of article twenty-three of the correction law to remove the disability under this section because of such conviction.

1-a. Notwithstanding the provision of subdivision one of this section, a corporation holding a license to traffic in alcoholic beverages shall not, upon conviction of a felony or any of the misdemeanors or offenses described in subdivision one of this section, be automatically forbidden to traffic in alcoholic beverages, but the application for a license by such a corporation shall be subject to denial, and the license of such a corporation shall be subject to revocation or suspension by the authority pursuant to section one hundred eighteen of this chapter, consistent with the provisions of article twenty-three-A of the correction law. For any felony conviction by a court other than a court of this state, the authority may request the board of parole to investigate and review the facts and circumstances concerning such a conviction, and

Printed in the U.S.A. ab

the board of parole shall, if so requested, submit its findings to the authority as to whether the corporation has conducted itself in a manner such that discretionary review by the authority would not be inconsistent with the public interest. The division of parole may charge the licensee or applicant a fee equivalent to the expenses of an appropriate investigation under this subdivision. For any conviction rendered by a court of this state, the authority may request the corporation, if the corporation is eligible for a certificate of relief from disabilities, to seek such a certificate from the court which rendered the conviction and to submit such a certificate as part of the authority's discretionary review process.

2. A person under the age of twenty-one years.

3. A person who is not a citizen of the United States or an alien lawfully admitted for permanent residence in the United States.

4. A copartnership or a corporation, unless each member of the partnership, or each of the principal officers and directors of the corporation, is a citizen of the United States or an alien lawfully admitted for permanent residence in the United States, not less than twenty-one years of age, and has not been convicted of any felony or any of the misdemeanors, specified in section eleven hundred forty-six of the former penal law as in force and effect immediately prior to September first, nineteen hundred sixty-seven, or of an offense defined in section 230.20 or 230.40 of the penal law, or if so convicted has received, subsequent to such conviction, an executive pardon therefor removing this disability* a certificate of good conduct granted by the board of parole, or a certificate of relief from disabilities granted by the board of parole or a court of this state pursuant to the provisions of article twenty-three of the correction law to remove the disability under this section because of such conviction; provided however that a corporation which otherwise conforms to the requirements of this section and chapter may be licensed if each of its principal officers and more than one-half of its directors are citizens of the United States or aliens lawfully admitted for permanent residence in the United States; and provided further that a corporation organized under the not-for-profit corporation law or the education law which otherwise conforms to the requirements of this section and chapter may be licensed if each of its principal officers and more than one-half of its directors are not less than twenty-one years of age and none of its directors are less than eighteen years of age; and provided further that a corporation organized under the not-for-profit corporation law or the education law and located on the premises of a college as defined by section two of the education law which otherwise conforms to the requirements of this section and chapter may be licensed if each of its principal officers and each of its directors are not less than eighteen years of age.

**So in original. Probably should be followed by a comma.*

5. (a) A person who shall have had any license issued under this chapter revoked for cause, until the expiration of two years from the date of such revocation.

(b) A person not licensed under the provisions of this chapter, who has been convicted of a violation of this chapter, until the expiration of two years from the date of such conviction.

6. A corporation or copartnership, if any officer and director or any partner, while not licensed under the provisions of this chapter, has been convicted of a violation of this chapter, or has had a license issued under this chapter revoked for cause, until the expiration of two years from the date of such conviction or revocation.

**§127. Surrender and cancellation of licenses; payment of refunds; notice to police officials.**

1. If a person holding a license to traffic in alcoholic beverages under the provisions of this chapter, against whom no complaint, prosecution or action is pending on account of any violation thereof, shall voluntarily, and before arrest or indictment for a violation of this chapter, cease to traffic in alcoholic beverages during the term for which the license fee is paid, such person may surrender such license to the liquor authority for cancellation and refund, provided that such license shall have at least one month to run at the time of such surrender. Such refund shall be computed for full months less thirty dollars, commencing with the first day of the month succeeding the one in which such license is surrendered, unless such surrender be on the first day of the month; and at the same time such person shall present to the liquor authority a verified petition setting forth all facts required to be shown by the liquor authority upon such surrender. The liquor authority shall thereupon compute the amount of refund then due on said license for the unexpired term thereof, and shall execute a receipt therefor showing the name of the person to whom such license was issued, the number thereof, date when issued, amount of license fee paid therefor, and the date when surrendered for cancellation, together with the amount of refund due thereon at such date as computed by it, and the name of the person entitled to receive the refund. Such receipt shall be delivered by the liquor authority to the person entitled thereto. If within thirty days from the date of such surrender and application, the person surrendering such certificate shall be arrested or indicted for a violation of this chapter, or proceedings shall be instituted for the cancellation of such certificate, or an action shall be commenced against him for penalties, such petition shall not be granted until the final determination of such proceedings or actions; and if the said petitioner be convicted, or said action or proceedings be determined against him, the authority may direct that any refund due thereunder be forfeited or may impose such other penalty or conditions it may deem appropriate in the circumstances but if such petitioner be acquitted, or such proceedings or action against him be dismissed on the merits or, if within such time, no such action or proceeding shall be brought against such person, then the liquor authority shall prepare an order for the payment of such refund, directed to the comptroller, to be paid him, on his audit, upon the surrender of the receipt theretofore given such person; provided, however,

that if any taxes or penalties imposed by article eighteen of the tax law or if any civil penalties imposed under this chapter are unpaid by such person, the amount of such taxes, penalties or civil penalties shall be deducted from the amount of such refund. Any refunds due on the surrender and cancellation of licenses pursuant to this section shall be paid by the comptroller from moneys in his custody, derived from license fees received pursuant to this chapter. ⑨*(1999, chgd. by chap. 98, eff. 8/21/99.)*

2. It shall be the duty of the liquor authority, upon the receipt of a license surrendered for cancellation and refund pursuant to this section, to immediately serve a written or printed notice upon the commissioner of police, chief of police, or chief police officer of the city, borough or village in which the place for which the surrendered license was issued is situated, or upon the sheriff of the county and a constable of the town, in case the license was issued for a place situated in a town and not within any city, borough or village, which notice shall include a statement of the number of the surrendered license, the name and place of residence of the holder of the license at the time of surrender, the location of the place for which the license was issued and was held at the time of surrender by street and number, if any, otherwise such apt description as will definitely locate the premises; the fact that such license has been surrendered; that the traffic in alcoholic beverages at said premises by any one is not authorized until a new license has been obtained therefor; and the date when such license was surrendered for cancellation. Such notice may be served by registered or certified mail, by inclosing the same in a post-paid sealed envelope, duly addressed to such officer.



### §127-a. Surrender and cancellation of permits; payment of refunds; notice to police officials.

The procedure prescribed by the provisions of section one hundred twenty-seven of this chapter shall be applicable to permits issued pursuant to this chapter. Notwithstanding anything to the contrary contained in this chapter, no refund shall be payable with respect to any special permit issued pursuant to section ninety-nine-c.

### §127-b. Payment of refunds on special permits and notice to police officers.

Where a special permit to remain open until three antemeridian has been issued under subdivision two of section ninety-nine of this chapter, in a county where a regulation of a local board further restricting the hours during which alcoholic beverages may be sold for on-premises consumption shall have been rescinded by such local board during the period for which the special permit was issued, the holder of such special permit shall be entitled to a refund computed for full months commencing with the first day of the month succeeding the month in which the rescission of the local regulation occurred. The procedure with reference to the payment of refunds and notice to police officials shall be as nearly as possible the same as outlined in section one hundred and twenty-seven of this chapter.

**§127-c. Refunds on licenses and permits erroneously or unlawfully cancelled, revoked or suspended.**

If a license or permit issued under this chapter is cancelled, revoked or suspended and thereafter the action of the state liquor authority effecting such cancellation, revocation or suspension is reversed or annulled, upon application made within six months of the date of such judgment of reversal or annulment there shall be refunded to such licensee or his assignee such proportion of the fee paid for such license or permit as the period that such licensee or permittee has not had the beneficial use of such license or permit by reason of such cancellation, revocation or suspension bears to the full period for which the license or permit was issued. The provisions of section one hundred twenty-seven of this chapter so far as they can be made applicable and are not inconsistent with this section, shall govern the procedure to be followed in making application for refunds under this section.

**§127-d. Refunds on over-payment of fees; permit not issued.**

Monies heretofore or hereafter received by the authority pursuant to this chapter may, within three years from the receipt thereof, be refunded to the applicant for the license or permit, on satisfactory proof that:

a. Such monies were in excess of the amount required by this chapter, to the extent of such excess.

b. The permit for which application was made has not been issued.

Such refunds shall, upon approval by the authority and after audit by the state comptroller, be paid from any monies in the custody of the comptroller, derived from fees received pursuant to this chapter.

**§128. Certain officials not to be interested in manufacture or sale of alcoholic beverages.**

1. Except as otherwise provided in section one hundred twenty-eight-a, it shall be unlawful for any police commissioner, police inspector, captain, sergeant, roundsman, patrolman or other police official or subordinate of any police department in the state, to be either directly or indirectly interested in the manufacture or sale of alcoholic beverages or to offer for sale, or recommend to any licensee any alcoholic beverages. A person may not be denied any license granted under the provisions of sections fifty-four, fifty-five, fifty-nine, sixty-three, sixty-four, seventy-nine, eighty-one, or article seven of this chapter solely on the grounds of being the spouse of a public servant described in this subdivision. The solicitation or recommendation made to any licensee, to purchase any alcoholic beverages by any police official or subordinate as hereinabove described, shall be presumptive evidence of the interest of such official or subordinate in the manufacture or sale of alcoholic beverages.

2. No elective village officer shall be subject to the limitations set forth in subdivision one of this section unless such elective village officer shall be assigned duties directly relating to the operation or management of the police department.

Printed in the U.S.A. ab

**●§128-a. Police officers allowed to work in licensed premises in certain cases.**

Notwithstanding any inconsistent provision of law to the contrary, the authority shall promulgate such rules and regulations as may be necessary to provide that it shall not be unlawful for a police officer employed in this state, having written permission and consent from his commanding officer, to work in a premises licensed to sell beer at retail for off-premises consumption under section fifty-four of this chapter or to work solely as a security guard or director of traffic on the premises of a volunteer firefighters' organization licensed to sell beer and wine at retail pursuant to a temporary permit for on-premises consumption under section ninety-seven of this chapter. ●*(2002, chgd. by chap. 678, eff. 12/20/2002.)*



**§129. Surrender of license; notice to police officials.**

Within three days after a license shall have been revoked pursuant to this chapter, notice thereof shall be given to the licensee by mailing such notice addressed to him at the premises licensed. Notice shall also be mailed to the owner of the premises licensed. The holder of such license shall thereupon surrender same to the liquor authority. The mailing thereof by the licensee to the liquor authority by registered mail or insured parcel post shall be deemed sufficient compliance with this section. The liquor authority, immediately upon giving notice of revocation, shall serve a written notice thereof upon the commissioner of police, chief of police or chief police officer of the city, or village in which the premises for which the revoked license was issued is situated, or upon the sheriff of the county or a constable of the town in case the license was issued for premises situated in a town and not within any city or village. Such notice shall include a statement of the number of such license, the name and place of residence of the holder thereof, the location of the licensed premises, and the date when such license was revoked. In case such license be not forthwith surrendered, the liquor authority shall issue a written demand for the surrender of such license and deliver said demand to the sheriff of the county in which the licensed premises are located, or to any representative of the liquor authority, and said sheriff or representative shall immediately take possession of such license and return the same to the liquor authority.

**§130. Penalties for violations of chapter.**

1. Any person who manufactures for sale or sells alcoholic beverages, other than the illicit alcoholic beverages as defined in section one hundred fifty, without having an appropriate license therefor, or whose license has been revoked, surrendered or cancelled, shall be guilty of a misdemeanor, and upon first conviction thereof shall be punished by a fine not more than two times the cost of a special on premises license in the county where the unlawful act took place or by imprisonment in a county jail or penitentiary for a term of not less than thirty days nor more than one year or both and upon second conviction thereof shall be punished by a fine not less than two times and not more than three times the

cost of a special on premises license in the county where the unlawful act took place or by imprisonment in a county jail or penitentiary for a term of not less than thirty days nor more than one year or both and upon all subsequent convictions thereof shall be punished by a fine not less than three times and not more than four times the cost of a special on premises license in the county where the unlawful act took place or by imprisonment in a county jail or penitentiary for a term of not less than thirty days nor more than one year or both provided, however, that in default of payment of any fine imposed, such person shall be imprisoned in a county jail or penitentiary for a term of not less than thirty days.

1-a. Any licensee, whose license has been suspended pursuant to the provisions of this chapter, who sells alcoholic beverages during the suspension period, shall be guilty of a misdemeanor, and upon conviction thereof shall be punished by a fine of not more than two hundred dollars or by imprisonment in a county jail or penitentiary for a term of not more than six months, or by both such fine and imprisonment.

2. Any person who shall make any false statement in the application for a license or a permit under this chapter shall be guilty of a misdemeanor, and upon conviction thereof shall be punishable by a fine of not more than two hundred dollars, or by imprisonment in a county jail or penitentiary for a term of not more than six months or both.

3. Any violation by any person of any provision of this chapter for which no punishment or penalty is otherwise provided shall be a misdemeanor, provided, however, that the provisions of this subdivision shall not apply to the prohibitions provided for in subdivision six-a of section one hundred six of this chapter.

4. In the city of New York, a summons shall be issued for a violation of the provisions of subdivision fourteen of section one hundred and five, section one hundred and five-a and subdivision five of section one hundred and six of this chapter in the same manner as provided by subdivision h of section one hundred and sixteen of the New York city criminal courts act.

5. Any violation by any person of the alcoholic beverage control law for which no punishment or penalty is otherwise provided shall be a misdemeanor, provided, however, that the provisions of this subdivision shall not apply to the prohibitions provided for in subdivision six-a of section one hundred six of this chapter.

## Article 9
## LOCAL OPTION

Sec.

**§140. Applicability of chapter before local option.**

Until such time as it shall become unlawful to sell alcoholic beverages in any town or city by the vote of the voters in such town or city in the manner provided in this article, all of the provisions of this chapter shall apply throughout the entire state. This article shall not apply to the Whiteface mountain ski center, owned by the state and located in the town of Wilmington, county of Essex.

**§141. Local option for towns.**

1. Not less than sixty days nor more than seventy-five days before the general election in any town at which the submission of the questions hereinafter stated is authorized by this article, a petition signed by electors of the town to a number amounting to twenty-five per centum of the votes cast in the town for governor at the then last preceding gubernatorial election, acknowledged by the signers or authenticated by witnesses as provided in the election law in respect of a nominating petition, requesting the submission at such election to the electors of the town of the questions contained in either group A or group B, may be filed with the town clerk:



**GROUP A**

Question 1. Selling alcoholic beverages to be consumed on the premises where sold. Shall any person be authorized to sell alcoholic beverages at retail to be consumed on premises licensed pursuant to the provisions of section sixty-four of this chapter?

Question 2. Selling alcoholic beverages to be consumed on the premises where sold. Shall any person be authorized to sell alcoholic beverages at retail to be consumed on premises licensed pursuant to the provisions of section sixty-four-a of this chapter?

Question 3. Selling alcoholic beverages not to be consumed on the premises where sold. Shall any person be authorized to sell alcoholic beverages at retail not to be consumed on the premises where sold in (here insert the name of the town)?

Question 4. Selling alcoholic beverages by hotel keepers only. Shall any person be authorized to sell alcoholic beverages at retail to be consumed on the premises where sold but only in connection with the business of keeping a hotel (here insert the name of the town), if the majority of the votes cast on the first question submitted are in the negative?

Question 5. Selling alcoholic beverages by summer hotel keepers only. Shall any person be authorized to sell alcoholic beverages at retail to be consumed on the premises where sold but only in connection with the business of keeping a summer hotel within the period from May first to October thirty-first, in (here insert the name of the town), if the majority of the votes cast on the first question submitted are in the negative?

### GROUP B

Question 1. Selling liquor or wine to be consumed on the premises where sold. Shall any person be authorized to sell liquor or wine at retail to be consumed on premises licensed pursuant to the provisions of section sixty-four of this chapter?

Question 2. Selling liquor or wine to be consumed on the premises where sold. Shall any person be authorized to sell liquor or wine at retail to be consumed on premises licensed pursuant to the provisions of section sixty-four-a of this chapter?

Question 3. Selling liquor or wine not to be consumed on the premises where sold. Shall any person be authorized to sell liquor or wine at retail not to be consumed on the premises where sold in (here insert the name of the town)?

Question 4. Selling liquor or wine by hotel keepers only. Shall any person be authorized to sell liquor or wine at retail to be consumed on the premises where sold but only in connection with the business of keeping a hotel in (here insert the name of the town), if the majority of the votes cast on the first question submitted are in the negative?

Question 5. Selling liquor or wine by summer hotel keepers only. Shall any person be authorized to sell liquor or wine at retail to be consumed on the premises where sold but only in connection with the business of keeping a summer hotel within the period from May first to October thirty-first, in (here insert the name of the town), if the majority of the votes cast on the first question submitted are in the negative?

2. Upon the due filing of such petition complying with the foregoing provisions, such questions shall be submitted in accordance therewith. If petitions praying for the submission of the questions contained in both group A and group B are filed, only the questions of the group mentioned in the petition first filed shall be submitted.

3. The town clerk shall, within five days from the filing of such petition in his office, prepare and file in the office of the board of elections, as defined by the election law, of the county, a certified copy of such petition. Such questions may be submitted only at the time of a general election. At least ten days before such general election, the board of elections shall cause to be printed and posted in at least four public places in such town, a notice of the fact that all of the local option questions provided for in group A or group B, as the case may be, will be voted on at such general election; and the said notice shall also be published at least five days before the vote is to be taken once in a newspaper published in the county in which such town is situated, which shall be a newspaper published in the town, if there be one. Whenever such questions are to be submitted under the provisions of this article the board of elections shall cause the proper ballot labels to be printed and placed on all voting machines used in the town in which such questions are to be submitted, in the form prescribed by the election law in respect of other propositions or questions, upon the face of which shall

be printed in full the said questions. Any elector qualified to vote for state officers shall be entitled to vote upon such local option questions. As soon as the election shall be held, a return of the votes cast and counted shall be made as provided by law and the returns canvassed by the inspectors of election. If a majority of the votes cast shall be in the negative on all or any of the questions, no person shall, after such election, sell alcoholic beverages in such town contrary to such vote or to the provisions of this chapter; provided, however, that the result of such vote shall not shorten the term for which any license may have been lawfully issued under this chapter or affect the rights of the licensee thereunder; and no person shall after such vote apply for or receive a license to sell alcoholic beverages at retail in such town contrary to such vote, until, by referendum as hereinafter provided for, such sale shall again become lawful.

4. If at such election the votes cast on question number one of either group be equal or a majority thereof be in the affirmative and a majority of the votes cast on question number two of either group be in the negative, alcoholic beverages or beer only, as the case may be, may nevertheless be sold in such town at retail not to be consumed on the premises by the holder of a license to sell such beverages in such town at retail to be consumed upon the premises.

5. Subject to the local option provisions of this section, a summer hotel open for business only within the period from May first to October thirty-first in each year, may be licensed in the manner provided in this chapter to sell one or more alcoholic beverages at retail to be consumed on the premises only.



**§142. Local option for cities.**

1. Not less than sixty days nor more than eighty days before the general election in the year nineteen hundred thirty-five in any city, and before any subsequent general election in the city at which the submission of the questions hereinafter stated is authorized by this article, a petition signed by electors of the city to a number amounting to twenty-five per centum of the votes cast in the city for governor at the then last preceding gubernatorial election, requesting the submission at such election to the electors of the city of the questions contained in either group A or group B of section one hundred forty-one, substituting however the word "city" for "town," may be filed with the city clerk or, in the city of New York, with the board of elections. If petitions praying for the submission of the questions contained in both group A and group B are filed, only the questions of the group mentioned in the petition first filed shall be submitted.

(a) Opposite and on the right of the name of each elector signing such petition shall be written his residence address by house number and street name, if any, and otherwise by an appropriate designation, and the date of his signing. Each signature shall be made personally by the one whose name is signed and not by another. No signature shall be valid or counted as to which any of such requirements is not complied with, nor as to which the date of signing is more than four months prior to the day of the election. No signature shall be withdrawn after the petition is filed.

(b) At the bottom of each sheet of the petition shall be a statement, signed by a duly qualified elector of the city, with his residence address, stating that every signature on that sheet of the petition is genuine and that to the best of his knowledge and belief every person so signing was at the time thereof a qualified elector of such city, that their respective residences are correctly stated therein and that each signer signed the same on the date set opposite his name. Such statement shall be sworn to before an officer authorized to administer oaths within such city.

(c) The same petition may be either in one document or prepared and signed in two or more documents. Such documents shall constitute one petition and be filed as a whole.

(d) The petition shall also appoint a committee upon whom or any of its members a summons, order or notice may be served in any proceeding respecting the validity of the petition or of an election held pursuant thereto, and shall also designate the chairman of such committee. The residence address of each member of the committee shall be stated. Such committee may fill a vacancy in its chairmanship or in its membership and notice of any such change shall promptly be filed with the officer with whom the petition is required to be filed; provided, however, that failure to file such notice shall not invalidate any proceeding under this chapter.

(e) Upon the due filing of such a petition, complying with the foregoing provisions, such questions shall be submitted in accordance therewith. If the petition be filed with the city clerk, he shall within five days from the filing thereof, prepare and file in the office of the board of elections of the county as defined by the election law, a certified copy thereof.

2. The method and manner of submission, preparation and provision of ballot labels, balloting by voting machine and conducting the election, canvassing the result and making and filing the returns and all other procedure with reference to the submission of and action upon any such question shall be the same as in the case of any other proposition to be submitted to the electors of a city at a general election as provided by law.

3. If a majority of the votes cast shall be in the negative on any or all of the questions, no person shall, after such election, sell alcoholic beverages in such city contrary to such vote or to the provisions of this chapter; provided, however, that the result of such vote shall not shorten the term for which any license may have been lawfully issued under this chapter or affect the rights of the licensee thereunder; and no person shall after such vote apply for or receive a license to sell alcoholic beverages at retail in such city contrary to such vote, until, by referendum as hereinafter provided for, such sale shall again become lawful.

4. If at such election the votes cast on question number one of either group be equal or a majority thereof be in the affirmative and a majority of the votes cast on question number two of either group be in the negative, alcoholic beverages or beer only, as the case may be, may nevertheless be sold in such city at retail not to be consumed on the premises by the holder of a license to sell such beverages in such city at retail to be consumed upon the premises.

**§143. Filing certificate of result with liquor authority.**
Whenever at an election a vote shall be taken on the local option questions pursuant to sections one hundred forty-one or one hundred forty-two in any town or city, the officer or board charged by law with the duty of filing a statement of the result and certificate of determination of such election shall file a duplicate thereof with the liquor authority.



**§144. Contesting validity of petition.**
Proceedings may be instituted and maintained to contest the validity, sufficiency or legality of any petition provided for in this article, in the manner provided by the election law, as though such petition were a certificate of nomination.

**§145. False statements and forgery.**
A person who forges the signature of any person upon any petition or statement provided for in this article shall be guilty of forgery in the third degree and on conviction thereof be punished accordingly.

**§146. Alcoholic beverages to be removed from place of former sale.**
A person engaged in the sale of alcoholic beverages at retail or of beer at retail only in a city or town when a local option vote is taken as provided in this article shall remove or cause to be removed all such beverages from the premises licensed to a place in which no grocery store, drug store, restaurant, hotel or club is conducted, at least ten days before the taking effect of such vote, if as a result of such vote the sale of such beverages at such premises will become unlawful. Failure to comply with the provisions of this section shall be presumptive evidence that such beverages are kept for the purpose of sale contrary to law.

**§147. Effective duration of local option determination.**
1. In any town or city in which a vote shall be taken on any one group of local option questions provided for in this article, no further vote shall be submitted upon the questions contained in such group before the third general election thereafter.

2. If at the time of any subsequent submission of such questions it shall be lawful to sell alcoholic beverages and a majority of the votes cast shall be in the negative on such questions, then all of the provisions of this article applicable thereto shall become effective.

## Article 10
## SPECIAL PROVISIONS RELATING TO ILLICIT ALCOHOLIC BEVERAGES AND STILLS



### §150. Definitions.

Whenever used in this article only, unless the context requires otherwise:

1.* "Illicit alcoholic beverage" means and includes any alcohol or distilled spirits owned, manufactured, distributed, bought, sold, bottled, rectified, blended, treated, fortified, mixed, processed, warehoused, possessed or transported on which any tax required to have been paid under any applicable federal law has not been paid.

**So in original. No subd. 2 has been enacted.*

### §151. Possession of illicit alcoholic beverages.

Any person who shall knowingly possess or have under his control any illicit alcoholic beverages is guilty of a misdemeanor.

### §152. Sale of illicit alcoholic beverages.

(a) Any person who shall knowingly barter or exchange with, or sell, give or offer to sell or to give another any illicit alcoholic beverage is guilty of a misdemeanor.

(b) Any person who shall possess or have under his control or transport any illicit alcoholic beverage with intent to barter or exchange with, or to sell or give to another the same or any part thereof is guilty of a misdemeanor. Such intent is presumptively established by proof that the person knowingly possessed or had under his control one or more gallons of illicit alcoholic beverages. This presumption may be rebutted.

### §153. Stills and distilling apparatus.

Any person who shall manufacture any illicit alcoholic beverage or who, not being duly licensed as a distiller under the provisions of the alcoholic beverage control law, shall own, operate, possess or have under his control any still or distilling apparatus is guilty of a felony. "Still" or "distilling apparatus" shall mean any apparatus designed, intended, actually used, or capable of being used for or in connection with the separating of alcoholic or spirituous vapors, or alcohol or spirituous solutions, or alcohol or spirits, from alcohol or spirituous solutions or mixtures, but shall not include stills used for laboratory purposes or stills used for distilling water or other nonalcoholic materials where the cubic capacity of such stills is one gallon or less.

Provided, however, that it shall not be unlawful for any person to own, possess or have under his control any still or distilling apparatus

(a) where the same has been duly registered in compliance with or has otherwise complied with the provisions of federal law and regulations issued pursuant thereto, or (b) where the same is not required to be registered under federal law, or (c) where the same is in the possession of a duly qualified manufacturer of stills under federal law.

The unlawful ownership, operation, possession, control or use of any still or distilling apparatus or illicit alcoholic beverage is a nuisance, and each such still and distilling apparatus and illicit alcoholic beverage is hereby declared to be a nuisance, and when any such still or distilling apparatus or illicit alcoholic beverage shall be taken from the possession of any person, the same shall be surrendered and forfeited to the sheriff of the county wherein the same shall be taken, except that in a city having a population of seventy-five thousand or more, the same shall be surrendered and forfeited to the police commissioner or other head of the police force or department of said city and except that in the county of Nassau, the same shall be surrendered and forfeited to the commissioner of the county police department.



**§154. Premises used for manufacture or storage of illicit alcoholic beverages.**

Any person who, being the owner, lessee, or occupant of any room, shed, tenement, booth or building, float or vessel, or part thereof, knowingly permits the same to be used for the manufacture, distribution, purchase, sale, bottling, rectifying, blending, treating, fortifying, mixing, processing, warehousing, transportation, distilling, or storage of an illicit alcoholic beverage, is guilty of a misdemeanor.

**§155. Punishment for second offenders.**

Any person who is convicted of violating section one hundred fifty-two or section one hundred fifty-four of this chapter and who has been previously convicted of a violation of either of these said sections or after the effective date of this article has been convicted in any other state or federal court of a crime which if committed in this state would constitute a violation of either of said sections, is guilty of a felony and shall be punishable for a felony.

## Article 11
## MISCELLANEOUS PROVISIONS; LAWS REPEALED; TIME OF TAKING EFFECT

Sec.



**§160. Construction of chapter.**

This chapter shall be so construed as to assure that the policy of the state and the intent and purpose thereof will be carried out.

**§161. Invalidity; effect of.**

If any part, provision or section of this chapter or the application thereof to any person or circumstances shall be held invalid by any court of competent jurisdiction, the remainder thereof or the application of such part, provision or section to any other person or circumstances shall not be affected thereby.

**§162. Laws repealed; effect of repeal; saving clause.**

1. Chapter one hundred eighty of the laws of nineteen hundred thirty-three, entitled "An act relating to the manufacture, sale, control, distribution and regulation of certain alcoholic beverages, constituting chapter three-b of the consolidated laws," and all acts amendatory thereof or supplemental thereto are hereby repealed.

2. The repeal of the acts specified in subdivision one hereof shall not operate or be construed to shorten or terminate the term of any license heretofore issued thereunder or the rights of any person holding such a license; nor shall it be construed to abolish the state alcoholic beverage control board or the several county alcoholic beverage control boards or the New York city alcoholic beverage control board, as presently constituted, and which were heretofore established and are now operating pursuant to such acts nor to invalidate or affect any action heretofore taken by either of such boards or their officers or employees; nor to require the discharge or the re-appointment of any employees of either of such boards.

3. This chapter shall not affect any action or proceeding now pending in any court.

**§163. Time of taking effect.**

This chapter shall take effect July first, nineteen hundred thirty-four except that the state liquor authority and the local alcoholic beverage control board may, prior to July first, nineteen hundred thirty-four, receive and entertain such applications for licenses or permits and take such other steps as may be necessary or appropriate to permit this chapter to become effective and operative on July first, nineteen hundred thirty-four.

**§164. Saving clause on repeal of article three.**

1. The repeal of article three by the chapter of the laws of nineteen hundred ninety-five which added this section shall not operate or be construed to invalidate or affect any action heretofore taken by the several county alcoholic beverage control boards or the New York city alcoholic beverage control board, as heretofore established by said article three, or by their boards or officers or employees, nor to require the discharge or the re-appointment of any of their employees.

2. Such chapter of the laws of nineteen hundred ninety-five shall not affect any action or proceeding now pending in any court on or before the effective date of this section.

*(1995, added by chap. 83, eff. 6/20/95.)*

*(Unless otherwise noted, all references are to sections of the Alcoholic Beverage Control Law.)*

Printed in the U.S.A. ab

Printed in the U.S.A. ab

This page intentionally left blank.